T0135281

Linked Data

Sherif Sakr • Marcin Wylot • Raghava Mutharaju •
Danh Le Phuoc • Irini Fundulaki

Linked Data

Storing, Querying, and Reasoning

 Springer

Sherif Sakr
College of Public Health &
Health Informatics
King Saud bin Abdulaziz University
for Health Sciences
Riyadh, Saudi Arabia

Marcin Wylot
Fakultät IV - Open Distributed Systems
Technische Universität Berlin
Berlin, Germany

Raghava Mutharaju
Knowledge Discovery Lab
GE Global Research
Niskayuna
New York, USA

Danh Le Phuoc
Fakultät IV - Open Distributed Systems
Technische Universität Berlin
Berlin, Germany

Irini Fundulaki
Foundation for Research
and Technology - Hellas (FORTH)
Institute of Computer Science (ICS)
Heraklion, Greece

ISBN 978-3-030-08803-3   ISBN 978-3-319-73515-3   (eBook)
https://doi.org/10.1007/978-3-319-73515-3

Printed on acid-free paper

This Springer imprint is published by Springer Nature
The registered company is Springer International Publishing AG
The registered company address is: Gewerbestrasse 11, 6330 Cham, Switzerland

Foreword

The Semantic Web has matured over the past years. Since the grand vision of an intelligent agent-based Web of machines that will involve agents acting on our behalf, as outlined in a seminal article by Tim Berners-Lee et al. in 2001, we have seen the development of proven standards, used in Enterprise applications and almost anywhere on the Web. We could—as researchers—well ask ourselves the question "Are we there yet?" and would probably find many reasons to give an affirmative answer. Linked Data and Semantic Web technologies have become mainstream in many Web applications, being used heavily by Web search engines, by big media companies, and very successfully in Healthcare & Life Sciences applications, or e-Science. As such, Linked Data and Sematic Web have become a cornerstone of many "Big Data" applications, providing the "glue" for "Data Lakes" of heterogeneous data or building backbones of large-scale distributed knowledge bases in the form of so-called Knowledge Graphs.

Particularly, on this journey over the past roughly 20 years of research, the focus of the Semantic Web has changed several times, from originally being very much on (1) Knowledge Representation and Reasoning towards (2) more lightweight vocabulary management and Linked Data publishing and—more recently—towards (3) distributed graph databases and scalable data management and processing of Semantic (Web) data, accessible as distributed Linked Data via query interfaces using SPARQL as a standard query language, so-called SPARQL endpoints.

Whereas other textbooks already cover the former two aspects in much detail, now is probably an excellent time for the latter aspect to be presented to a wider audience as it is done in this volume. The success of the Semantic Web has always been driven by enthusiasts who carried the idea forward in education, with preparing and teaching materials for academics and third-level education in general. The availability of good entry-level materials to teach techniques and the state of the art in research is important for both practitioners and researchers approaching the field in order to advance research and our knowledge itself.

This book will provide people with little or no Semantic Web background an entrance, but also covers current hot topics and recent trends about querying and efficient storage of Linked Data at scale. After providing an overview of the relevant standards, the reader will learn how RDF and Linked Data can be stored and queried efficiently, also using recent techniques from NoSQL databases. Next, the processing of and reasoning about dynamic, streaming data is covered as well as distributed techniques for storing and reasoning about Semantic Web data. Last but not least, the book provides information about state-of-the-art benchmarks for systems to store and query such data. A final chapter explains the importance of storing and using provenance data in the context of linked data and how such provenance information can be leveraged in Semantic data management.

Overall, I recommend this book to anyone interested in Semantic Web beyond just data publishing and querying SPARQL endpoints for gaining a deeper insight on what efficient management of Linked Data means under the surface and how it can be implemented and realized using modern NoSQL database systems.

Vienna University of Economics and Business   Axel Polleres
Vienna, Austria

Preface

The World Wide Web is an interlinked collection of documents that are generally devoid of any structure and primarily meant for human consumption. In 2006, Sir Tim Berners-Lee, the inventor of the Web, proposed and described the Semantic Web vision as an extension of the World Wide Web where structure and meaning are provided to the data. This makes the information in the interlinked documents machine understandable. In practice, the nature of the World Wide Web has evolved from a web of linked documents to a web including Linked Data. Traditionally, we were able to publish documents on the Web and create links between them. Those links, however, only allowed the document space to be traversed without understanding the relationships between the documents and without linking to particular pieces of information. In principle, Linked Data allows meaningful links to be created between pieces of data on the Web. The adoption of Linked Data technologies has shifted the Web from a space of connecting documents to a global space where pieces of data from different domains are semantically linked and integrated to create a global Web of Data. Linked Data enables operations to deliver integrated results as new data is added to the global space. This opens new opportunities for applications such as search engines, data browsers, and various domain-specific applications.

In practice, the Web of Linked Data is rapidly growing from a dozen data collections in 2007 to a space of hundreds of data sources in April 2014. In particular, the number of linked datasets doubled between 2011 and 2014, which shows an accelerating trend of data integration on the Web. The Web of Linked Data contains heterogeneous data coming from multiple sources and various contributors, produced using different methods and degrees of authoritativeness, and gathered automatically from independent and potentially unknown sources. Thus, there is a growing momentum to harness the power of linked data in several application domains. This book is intended to take you in a journey for describing efficient and effective techniques for harnessing the power of Linked Data by tackling the various aspects for managing the growing amounts of Linked Data: storing, querying, reasoning, provenance management, and benchmarking.

Organization of the Book

The World Wide Web is an interlinked collection of documents that are generally devoid of any structure and primarily meant for human consumption. The Semantic Web is an extension of the World Wide Web where structure and meaning are provided to the data. The adoption of Linked Data technologies has shifted the Web from a space of connecting documents to a global space where pieces of data from different domains are semantically linked and integrated to create a global Web of Data. Chapter 1 introduces the main concepts of Semantic Web and Linked Data and provides the book roadmap.

All concepts underpinning Linked Data are standardized by the World Wide Web Consortium. The Consortium publishes recommendations defining and describing in detail the technologies behind Linked Data. Chapter 2 briefly introduces the basic concepts underpinning Linked Data technologies and that are necessary to follow the course of this book. We present a data model, a query language, vocabularies, and a data exchange format. In addition, the chapter provides an overview of emerging big data storage and processing frameworks that are frequently used for RDF data management (e.g., NoSQL databases, Hadoop, Spark).

The wide adoption of the RDF data model has called for efficient and scalable RDF query processing schemes. As a response to this call, a number of centralized RDF query processing systems have been designed to tackle this challenge. In these systems, the storage and query processing of RDF datasets are managed on a single node. Chapter 3 gives an overview of various techniques and systems for centrally querying RDF datasets.

With increasing sizes of RDF datasets, executing complex queries on a single node has turned to be impractical especially when the node's main memory is dwarfed by the volume of the dataset. Therefore, there was a crucial need for distributed systems with a high degree of parallelism that can satisfy the performance demands of complex SPARQL queries. Chapter 4 provides an overview of various techniques and systems for efficiently querying large RDF datasets in distributed environments.

We are witnessing a paradigm shift, where real-time, time-dependent data is becoming ubiquitous. As Linked Data facilitates the data integration process among heterogeneous data sources, RDF Stream Data has the same goal with respect to data streams. It bridges the gap between stream and more static data sources. To support the processing of RDF stream data, there is a need of investigating how to extend RDF to model and represent stream data. Then, from the RDF-based data representation, the query processing models need to be defined to build the stream processing engine that is tailored for streaming data. Chapter 5 provides an overview on how such requirements are addressed in the current state of the art of RDF Stream Data processing.

Large RDF interconnected datasets, especially in the form of open as well as enterprise knowledge graphs, are constructed and consumed in several domains. Reasoning over such large knowledge graphs poses several performance challenges. In practice, although there has been some prior work on scalable approaches to RDF reasoning, the interest in this field started gathering momentum with the rising popularity of modern big data processing systems (e.g., Hadoop, Spark). Chapter 6 covers five main categories of distributed RDF reasoning systems: (1) Peer-to-Peer RDF reasoning systems, (2) NoSQL-based RDF reasoning systems, (3) Hadoop-based RDF reasoning systems, (4) Spark-based RDF reasoning systems, and (5) shared-memory RDF reasoning systems.

Standards and benchmarking have traditionally been used as the main tools to formally define and provably illustrate the level of the adequacy of systems to address the new challenges. Chapter 7 discusses benchmarks for RDF query engines and instance matching systems. In practice, benchmarks are used to inform users of the strengths and weaknesses of competing tools and approaches, but more importantly, they encourage the advancement of technology by providing both academia and industry with clear targets for performance and functionality.

Chapter 8 discusses the provenance management for Linked Data and presents the different provenance models developed for the different fragments of the SPARQL standard language for querying RDF datasets. In addition, we discuss the different models for relational provenance that set the basis for RDF provenance models and proceed with a thorough presentation of the various provenance models for the different fragments of the SPARQL query language.

Chapter 9 briefly summarizes the book journey before providing some insights and highlights on some of the open challenges and research directions for advancing the state of the art of Linked Data towards achieving the ultimate vision of the Semantic Web Domain.

Target Audience

This book is mainly targeting students and academic researchers who are interested in the Linked Data domain. The book provides readers with an updated view of methods, technologies, and systems related to Linked Data.

For Students This book provides an overview of the foundations and underpinning technologies and standards for Linked Data. We comprehensively cover the state of the art and discuss the technical challenges in depth.

For Researchers The material of this book will provide you with a thorough coverage for the emerging and ongoing advancements on Linked Data storing, querying, reasoning, and provenance management systems. You can use this book as a starting point to tackle your next research challenge in the domain of Linked Data management.

Riyadh, Saudi Arabia   Sherif Sakr
Berlin, Germany   Marcin Wylot
Niskayuna, NY, USA   Raghava Mutharaju
Berlin, Germany   Danh Le Phuoc
Heraklion, Greece   Irini Fundulaki

Acknowledgments

The authors are grateful to many collaborators for their contribution to this book. In particular, we would like to mention Manfred Hauswirth, Martin Grund, Philippe Cudre-Mauroux, Floris Geerts, Vassilis Christophides, Grigoris Karvounarakis, Anastasios Kementsietsidis, Giorgos Flouris, Evangelia Daskalaki, Venelin Kotsev, Peter Boncz, Axel Ngonga-Ngomo, and Paul Groth. Thank you all!

Thanks to Marie Sklodowska-Curie Programme H2020-MSCA-IF-2014 which is supporting one of the authors under his Individual Fellowship, Grant No. 661180.

Thanks to Springer-Verlag for publishing this book. Ralf Gerstner has greatly encouraged and supported us to write this book. Thanks Ralf!

Contents

About the Authors

Sherif Sakr is a professor of computer and information science in the Health Informatics department at King Saud bin Abdulaziz University for Health Sciences. He is also affiliated with the University of New South Wales and DATA61/CSIRO. He received his PhD in Computer and Information Science from the University of Konstanz, Germany, in 2007. He received his BSc and MSc in Computer Science from the Faculty of Computers and Information in Cairo University, Egypt, in 2000 and 2003, respectively. In 2013, Sherif has been awarded the Stanford Innovation and Entrepreneurship Certificate. Sherif's research interests revolve around the areas of efficient and scalable Big Data Management, Processing, and Analytics. He coauthored and coedited seven books covering various fundamental aspects in the field of Data Management. Prof. Sakr is an ACM and IEEE Distinguished Speaker. He is currently serving as the Editor-in-Chief of the Springer Encyclopedia of Big Data Technologies. Homepage: http://www.cse.unsw.edu.au/~ssakr/.

Marcin Wylot is a postdoctoral researcher at TU Berlin in the ODS group. He received his PhD at the University of Fribourg in Switzerland in 2015, with the supervision of Professor Philippe Cudré-Mauroux. He obtained his MSc in Computer Science at the University of Lodz in Poland in 2010, doing part of his studies at the University of Lyon in France. During his studies he was also gaining professional experience working in various industrial companies. His main research interests revolve around database systems for Semantic Web data, provenance in Linked Data, Internet of Things, and Big Data processing. Homepage: http://mwylot.net.

Raghava Mutharaju is a Research Scientist in the AI & Machine Learning Systems division of GE Global Research in Niskayuna, NY, USA. He received his PhD in Computer Science and Engineering from Wright State University, Dayton, OH, USA, in 2016. His dissertation work involved investigating various approaches to distributed reasoning of OWL ontologies. He received his Master of Technology (M.Tech) and Bachelor of Technology (B.Tech) in Computer Science from Motilal

Nehru National Institute of Technology (MNNIT), Allahabad, India, and Jawaharlal Nehru National Institute of Technology (JNTU), Hyderabad, India, respectively. His research interests are in ontology modeling and reasoning, scalable SPARQL query processing, Big Data, and Semantic Web and its applications. He has published at several venues such as ISWC, ESWC, ECAI, and WISE. He cochaired workshops at WebSci 2017 and ISWC 2015. He has co-organized tutorials at IJCAI 2016, AAAI 2015, and ISWC 2014. He has been on the Program Committee of several Semantic Web conferences such as ISWC, ESWC, K-CAP, and SEMANTiCS. Homepage: http://raghavam.github.io/.

Danh Le Phuoc is a Marie Sklodowska-Curie Fellow at the Technical University of Berlin. He received his PhD in Computer Science from the National University of Ireland. He is working on Pervasive Analytics which includes Linked Data/Semantic Web, Pervasive Computing, Future Internet, and Big Data for Internet of Everything. Before joining TUB, he was a Principal Investigator, Research Fellow, and Project Lead of the Insight Centre of Data Analytics or Digital Enterprise Research Institute (DERI) at the National University of Ireland, Galway. Before doing PhD, he spent 8 years working in several industrial positions.

Irini Fundulaki is a Principal Researcher at the Institute of Computer Science of the Foundation for Research and Technology-Hellas. She received her PhD in Computer Science from the Conservatoire National des Arts et Métiers, Paris, France, in 2003. She received her BSc and MSc in Computer Science from the Computer Science Department of the University of Crete, Greece, in 1994 and 1996, respectively. After her PhD she worked as a postdoc and subsequently became a Member of Technical Staff in Bell Laboratories, USA, at the Network Data and Services Research Department. She was also a Research Fellow at the Database Group, Laboratory for Foundations of Computer Science, School of Informatics, University of Edinburgh, UK. Irini's research interests are related to Web Data Management and more specifically the development of benchmarks for RDF engines, instance matching and link discovery systems, the management of provenance for Linked Data, access control for RDF datasets, bias in online information providers, and finally data integration. She has authored a large number of articles and journals and has served as chair of three international workshops.

Chapter 1
Introduction

1.1 Semantic Web

The World Wide Web is an interlinked collection of documents that are generally devoid of any structure and primarily meant for human consumption. On the other hand, the Semantic Web, as proposed by Tim Berners-Lee and described in the well-known *Scientific American* article titled "The Semantic Web" [40], is an extension of the World Wide Web where structure and meaning are provided to the data. This makes the information in the interlinked documents machine understandable. The goal is to make the machines (or software agents as indicated in [40]) to not only parse but also to comprehend the vast amount of data on the Web. This allows software agents to integrate data from different sources, infer hidden facts, and respond to complex queries easily. Software agents can then work together with humans and learn from them. They can interact with humans by voice or text and perform tasks such as booking appointments given certain constraints such as distance and ratings of the place. Software agents should also be able to explain how they arrived at a particular conclusion or recommendation.

This vision of the Semantic Web by Tim Berners-Lee et al. was published in 2001. Now, after 16 years, in 2017, software agents, which are typically our smartphones, can perform most of the tasks [40]. Along with the Semantic Web, advances in several other fields such as Machine Learning, Deep Learning, Natural Language Processing, Computer Vision, and Information Retrieval and also the reduced cost of hardware have contributed in realizing most of the Semantic Web vision. Our smartphones can, for example, suggest nearby service providers (restaurants, doctors, etc.), book appointments based on our calendar, interact with humans through voice, and provide answers to complex queries. An example of such a query "What was the US population when Michael Jordan was born?" is given in

© Springer International Publishing AG 2018
S. Sakr et al., *Linked Data*, https://doi.org/10.1007/978-3-319-73515-3_1

Fig. 1.1 A search engine can now answer a complex query such as "What was the US population when Michael Jordan was born?"

Fig. 1.1. This query can be considered complex because the search engine needs to understand and find information about a number of things such as:

(a) The string "Michael Jordan" is a person and should be disambiguated from other people named "Michael Jordan."
(b) The year of birth of "Michael Jordan," which is 1963.
(c) The string "US" refers to a country.
(d) The population of the US in 1963.

The information required to answer this query can be obtained from various semi-structured and structured sources such as Wikipedia Infobox,[1] DBpedia [230], Wikidata [401], etc. After collecting the information, the search engine then has to integrate data from different sources, filter them, and mark the most appropriate result as the answer(s). Apart from the scenarios discussed so far, Semantic Web plays a crucial role in applications across several domains such as health care, life science, geo-science, e-governance, Internet of Things, etc.

The technologies that played a key part in shaping and realizing the Semantic Web vision are part of the Semantic Web stack, also called as the layer cake. The Semantic Web stack has evolved over the years as shown in Figs. 1.2, 1.3, and 1.4. In principle, the Semantic Web stack shows the use of multiple languages and technologies where each layer makes use of the layer below it. Several technologies shown in the stack are standardized by the W3C such as XML, OWL, RDF, SPARQL, and RIF. The layers in the stack (Fig. 1.4) can be divided into three categories:

(a) *Hypertext Web technologies*: These technologies are used in the hypertext web and provide the base on which Semantic Web technologies are built.

---

[1] https://en.wikipedia.org/wiki/Help:Infobox.

Fig. 1.2 Semantic Web layer cake in 2002. ©2009 W3C (MIT, ERCIM, Keio), All Rights Reserved. Reprinted with Permission

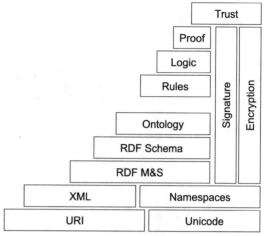

Fig. 1.3 Semantic Web layer cake in 2004. ©2009 W3C (MIT, ERCIM, Keio), All Rights Reserved. Reprinted with Permission

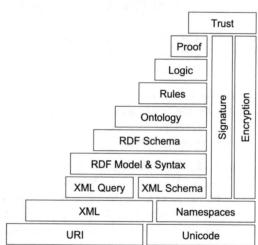

- *Internationalized Resource Identifier (IRI)*: It represents an extension of the Uniform Resource Identifier (URI) which is used to identify a resource uniquely. URIs can only contain a subset of ASCII character set, whereas IRIs can contain characters from the Universal character set.
- *Unicode*: It is used to represent text in multiple languages. The most commonly used Unicode encodings are UTF-8, UTF-16, and UCS-2.
- *Extensible Markup Language (XML)*: It is used to encode documents in structured format. XML namespace provides a unique name to the elements and attributes in an XML document. This is useful when referencing elements or attributes from multiple sources. Semantic Web uses XML extensively to serialize the data.

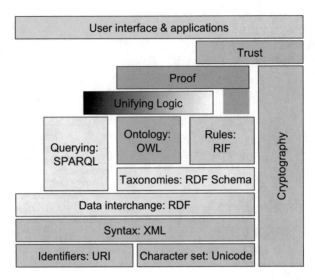

Fig. 1.4 Semantic Web layer cake in 2007. ©2009 W3C (MIT, ERCIM, Keio), All Rights Reserved. Reprinted with Permission

(b) *Semantic Web technologies*: The technologies in the middle layer are standard-ized by the W3C and are useful to build Semantic Web applications. Most of these technologies are discussed in detail in later chapters. Here, we provide only a brief introduction.

- *RDF*: Resource Description Framework (RDF) is a framework for represent-ing information on the Web. Any resource on the Web can be represented by an IRI and can be described in the form of a triple—a subject, a predicate, and an object. This forms a directed labeled graph with a subject and an object as nodes and a predicate as a labeled edge between the nodes.
- *RDFS*: RDF Schema provides a vocabulary for RDF. RDFS can be used, among other things, to describe groups of related resources and the relation-ships between these resources.
- *OWL*: Web Ontology Language (OWL) provides more advanced constructs than RDFS to model rich and complex knowledge of things on the Web. The formal underpinnings for OWL are provided by Description Logics which are a family of knowledge representation languages that are mostly decidable fragments of first-order logic.
- *SPARQL*: It is a query language for RDF. SPARQL provides triple patterns to query RDF graphs. The results of SPARQL queries can be either RDF graphs or result sets.
- *RIF*: Rule Interchange Format (RIF) provides a standard to exchange rules between the rule systems. RIF can be used to specify declarative rules (rules that specify facts about the domain) and production rules (rules that specify action based on a condition).

(c) Other technologies: These are the technologies that do not fall under either of the above two categories and are not standardized as well.

- *Cryptography*: This is important for secure communication and also to verify that the RDF statements are sent by a trusted source. Statements can be encrypted to achieve secure communication and digital signatures can be used to verify the authenticity of the statements.
- *Trust*: We must be able to verify that the Semantic Web statements are generated by a trusted source. Once verified, this provenance information can be retained in the triple by adding a fourth component to the triple and now it becomes a quad.
- *User interface*: This is the top most layer and it provides a convenient access to the applications that use Semantic Web technologies.

1.2 Linked Data

The nature of the World Wide Web has evolved from a web of linked documents to a web including Linked Data [180]. Traditionally, we were able to publish documents on the Web and create links between them. Those links, however, only allowed the document space to be traversed without understanding the relationships between the documents and without linking to particular pieces of information. Linked Data allows meaningful links to be created between pieces of data on the Web [40]. The adoption of Linked Data technologies has shifted the Web from a space of connecting documents to a global space where pieces of data from different domains are semantically linked and integrated to create a global Web of Data [180]. Linked Data enables operations to deliver integrated results as new data is added to the global space. This opens new opportunities for applications such as search engines, data browsers, and various domain-specific applications [180].

The Web of Linked Data is rapidly growing from a dozen data collections in 2007 to a space of hundreds of data sources in April 2014 [26, 46, 343]. The number of linked datasets doubled between 2011 and 2014 [343], which shows an accelerating trend of data integration on the Web. The Web of Linked Data contains heterogeneous data coming from multiple sources and various contributors, produced using different methods and degrees of authoritativeness, and gathered automatically from independent and potentially unknown sources. Figure 1.5 shows the Linking Open Data cloud diagram created in August 2014; it depicts the scale and heterogeneity of Linked Data on the Web. Such data size and heterogeneity bring new challenges for Linked Data management systems (i.e., systems which allow Linked Data to be stored and to be queried). While small amounts of Linked Data can be handled in-memory or by standard relational database systems, big Linked Data graphs, which we nowadays have to deal with, are very hard to manage. Modern Linked Data management systems have to face large amounts of

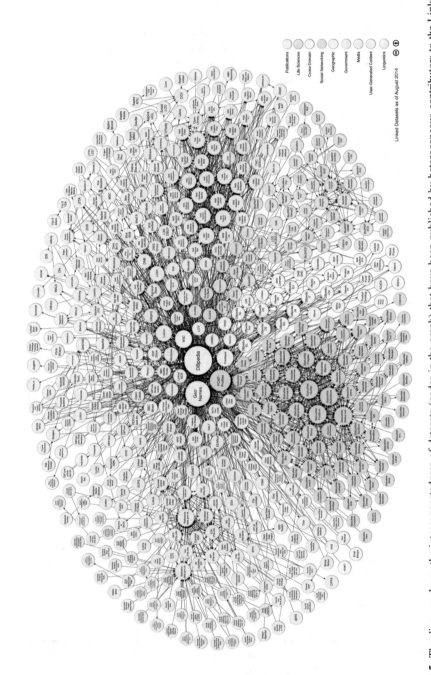

Fig. 1.5 The diagram shows the interconnectedness of datasets (nodes in the graph) that have been published by heterogeneous contributors to the Linking Open Data community project. It is based on research conducted in August 2014 [3]

heterogeneous, inconsistent, and schema-free data. Such large linked RDF graphs provide several challenges:

(a) Scalable techniques are required to query and reason over large RDF graphs.
(b) With sensors getting deployed everywhere, the availability of streaming data is increasing. Handling such time-dependent data presents some unique challenges.
(c) Along with RDF triples, sometimes provenance information such as source of the data, date of creation, or last modification is also captured. This information helps in setting privacy policies and also to measure the quality of the data. In large RDF graphs, adding provenance information would only make the graph larger. Suitable mechanisms are needed to handle and manage provenance information.
(d) In order for a field to grow and mature, it is necessary for the community to develop efficient tools that help in user adoption of the technologies. An important aspect in the development of tools is the presence of good benchmarks. They push developers to keep improving their systems.

In this book, we provide a comprehensive discussion of all these topics, including the challenges and existing solutions.

1.3   Book Roadmap

Chapter 2 provides the reader with background information that is necessary to follow the course of this book. We introduce the fundamentals of Linked Data, RDF data model, and the query language (SPARQL). We also introduce the OWL ontology language, the reasoning based on the ontologies, and various ontology profiles. Furthermore, we describe data processing frameworks that are leveraged to store and query Linked Data.

Chapter 3 discusses the details of the design and implementation for different schemes of scalable centralized RDF query engines. In principle, we present a set of RDF storage and querying systems that relies mainly on the relational systems with various design decisions for data models (statement table, property tables, and vertical partitioning) and the index permutation schemes. Furthermore, we discuss systems that store and query RDF data as a graph-based model or using a compact in-memory representation.

As the centralized systems are limited in their physical capacity to handle increasing amounts of data, the Linked Data community developed a number of distributed systems with a high degree of parallelism to tackle the challenges of providing scalable SPARQL query engines over massive amounts of RDF data. Chapter 4 provides an overview of various techniques and systems for efficiently querying large RDF datasets in distributed environments. In particular, we introduce systems that leverage existing data processing frameworks (i.e., NoSQL, Hadoop, Spark). In addition, we discuss systems that have been designed to work in main memory and systems that go beyond this classification. Finally, we describe systems that are designed to handle highly distributed Linked Data published by various uncoordinated data providers, namely, federated query processing systems.

Chapter 5 discusses the challenges of dealing with RDF stream data. We present the design and implementation of RDF stream processing and RDF-based complex event processing engines. We discuss how to model and represent the stream data using RDF and how to design a query language (e.g., as an extension of SPARQL) to query stream data continuously. Along with theoretical foundations, we present the design principles and the important implementation aspects of RDF stream processing systems such as time management, scheduling, and memory management. Finally, we provide an overview of popular systems in this domain.

Chapter 6 discusses different approaches to distributed RDF reasoning. This chapter describes the process of rule-based RDF reasoning and it discusses different scalable algorithms used by RDF reasoning systems. We categorize these systems into five: Peer-to-Peer systems, Hadoop-based systems, RDF reasoning systems based on NoSQL databases, Spark-based systems, and shared-memory RDF reasoning systems. Finally, we briefly describe similar techniques for rule-based reasoning in other Semantic Web languages.

Benchmarks are essential for assessing the ability of systems to address technical difficulties, also known as *choke points*, and can be used to improve the systems' performance. Chapter 7 discusses the most popular benchmarks that have been developed over the last years for RDF query engines and instance matching systems for linked data. We present the principles described in the literature for benchmark development and the existing benchmark frameworks. In addition, we provide an in-depth overview of the different frameworks for benchmarking query engines as well as instance matching systems for linked data.

Chapter 8 provides an overview of the different provenance models for Linked Data. In general, provenance is versatile and could include various types of information such as the source of the data, information on the processes that led to a certain result, date of creation or last modification, and authorship. In practice, recording and managing the provenance of data is of paramount importance as it allows the models to support trust mechanisms, privacy policies, and quality management among other crucial applications in the Linked Data Cloud. In this chapter, we cover the provenance models for all the fragments of the SPARQL language including the models for SPARQL updates. We also discuss various systems that have been designed to implement provenance models for Linked Data.

Finally, we provide some conclusions and an outlook for future research challenges in Chap. 9.

Chapter 2
Fundamentals

Linked Data refers to links between data sources, as well as the practice of connecting data on the Web. In contrast to the isolated data silos of the conventional Web, the Semantic Web aims to interconnect these data so that all datasets contribute to a global data integration, connecting data from diverse domains and sources. In practice, all concepts underpinning Linked Data are standardized by the World Wide Web Consortium. The Consortium publishes recommendations defining and describing in detail the technologies behind Linked Data. This chapter briefly introduces the basic concepts underpinning Linked Data technologies and that are necessary to follow the course of this book. We present a data model, a query language, vocabularies, and a data exchange format. In addition, we provide an overview of emerging big data storage and processing frameworks that are frequently used for RDF data management (e.g., NoSQL databases, Hadoop, Spark).

2.1 Linked Data

Linked Data extends the principles of the World Wide Web from linking documents to that of linking pieces of data and creating a Web of Data; it specifies data relationships and provides machine-processable data to the Internet. It is based on standard Web techniques but extends them to provide data exchange and integration. The four main principles of the Web of Linked Data, as defined by Tim Berners-Lee [39], are:

- Use URIs (Uniform Resource Identifier)[1] as names for things.
- Use HTTP (Hypertext Transfer Protocol)[2] URIs so that people can look up those names.

---

[1] http://www.w3.org/Addressing/.
[2] http://www.w3.org/Protocols/.

© Springer International Publishing AG 2018
S. Sakr et al., *Linked Data*, https://doi.org/10.1007/978-3-319-73515-3_2

- When someone looks up a URI, provide useful information, using standards (Resource Description Framework,[3] SPARQL Query Language.[4])
- Include links to other URIs, so that they can discover more things.

Linked Data in general is a static snapshot of information, though it can express events and temporal aspects of entities with specific vocabulary terms.[5] A snapshot of the state can be seen as a separate (named) RDF graph containing the current state of the universe. Changes in data typically concern relationships between resources; IRIs and Literals are constant and rarely change their value. In general, Linked Data allows data to be combined and processed from many sources [39]. The basic triple representation of pieces of data when combined together results in large RDF graphs. Such large amounts of data are made available as Linked Data where datasets are interlinked and published on the Web.

In practice, Linked Data can be serialized in a number of formats that are logically equivalent. The data can be stored in the following formats:

- **N-Triples**[6]: It provides a simple, plain-text way to serialize Linked Data. Each line in a file represents a triple; the period at the end signals the end of a statement (triple). This format is often used to exchange large amounts of Linked Data and for processing graphs with stream-oriented tools.

```
<http://ex/sbj1> <http://ex/pred1> <http://ex/obj1> .
<http://ex/sbj1> <http://ex/pred2> <http://ex/obj2> .
<http://ex/sbj2> <http://ex/pred3> <http://ex/obj1> .
```

- **N-Quads**[7]: It is a simple extension of N-Triples. It allows a fourth optional element to be added in a line denoting a named graph IRI, which the triple belongs to.

```
<http://ex/sbj1> <http://ex/pred1> <http://ex/obj1> <graph1> .
<http://ex/sbj1> <http://ex/pred2> <http://ex/obj2> <graph1> .
<http://ex/sbj2> <http://ex/pred3> <http://ex/obj1> <graph2> .
```

- **Turtle**[8]: It is an extension of N-Triples; it introduces a number of syntactic shortcuts, such as prefixes, lists, and shorthands for data-typed literal. It provides a trade-off between ease of writing, parsing, and readability. It does not support the notion of named graphs.

```
@base <http://example.org/> .
@prefix rdf: <http://www.w3.org/1999/02/22-rdf-syntax-ns#> .
@prefix rdfs: <http://www.w3.org/2000/01/rdf-schema#> .
@prefix foaf: <http://xmlns.com/foaf/0.1/> .
@prefix rel: <http://www.perceive.net/schemas/relationship/> .
```

---

[3]http://www.w3.org/RDF/.

[4]http://www.w3.org/TR/sparql11-query/.

[5]https://www.w3.org/TR/rdf11-concepts/.

[6]https://www.w3.org/TR/n-triples/.

[7]https://www.w3.org/TR/n-quads/.

[8]https://www.w3.org/TR/turtle/.

```
<#green−goblin>
    rel : enemyOf  <#spiderman> ;
    a  foaf : Person  ;       # in  the  context  of  the  Marvel  universe
    foaf : name  "Green␣Goblin"  .

<#spiderman>
    rel : enemyOf  <#green−goblin> ;
    a  foaf : Person  ;
    foaf : name  "Spiderman" ,  "−"@ru  .
```

- **TriG**[9]: It extends Turtle to support multiple named graphs.

```
# This  document  contains  a  default  graph  and  two  named  graphs .

@prefix  rdf :  <http ://www.w3.org/1999/02/22 − rdf−syntax−ns#>  .
@prefix  dc :  <http :// purl . org/dc/terms/>  .
@prefix  foaf :  <http :// xmlns .com/foaf /0.1/>  .

# default  graph
    {
        <http :// example . org /bob>  dc : publisher  "Bob"  .
        <http :// example . org/ alice >  dc : publisher  "Alice"  .
    }

<http :// example . org /bob>
    {
        _:a  foaf : name  "Bob"  .
        _:a  foaf : mbox  <mailto : bob@oldcorp. example . org>  .
        _:a  foaf : knows  _:b  .
    }

<http :// example . org / alice >
    {
        _:b  foaf : name  "Alice"  .
        _:b  foaf : mbox  <mailto : alice@work . example . org>  .
    }
```

- **JSON-LD**[10]: It provides a JSON syntax for Linked Data. It can be used to transform JSON documents into Linked Data and offers universal identifiers for JSON objects and a way in which a JSON document can link to an object in another document.

```
{
    "@context":  "http :// json−ld . org / contexts / person . jsonld" ,
    "@id":  "http :// dbpedia . org / resource / John_Lennon" ,
    "name":  "John␣Lennon" ,
    "born":  "1940−10−09" ,
    "spouse":  "http :// dbpedia . org / resource / Cynthia_Lennon"
}
```

---

[9]https://www.w3.org/TR/trig/.
[10]https://json-ld.org/.

- **RDFa**[11]: It is a syntax used to embed Linked Data in HTML and XML documents. This enables the aggregation of data from web pages where it can be used to enrich search results or presentation.

```
<html xmlns=" http ://www.w3.org/1999/xhtml">
  <head>
    <title >Homepage </title >
    <meta name="author" content="John_Smith" />
    <link rel="prev" href="intro.html" />
    <link rel="next" href="bio.html" />
  </head>
  <body >... </body>
</html>
```

- **RDF/XML**[12]: It provides an XML syntax for Linked Data.

```
<rdf:Description >
  <ex:editor >
    <rdf:Description >
      <ex:homePage >
        <rdf:Description >
        </rdf:Description >
      </ex:homePage >
    </rdf:Description >
  </ex:editor >
</rdf:Description >
```

2.2 RDF

Linked Data uses RDF, the Resource Description Framework, as its basic data model. RDF provides the means to describe resources in a semi-structured manner. The information expressed using RDF can be exchanged and processed by applications. The ability to exchange and interlink data on the Web means that it can be used by applications other than those for which it was originally created and that it can be linked to further pieces of information to enrich existing data. It is a graph-based format, optionally defining a data schema, to represent information about resources. RDF allows statements to be created in the form of triples consisting of *Subject, Predicate, Object*. A statement expresses a relationship (defined by a predicate) between resources (subject and object). The relationship is always from subject to object (it is directional). The same resource can be used in multiple triples playing the same or different roles, for example, it can be used as the subject in one triple and as the object in another. This ability enables multiple connections to be defined between the triples, hence creating a connected graph of data. The graph can

---

[11]https://www.w3.org/TR/rdfa-syntax/.

[12]https://www.w3.org/TR/rdf-syntax-grammar/.

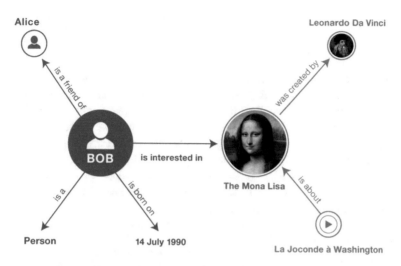

Fig. 2.1 An exemplary graph of triples [418]. ©2009 W3C (MIT, ERCIM, Keio), All Rights Reserved. Reprinted with Permission

be represented as nodes representing resources and edges representing relationships between the nodes. Figure 2.1 depicts a simple example of RDF graphs.

Data depicted in Fig. 2.1 describes two main recourses *Bob* and *The Mona Lisa* and their relation *Bob* → *is interested in* → *The Mona Lisa*. In this relation, *Bob* is a subject, *is interested in* is a predicate, and *The Mona Lisa* is an object. The data from Fig. 2.1 can be encoded in the form of triples (*Subject, Predicate, Object*) as follows:

```
<Bob> <is_a> <Person> .
<Bob> <is_a_friend_of> <Alice> .
<Bob> <in_born_on> "14 July 1990" .
<Bob> <is_interested_in> <The_Mona_Lisa> .
<The_Mona_Lisa> <was_created_by> <Leonardo_Da_Vinci> .
<La_Jaconde_a_Washington> <is_about> <The_Mona_Lisa> .
```

Elements appearing in the triples (subjects, predicates, objects) can be of one of the following types:

- **IRI (Internationalized Resource Identifier)** identifies a resource. It provides a global identifier for a resource without implying its location or a way to access it. The identifier can be reused by others to identify the same resource. IRI is a generalization of URI (Uniform Resource Identifier) allowing non-ASCII characters to be used. IRI can appear at all three positions in a triple (subject, predicate, object).
- **Literal** is a basic string value that is not an IRI. It can be associated with a data type and thus can be parsed and correctly interpreted. It is allowed only as the object of a triple.

- **Blank node** is used to denote a resource without assigning a global identifier with an IRI; it is a local unique identifier used within a specific RDF graph. It is allowed as the subject and the object in a triple.

The framework provides a way to co-locate triples in a subset and to associate such subsets with an IRI.[13] A subset of triples constitutes an independent graph of data (named graph). In practice, it provides data managers with a mechanism to create a collection of triples. A dataset can consist of multiple named graphs and no more than one unnamed (default) graph. For example, data depicted in Fig. 2.1 can be divided into two named graphs, one with the main subject *Bob* and the other with *The Mona Lisa*; the resources remain linked. The modified data can be encoded in the form of N-Quads (*Subject, Predicate, Object, graph*) as follows:

```
<Bob> <is_a> <Person> <Graph1_Bob> .
<Bob> <is_a_friend_of> <Alice> <Graph1_Bob> .
<Bob> <in_born_on> "14 July 1990" <Graph1_Bob> .
<Bob> <is_interested_in> <The_Mona_Lisa> <Graph1_Bob> .
<The_Mona_Lisa> <was_created_by> <Leonardo_Da_Vinci> <
    Graph2_MonaLisa> .
<La_Jaconde_a_Washington> <is_about> <The_Mona_Lisa> <
    Graph2_MonaLisa> .
```

Even though RDF does not require any naming convention for IRIs and does not impose any schema on data, it can be used in combination with vocabularies provided by the RDF Schema language.[14] RDFS is a semantic extension of RDF enabling to specify semantic characteristics of RDF data. It provides a data-modeling vocabulary for RDF data. Additionally, it allows the ability to state that an IRI is a property and that a subject and an object of the IRI have to be of a certain type. RDF schema allows the classification of resources with categories (i.e., classes, types). We can use the property *rdf:type* to specify that a resource is of a certain type.

```
<Person> <rdf:type> <rdfs:Class> .
<Bob> <rdf:type> <Person> .
```

Classes allow to regroup resources. Members of a class are called instances, while classes are also resources and can be described with triples. RDFS allows classes and properties to be hierarchical as a class can be a subclass of a more generic class. In the same way, properties can be defined as a specific property (sub-property) of a more generic one. Below we present an example of class hierarchy, depicted also in Fig. 2.2.

```
<Person> <rdf:type> <rdfs:Class> .
<Artist> <rdfs:subClassOf> <Person> .
<Cruck> <rdfs:subClassOf> <Person> .
<Researcher> <rdfs:subClassOf> <Person> .
<Noble prize winner> <rdfs:subClassOf> <Researcher> .
```

---

[13]https://www.w3.org/TR/rdf11-datasets/.

[14]https://www.w3.org/TR/2014/PER-rdf-schema-20140109/.

Fig. 2.2 "subClassOf"
relations between RDF
classes

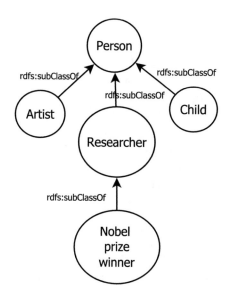

RDFS also provides the ability to specify a domain and a range of a predicate, that is, types of resources allowed as subjects and objects. With the *rdfs:domain* property, we can define what types of subjects are related with a predicate. The property *rdfs:range* defines what kinds of objects are related with a predicate. For example, we can define that the predicate *:takesCourse* takes as subjects instances of the class *:Student* and as objects instances of the class *:Course*:

```
<:takesCourse > <rdfs:domain> <:Student> .
<:takesCourse > <rdfs:range> <:Course> .
<:givesCourse > <rdfs:domain> <:Lecturer> .
<:givesCourse > <rdfs:range> <:Course> .
<:Student1 > <:takesCourse> <:Course1> .
<:Lecturer1 > <:givesCourse> <:Course1> .
```

The properties *rdfs:domain* and *rdfs:range* allow us to execute some reasoning. From the example above, we can deduce that *Student1* is of type *Student* and *Course1* is of type *Course*. The triples below can be inferred even though they are not explicitly stated in the data:

```
<:Student1 > <rdf:type> <:Student> .
<:Course1 > <rdf:type> <:Course> .
```

Properties are also resources that can be described by triples. They can be used as subjects in conjunction with domain and range or to define hierarchy of properties. They can also be used with user-defined properties to introduce enhanced semantics.

An instance can be associated with several independent classes specifying different sets of properties. One can define, for example:

```
<:John> <rdf:type> <:Student> .
<:John> <rdf:type> <:Lecturer> .
```

RDFS also provides a set of utility properties allowing it to link pieces of data like:

- *seeAlso* to indicate a resource providing additional information about the resource of a subject
- *rdfs:isDefinedBy* to indicate a resource providing a definition of the subject
- *rdf:value* which may be used to describe structured values

Another interesting vocabulary set defined by RDFS is reification, which allows the ability to write statements about statements. Reification can be used to provide additional metadata about a triple (e.g., provenance, timestamp, version). Let us use one of our previous example triples:

```
<:John>  <rdf:type>  <:Student>  .
```

Using reification we create a unique ID for this triple and we describe it with the following triples:

```
_:triple1  <rdf:type>  <rdf:Statement>  .
_:triple1  <rdf:subject>  <:John>
_:triple1  <rdf:predicate>  <rdf:type>
_:triple1  <rdf:object>  <:Student>  .
```

With the above triple, we can now provide additional information about this triple, for example:

```
_:triple1  <prov:wasDerivedFrom>  _:triple99
_:triple1  <prov:wasGeneratedBy>  <FacultyOfCS>
_:triple1  <prov:generatedAtTime>  "2012−04−03T13:35:23Z"^^xsd:
    dateTime;
```

Richer vocabularies or ontology languages (e.g., OWL) enable to express logical constraints on Web data. The OWL 2 Web Ontology Language[15] provides the ability to define ontologies to give a semantic meaning to the data. An ontology provides classes, properties, and data values. An ontology is exchanged along with the data as an RDF document and defines vocabularies and relationships between terms, often covering a specific domain shared by a community. An ontology can also be seen as an RDF graph, where terms are represented by nodes and relationships between them are expressed by edges. We describe OWL and ontologies in Sect. 2.4.

2.3 SPARQL

To facilitate querying and manipulating Linked Data on the Web, a semantic query language is needed. Such a language, named SPARQL Protocol and RDF Query Language, was introduced by the World Wide Web Consortium. In general, RDF is a directed labeled graph data format. Therefore, SPARQL is mainly a graph-matching

---

[15]https://www.w3.org/TR/owl2-overview/.

query language. SPARQL[16] can be used to formulate queries ranging from simple graph patterns to very complex analytic queries. Given an RDF database D, a query Q consists of a pattern which is matched against D, and the values obtained from this matching are processed to give the answer. The database D to be queried can be composed of multiple sources. SPARQL queries contain a set of triple patterns called *basic graph patterns*, which are like RDF triples except that each of the subject, predicate, and object could be a variable. A basic graph pattern matches a subgraph of the RDF graph and when the variables in the basic graph pattern are replaced by values from the RDF graph, it results in an RDF (sub) graph. This resultant RDF (sub) graph can be further queried or joined with the results of other basic graph patterns in the query. An example of a SPARQL SELECT query with a basic graph pattern is given below.

```
SELECT ?countryName
WHERE {
    ?country a type:LandLockedCountries .
    ?country rdfs:label ?countryName .
}
```

This SPARQL query asks for a list of countries that do not have a coastline and are surrounded entirely by land. It has two basic graph patterns—the first graph pattern asks for countries that are landlocked and the second graph pattern gets the human readable label for each country. Queries may include unions, optionals, filters, value aggregations, path expressions, sub-queries, value assignment, etc. An extension of the previous example that asks for a list of landlocked countries with a population of more than 15 million is given below.

```
SELECT ?countryName
WHERE {
    ?country a type:LandLockedCountries .
    ?country rdfs:label ?countryName .
    ?country prop:populationEstimate ?population .
    FILTER (?population > 15000000) .
}
```

In the above two examples, `rdfs`, `type`, and `prop` are convenient short forms for the following IRIs:

```
<http://www.w3.org/2000/01/rdf-schema#>
<http://dbpedia.org/class/yago/> and
<http://dbpedia.org/property/>
```

These short forms (local part of a namespace) can be declared using the PREFIX keyword. The complete example query with the PREFIX labels mapped to IRIs is given below.

---

[16]https://www.w3.org/TR/sparql11-overview/.

```
PREFIX rdfs: <http://www.w3.org/2000/01/rdf-schema#>
PREFIX type: <http://dbpedia.org/class/yago/> and
PREFIX prop: <http://dbpedia.org/property/>
SELECT ?countryName
WHERE {
    ?country a type:LandLockedCountries .
    ?country rdfs:label ?countryName .
    ?country prop:populationEstimate ?population .
    FILTER (?population > 15000000) .
}
```

In general, a SPARQL query Q specifies a graph pattern P which is matched against an RDF graph G. The query matching process is performed via matching the variables in P with the elements of G such that the returned graph is contained in G (pattern matching). In practice, most RDF stores can be searched using queries that are composed of *triple patterns*. A triple pattern is much like a triple, except that S, P, and O can be replaced by variables. Similar to triples, triple patterns are modeled as directed graphs. In general, a set of triple patterns is called a *basic graph pattern (BGP)* and SPARQL queries that only include such type of patterns are called BGP queries. In practice, SPARQL BGP queries can have different shapes (Fig. 2.3):

- *Star* query: only consists of subject-subject joins where a join variable is the subject of all the triple patterns involved in the query.
- *Chain* query: consists of subject-object joins where the triple patterns are consecutively connected like a chain.
- *Tree* query: consists of subject-subject joins and subject-object joins.
- *Cycle* query: contains subject-subject joins, subject-object joins, and object-object joins.
- *Complex* query: consists of a combination of different shapes.

Apart from SELECT queries, the SPARQL language also supports other constructs such as:

- **ASK** query to retrieve binary "yes/no" answer to a query
- **CONSTRUCT** query to construct new RDF graphs from a query result
- **DESCRIBE** query to return a single result (RDF graph) that contains details of a resource

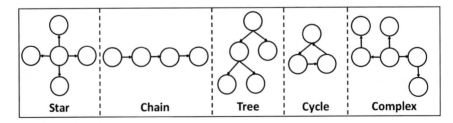

Fig. 2.3 Shapes of SPARQL BGP Queries

For more details of the different features of the SPARQL language, we refer the reader to the SPARQL overview and specifications document [415]. Chapters 3 and 4 discuss various *centralized* and *distributed* techniques for scalable processing of SPARQL queries over RDF databases, respectively.

2.4 OWL

OWL is a Semantic Web language used to build ontologies [364] which in turn represent the knowledge about things, groups of things, and the relations between them [184]. It is used to formally encode domain knowledge, that is, knowledge about some part of the world which is often referred to as the domain of interest. In order to build an ontology, it is important to come up with the vocabulary of the domain, that is, a set of terms and the relationships between them. These form the axioms in an ontology. The process of building an ontology and maintaining it over the course of its lifetime is referred to as *ontology engineering* [140]. Building an ontology is an iterative process and involves the following steps:

- *Domain and scope*: The first step is to determine the domain of the ontology and then, in consultation with the domain experts, determine the scope of the ontology. If the scope is not restricted, then the ontology engineering process would be never-ending.
- *Competency questions*: As part of setting the scope of an ontology, it is important to come up with competency questions with the help of domain experts. These are the questions that the applications would ask of the knowledge base. Competency questions would also be useful later on to assess the ontology.
- *Reuse*: One of the best practices in ontology engineering is to reuse, fully or partially, existing ontologies. This not only saves time and effort but also helps to interconnect data across different sources. We can search for existing ontologies in several well-known ontology repositories such as the NCBO BioPortal,[17] OBO Foundry,[18] Ontology Design Patterns,[19] Linked Open Vocabularies,[20] and the Manchester OWL Repository.[21]
- *Domain vocabulary*: The next step, in conjunction with the domain experts, is to come up with a list of terms that are frequently used in the domain. We can take notes or record the statements that a domain expert uses when describing the domain of interest. This could be iterative and the statements can be recorded across several sessions. After getting a list of statements, noun phrases (including

---

[17]http://bioportal.bioontology.org/ontologies.

[18]http://obofoundry.org/.

[19]http://ontologydesignpatterns.org/.

[20]http://lov.okfn.org/dataset/lov/.

[21]http://mowlrepo.cs.manchester.ac.uk/.

nouns) and verb phrases (including verbs) can be identified. This is useful for the next step.

- *Define classes and properties*: Among the terms, nouns become the classes, especially if the nouns are collection of elements that have similar properties, and verbs become the properties. After the classes are identified, the next step is to identify any specialization-generalization, partonomy relations among the classes and properties. This helps us to create the class and property hierarchy.

Some of the steps mentioned above can be repeated as needed while building an ontology. Several tools are available to assist in ontology engineering, such as ontology editors (e.g., Protégé[22]), ontology visualization tools (e.g., WebVOWL[23]), reasoners (next section), and triple stores (e.g., Virtuoso[24]).

Description Logics (DLs) are a family of knowledge representation languages and they provide a formal underpinning for OWL [226]. Most of the DLs are decidable fragments of first-order logic. DLs have a trade-off between expressivity and tractability of reasoning. In the latest version of OWL, referred to as OWL 2, three profiles (OWL 2 EL, OWL 2 QL, OWL 2 RL) that offer tractable reasoning were developed. These three profiles are discussed in more detail in Sect. 2.6. The DLs underlying OWL 2 EL and OWL 2 QL are $\mathcal{EL}^{++}$ [31] and DL-Lite [64]. OWL 2 RL is inspired by DLP [152] and pD* [379]. Some of the terminology used in the Semantic Web comes from the Description Logics parlance. We describe these terminologies next.

DL ontologies have three types of building blocks: (1) *Individuals* are instances in the domain and are the same as constants in first-order logic. In OWL also, they are called by the same name. (2) *Concepts* are groups of individuals that share similar characteristics. They are the same as unary predicates in first-order logic and are called classes in OWL. (3) *Roles* represent binary relations between the individuals. They are the same as binary predicates in first-order logic and are called properties in OWL. The knowledge or the axioms in an ontology can be categorized into TBox, ABox, and RBox. The terminological knowledge or TBox defines the general notions or the conceptualization of the domain, whereas the assertional knowledge or ABox defines the concrete notions or facts of the domain. RBox are the relational axioms that represent the properties on roles. In a database setting, TBox corresponds to the schema and ABox corresponds to the data [32]. Examples of axioms that belong to ABox, TBox, and RBox in DL as well as in RDFS syntax are given below.

Person(mary)	:mary rdf:type :Person
hasWife(john,mary)	:john :hasWife :mary
Women ⊑ Person	:Women rdfs:subClassOf :Person
hasSon ⊑ hasChild	:hasSon rdfs:subPropertyOf :hasChild

---

[22]https://protege.stanford.edu/.

[23]http://vowl.visualdataweb.org/webvowl.html.

[24]https://virtuoso.openlinksw.com/.

The first two statements are ABox axioms. `Person(mary)` is a concept assertion that states that `mary` is an individual and it is an instance of concept `Person`. `hasWife(john,mary)` is a role assertion that states that the individual `john` is in a relation named `hasWife` with the individual `mary`. Simply put, this assertion states that `john hasWife mary` which is given in the corresponding RDFS syntax. The third statement `Women ⊑ Person` is a TBox axiom. It is a concept inclusion which states that the concept `Women` is subsumed by the concept `Person`. The last statement from the example `hasSon ⊑ hasChild` is an RBox axiom. It is a role inclusion which states that the role `hasSon` is a subrole of the role `hasChild`. This means that every pair of individuals that is related by `hasSon` is also related by `hasChild`. More examples and details of other relations are available in [226].

There are two main assumptions that DLs and OWL follow—*Open World Assumption* and *Unique Name Assumption* [183]. In practice, DLs and, as a consequence, OWL are designed to deal with incomplete information in the form of *Open World Assumption*. The open world assumption makes the assumption that what is not known is simply unknown rather than be false, which is the theory followed by Closed World Assumption. Relational databases follow closed world assumption where querying on the data that is absent in the database returns a false. On the other hand, a similar query on an OWL knowledge base would return an *unknown*. The other assumption that most of the DLs and OWL make is called the *Unique Name Assumption*. It states that individuals that have different names need not necessarily refer to different individuals. In order to indicate that two differently named individuals are indeed different, it has to be explicitly asserted in the knowledge base that the two individuals are different.

2.5 Reasoning

The term *knowledge base* is often associated with models having different levels of semantics, starting with a loose vocabulary of terms and going up to a formal OWL model. In this book, we consider RDF and OWL models as knowledge bases. Reasoning is one of the important operations that can be performed over a knowledge base (ontology). Since OWL is a declarative language, it does not specify how reasoning should be done. This task is performed by the reasoner. Reasoning is required to infer logical consequences and check the consistency of the knowledge base. These are two standard reasoning tasks. The reasoning task that is of interest to us is called *classification*, which is the computation of the complete subclass relation hierarchy for each concept in the ontology. Consider the following related facts:

1. John is a US citizen.
2. Someone who is a US citizen has a US passport.
3. Someone who has a US passport does not require an EU visa.

After reasoning on these facts, among other things, the following logical consequences are derived:

(a) Each US citizen does not require an EU visa.
(b) John does not require an EU visa.

After deriving these logical consequences, it is easy to answer questions such as "does John require an EU visa?" which cannot be answered based on just the given three facts. From the three given facts, it is trivial for a human to come up with the derived conclusions. A reasoner allows a machine to not only automatically derive the conclusions from the given knowledge but also do it at a larger scale. There are currently several well-known and efficient reasoners such as ELK [211], Konclude [365], Pellet [359], HermiT [138], FaCT++ [383], Snorocket [262], etc. Reasoners either use tableau algorithms which involve constructing models [30] or use inference rules to derive logical consequences [357]. Chapter 6 considers the rule-based approach where we apply a set of inference rules on the given ontology until no new logical consequence can be derived. This is known as fixpoint iteration.

Two of the well-known inferencing approaches are forward chaining and backward chaining [326]. In forward chaining, we start with the available facts in the knowledge base and apply inference (also called entailment) rules to derive new inferences. This process is continued iteratively until a goal is reached, which in this case is complete materialization of all possible inferences. This iterative process is also known as fixpoint iteration and is described in Algorithm 1.

Example Consider the following RDF triples as the knowledge base.

```
<MotorVehicle> <rdf:type> <rdfs:Class> .
<PassengerVehicle> <rdfs:subClassOf> <MotorVehicle> .
<Truck> <rdfs:subClassOf> <MotorVehicle> .
<Van> <rdfs:subClassOf> <MotorVehicle> .
<MiniVan> <rdfs:subClassOf> <PassengerVehicle> .
<KiaSedona> <rdf:type> <MiniVan> .
```

The rule set is as follows:

r_1 If <uuu> <rdfs:subClassOf> <xxx> and <vvv> <rdf:type> <uuu> then
       <vvv> <rdf:type> <xxx>

r_2 If <uuu> <rdfs:subClassOf> <vvv> and <vvv> <rdfs:subClassOf> <xxx> then
       <uuu> <rdfs:subClassOf> <xxx>

Algorithm 1 Algorithm for inferencing using the forward-chaining approach

---

Require: Knowledge Base (KB), rule set (R)
1: newKB ← KB
2: **repeat**
3:     oldKB ← newKB
4:     **for all** r ∈ R **do**
5:         inferredSet ← applyRule(r, newKB)
6:         newKB ← newKB ∪ inferredSet   ▷ Add inferred facts to newKB
7:     **end for**
8: **until** oldKB == newKB

Here <uuu>, <vvv>, <xxx> are variables and can be replaced by values from the knowledge base such as <MiniVan>, <PassengerVehicle>, <KiaSedona>, etc.

Following steps 4–7 in Algorithm 1, we apply rules r_1 and r_2 on the given knowledge base to produce the following triples:

<KiaSedona> <rdf:type> <PassengerVehicle>
<MiniVan> <rdfs:subClassOf> <MotorVehicle>

After adding these inferred triples back to the knowledge base, as indicated in step 6 of Algorithm 1 and applying rules r_1, r_2 again on the knowledge base, the triple <KiaSedona> <rdf:type> <MotorVehicle> is inferred. After adding this triple to the knowledge base, the two rules are again applied. This does not produce any new triples. So the iterative process stops here.

Backward chaining, on the other hand, starts with the goal (often a query on the knowledge base) and works backwards by chaining through inference rules to find known facts. This process is described in Algorithm 2.

Example Consider the same knowledge base and rules as were used for forward chaining. The query in this case is "Is KiaSedona a MotorVehicle?". The first step in the backward-chaining algorithm is to check whether the given query is already in the data (ABox) of the knowledge base. The only data present in our knowledge base is <KiaSedona> <rdf:type> <MiniVan> and this does not match the query. The *matchesAfterSubstitution* function replaces the variables (if any) in the first argument with the constants from the second argument and then checks if the two arguments match. In the case of the previous step, as indicated, it does not match. So we go through steps 10–17 in Algorithm 2 by checking the consequents (*then* part of the rule). The consequent of rule r_1 (<vvv> <rdf:type> <xxx>) matches

---

Algorithm 2 Algorithm for inferencing using the backward-chaining approach

Require: Knowledge Base (KB), rule set (R), and query (q)
1: fs ← facts(KB)
2: results ← ∅
3: **function** MATCHGOAL(q)
4:     **for all** f ∈ fs **do**
5:         **if** matchesAfterSubstitution(f, q) **then**
6:             results ← results ∪ {f}
7:             **return** results
8:         **end if**
9:     **end for**
10:    **for all** r ∈ R **do**
11:        c ← consequent(r)
12:        **if** matchesAfterSubstitution(c, q) **then**
13:            a ← antecedent(r)
14:            res ← MATCHGOAL(a)
15:            results ← results ∪ res
16:        **end if**
17:    **end for**
18:    **return** results
19: **end function**

the given query. After substitution, we get <KiaSedona> <rdf:type> <MotorVehicle>. Making the same substitutions in the antecedent (*If* part of the rule), we get <uuu > <rdfs:subClassOf> <MotorVehicle> and <KiaSedona> <rdf:type> <uuu>. Now, we need to continue with the recursive call (step 14) with these two antecedents separately and match them first with the data and, in case of not finding any match, check the consequents of the rules. <KiaSedona> <rdf:type> <uuu> matches the data <KiaSedona > <rdf:type> <MiniVan>. So <uuu> can be replaced with <MiniVan>. Using the same substitution in the other antecedent, we get <MiniVan> <rdfs:subClassOf> <MotorVehicle >. We repeat the process of matching this with the consequents of the rules and find the consequent of rule r_2 as a result. After substitution of <uuu> with <MiniVan > and <xxx> with <MotorVehicle>, the antecedents are <MiniVan> <rdfs:subClassOf> <vvv> and <vvv> <rdfs:subClassOf> <MotorVehicle>. <MiniVan> <rdfs:subClassOf> <vvv> matches with <MiniVan> <rdfs:subClassOf> <PassengerVehicle> in the knowledge base after substituting <vvv> with <PassengerVehicle>. The same substitution can also be made in the other antecedent <vvv> <rdfs:subClassOf> <MotorVehicle> and it would match <PassengerVehicle> <rdfs:subClassOf> <MotorVehicle> present in the knowledge base. At this point, we can stop the backward-chaining process since all the substitutions have been made. We can conclude that <KiaSedona> <rdf:type> <MotorVehicle>, that is, "KiaSedona is a MotorVehicle".

As shown in Fig. 2.4, a reasoner is invisible to the application interacting with the knowledge base. It makes the implicit knowledge explicit, which in turn helps the applications to get more complete answers. The reasoner in Fig. 2.4 can be either a forward-chaining reasoner or a backward-chaining reasoner. In the case of forward-chaining reasoner, all the implicit facts are inferred and materialized offline. But in the case of backward-chaining reasoner, depending on the query submitted by the application, reasoning happens on the fly.

Fig. 2.4 Reasoner makes the implicit knowledge in the knowledge base explicit

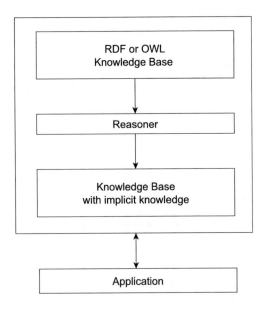

2.6   OWL 2 Profiles

With the focus on tractability and scalability, the most recent version of OWL, referred to as OWL 2, provides three profiles or fragments, namely, OWL 2 EL, OWL 2 QL, and OWL 2 RL [184, 271]. Each profile offers different expressivity features and hence is useful in different application scenarios. They provide different aspects of expressivity in order to obtain different computational and implementation benefits. None of these profiles is a subset of each other, but there is some overlap among them as indicated in Fig. 2.5.

OWL 2 EL is useful in domains where there are complex descriptions and a very large number of concepts and relations. The description logic underlying this profile is $\mathcal{EL}^{++}$ [31]. This profile provides existential quantification and hence the name EL. Several large biomedical ontologies such as SNOMED CT, NCI Thesaurus, Galen, etc., are in this profile. It can also be used in modeling other complex domains such as system configurations, product inventories, and other scientific domains. Compared to the other two profiles, this profile has comparatively expressive class expressions. This profile also has fairly expressive property expressions, including property chains. But it does not support negation, disjunction, universal quantification, or inverse properties. All the standard reasoning tasks take polynomial time with respect to the size of the ontology.

OWL 2 QL is useful in applications that have large instance data (ABox) and where the primary reasoning task is query answering. This profile is suitable for representing database schemas (entity relationships). Different databases can be integrated by designing a higher-level ontology. The process of using an ontology to describe, query, and integrate databases is called ontology-based data access (OBDA) [221]. Queries, referred to as conjunctive queries [216], written with respect to the ontology can be rewritten to a relational query language. This is the basis for the profile's name. Sound and complete conjunctive query answering can be performed in LOGSPACE (more precisely AC^0) with respect to the size of the

Fig. 2.5 OWL 2 profiles.

data (assertional knowledge). The description logic underlying this profile is DL-Lite [64]. OWL 2 QL does not allow existential quantification of roles to a class expression. But unlike OWL 2 EL, it supports inverse properties.

The OWL 2 RL profile is suitable for enriching RDF data with rules. It also allows for scalable reasoning without giving up too much of expressivity. Reasoning in this profile can be implemented using a standard rule language. This is the reason behind naming this profile OWL 2 RL. The design of this profile is inspired from Description Logic Programs (DLP) [152] and pD* [379]. All the standard reasoning tasks can be performed in polynomial time with respect to the size of the ontology. Among other things, existential quantification is not supported in this profile.

For further details related to Linked Data, we refer the reader to the following documents:

- RDF 1.1 Primer [418]
- RDF 1.1 Concepts and Abstract Syntax [416]
- RDF Schema 1.1 [419]
- RDF 1.1: On Semantics of RDF Datasets [417]
- OWL 2 Web Ontology Language [414]
- SPARQL 1.1 Overview [415]

2.7 Modern Big Data Storage and Processing Systems

The new scale of Big Data has been attracting a lot of interest from both the research and industrial communities with the aim of creating the best means to process and analyze these data in order to make the best use of them [329]. In this section, we introduce two popular big data processing systems, namely, **Hadoop** and **Spark**, which have been widely exploited for building scalable RDF processing systems. Several parts of this book discuss the use of big data storage and processing systems for building scalable storage and querying engines over RDF databases (Chap. 4) in addition to building scalable reasoning systems over RDF databases (Chap. 6).

2.7.1 NoSQL Databases

The ever-growing requirement for scalability combined with new application specifications has created unprecedented challenges for traditional relational database systems. In addition to the rapid growth of information, data has become increasingly semi-structured and sparse in nature. Such emerging requirements challenged the traditional data management architectures in their need for upfront schema definition and the relational-based data organization in many scenarios. In response, we have experienced the emergence of a new generation of *distributed* and scalable data storage system, referred to as NoSQL (Not Only SQL) database systems.[25] A majority of these systems are originally designed and built to support distributed environments with the need to improve performance by adding new nodes to the existing ones [438]. One key principle of NoSQL systems is to compromise the consistency to trade for high availability and scalability. Basically, the implementation of a majority NoSQL systems share some common design features:

- High scalability, which requires the ability to scale up horizontally over a large cluster of nodes
- High availability and fault tolerance, which is supported by replicating and distributing data over distributed servers
- Flexible data models, with the ability to dynamically define and update attributes and schemas
- Weaker consistency models, which abandoned the ACID transactions and are usually referred to as BASE models (Basically Available, Soft state, Eventually consistent) [313]
- Simple interfaces, which are normally single call-level interfaces or protocol in contrast to the SQL bindings

For different scenarios and focus of usage, several NoSQL systems have been developed based on different data models. These NoSQL systems can be generally classified into three main classes [69, 331]:

- **Key-Value stores**: The systems of this class use a simple data model where data are considered as a set of Key-Value pairs. Keys are unique IDs for each data and also work as indexes during accessing the data. Values are attributes or objects which contain the actual information of data. Examples for systems of this class include **DynamoDB**[26] and **Project Voldemort.**[27]
- **Extensible-Record/Column-Family stores**: In these systems, data are considered as tables with rows and column families in which both rows and columns can be split over multiple nodes. Correlated fields/columns (named as column families) are located on the same partition to facilitate query performance. Normally, column families are predefined before creating a data table. However, this is not a big limitation as new columns and fields can always be dynamically added to the existing tables. Examples for systems of this class include **HBase**[28] and **Cassandra.**[29]
- **Document stores**: This class provides a more complex data structure and richer capabilities than Key-Value and Column-Family systems. In document stores, the unit of data is called a *document* which is actually an object that can contain

---

[25]http://nosql-database.org/.

[26]https://aws.amazon.com/dynamodb/.

[27]http://www.project-voldemort.com/voldemort/.

[28]https://hbase.apache.org/.

[29]http://cassandra.apache.org/.

an arbitrary set of fields, values, and even nested objects and arrays. Document stores normally do not have predefined schemas for data and support search and indexing by document fields and attributes. Examples for systems of this class include MongoDB[30] and CouchDB.[31]

2.7.2 MapReduce/Hadoop

In 2004, Google introduced the MapReduce framework as a simple and powerful programming model that enables easy development of scalable parallel applications to process vast amounts of data on large clusters of commodity machines [97]. In particular, the implementation described in the original paper is mainly designed to achieve high performance on large clusters of commodity PCs. One of the main advantages of this approach is that it isolates the application from the details of running a distributed program, such as issues on data distribution, scheduling, and fault tolerance. In this model, the computation takes a set of key/value pairs as input and produces a set of key/value pairs as output. The user of the MapReduce framework expresses the computation using two functions: *Map* and *Reduce*. The Map function takes an input pair and produces a set of intermediate key/value pairs. The MapReduce framework groups together all intermediate values associated with the same intermediate key I and passes them to the Reduce function. The Reduce function receives an intermediate key I with its set of values and merges them together. Typically just zero or one output value is produced per Reduce invocation. The main advantage of this model is that it allows large computations to be easily parallelized and re-executed to be used as the primary mechanism for fault tolerance.

Hadoop[32] is an open-source Java library [409] that supports data-intensive distributed applications by realizing the implementation of the MapReduce framework.[33] It has been widely used by a large number of business companies for production purposes.[34] On the implementation level, the Map invocations of a MapReduce job are distributed across multiple machines by automatically partitioning the input data into a set of M splits. The input splits can be processed in parallel by different machines. Reduce invocations are distributed by partitioning the intermediate key space into R pieces using a partitioning function (e.g., hash(key) mod R). The number of partitions (R) and the partitioning function are specified

---

[30]https://www.mongodb.com/.

[31]http://couchdb.apache.org/.

[32]http://hadoop.apache.org/.

[33]In the rest of this article, we use the two names MapReduce and Hadoop interchangeably.

[34]http://wiki.apache.org/hadoop/PoweredBy.

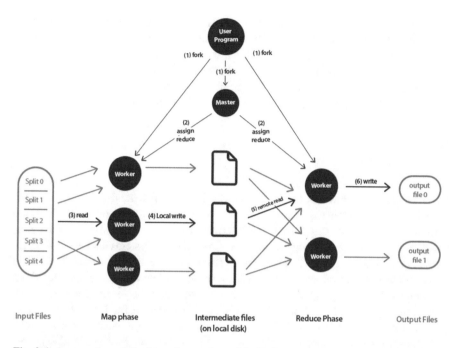

Fig. 2.6 An overview of the flow of execution a MapReduce operation [329]. ©The Author(s) 2016. Reprinted with Permission

by the user. Figure 2.6 illustrates an example of the overall flow of a MapReduce operation which goes through the following sequence of actions:

- The input data of the MapReduce program is split into M pieces and starts up many instances of the program on a cluster of machines.
- One of the instances of the program is elected to be the *master* copy while the rest are considered as *workers* that are assigned their work by the master copy. In particular, there are M map tasks and R reduce tasks to assign. The master picks idle workers and assigns each one or more map tasks and/or reduce tasks.
- A worker who is assigned a map task processes the contents of the corresponding input split and generates key/value pairs from the input data and passes each pair to the user-defined Map function. The intermediate key/value pairs produced by the Map function are buffered in memory.
- Periodically, the buffered pairs are written to local disk and partitioned into R regions by the partitioning function. The locations of these buffered pairs on the local disk are passed back to the master, who is responsible for forwarding these locations to the reduce workers.
- When a reduce worker is notified by the master about these locations, it reads the buffered data from the local disks of the map workers which is then sorted by the intermediate keys so that all occurrences of the same key are grouped together. The sorting operation is needed because typically many different keys map to the same reduce task.

- The reduce worker passes the key and the corresponding set of intermediate values to the user's Reduce function. The output of the Reduce function is appended to a final output file for this reduce partition.
- When all map tasks and reduce tasks have been completed, the master program wakes up the user program. At this point, the MapReduce invocation in the user program returns the program control back to the user code.

2.7.3 Spark

The Hadoop framework has pioneered the domain of general-purpose data processing systems. However, one of the main performance limitations of the Hadoop framework is that it materializes the intermediate results of each Map or Reduce step on HDFS before starting the next one. Several other systems have been recently developed to tackle the performance problem of the Hadoop framework. The Spark project has been introduced as a general-purpose big data processing engine which can be used for many types of data processing scenarios [429]. In principle, Spark was initially designed for providing efficient performance for interactive queries and iterative algorithms, as these were two major use cases which were not well supported by the MapReduce framework. Spark, written in Scala[35] [297], was originally developed in the AMPLab at UC Berkeley[36] and open sourced in 2010 as one of the new generation data flow engines that was developed to overcome the limitations of the MapReduce framework.

In general, one of the main limitations of the Hadoop framework is that it requires that the entire output of each map and reduce task be materialized into a local file on the Hadoop Distributed File System (HDFS) before it can be consumed by the next stage. This materialization step allows for the implementation of a simple and elegant checkpoint/restart fault-tolerant mechanism; however, it dramatically harms the system performance. Spark takes the concepts of Hadoop to the next level by loading the data in distributed memory and relying on less expensive shuffles during the data processing (Fig. 2.7). In particular, the fundamental programming abstraction of Spark is called *Resilient Distributed Datasets* (RDD) [429] which represents a logical collection of data partitioned across machines that are created by referencing datasets in external storage systems or by applying various and rich coarse-grained transformations (e.g., *map, filter, reduce, join*) on existing RDDs rather than the two simple programming abstractions, *map* and *reduce*, of the Hadoop framework. For instance, the *map* transformation of Spark applies a transformation function to each element in the input RDD and returns a new RDD with the elements of the transformation output as a result, the *filter* transformation applies a filtration predicate on the elements of an RDD and returns a new RDD

---

[35]http://www.scala-lang.org/.

[36]https://amplab.cs.berkeley.edu/.

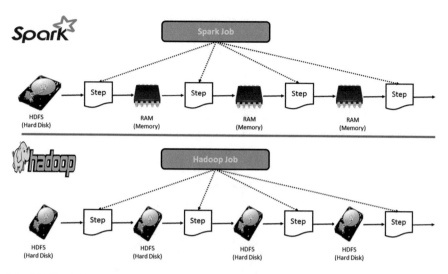

Fig. 2.7 Spark framework vs Hadoop framework [329]. ©The Author(s) 2016. Reprinted with Permission

with only the elements which satisfy the predicate conditions, while the *union* transformation returns all elements of two input RDDs in a new RDD.

Figure 2.8 illustrates the execution flow of operations of Spark jobs. In principle, having RDD as an in-memory data structure gives the power to Spark's functional programming paradigm by allowing user programs to load data into a cluster's memory and query it repeatedly. In addition, users can explicitly cache an RDD in memory across machines and reuse it in multiple MapReduce-like parallel operations. In particular, RDDs can be manipulated through operations like map, filter, and reduce, which take functions in the programming language and ship them to nodes on the cluster. This simplifies programming complexity because the way applications manipulate RDDs is similar to that of manipulating local collections of data. During the execution phase, Spark follows a lazy mechanism for the evaluation of program operations where RDDs are not always immediately materialized. Instead, data in RDDs is not processed and is not materialized in memory until an *action* function (e.g., *first, count, countByValue, reduce*) is performed over it after which the Spark engine launches a computation to materialize the new RDD. For example, the *first* action returns the first element in an RDD, the *count* action returns the number of elements in an RDD, while the *reduce* action combines the elements on an RDD together according to an aggregate function. Spark can interface with a wide variety of distributed storage implementations, including Hadoop Distributed File System (HDFS) [356], Cassandra,[37] and Amazon S3.[38] RDDs can be also

---

[37] http://cassandra.apache.org/.

[38] http://aws.amazon.com/s3/.

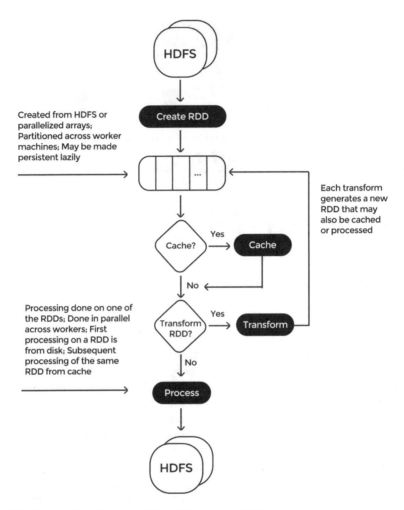

Fig. 2.8 An overview of the flow of execution spark operations

created by distributing a collection of objects (e.g., a list or set) which are loaded in memory or by applying coarse-grained transformations (e.g., map, filter, reduce, join) on existing RDDs.

Chapter 3
Centralized RDF Query Processing

The wide adoption of the RDF data model has called for efficient and scalable RDF query processing schemes. As a response to this call, a number of centralized RDF query processing systems have been designed to tackle this challenge. In these systems, the storage and query processing of RDF datasets are managed on a single node. Therefore, a main property of such systems is that they do not incur any communication overhead (i.e., they process all data locally). On the other hand, they remain limited by the computational power and memory capacities of a single machine. In this chapter, we give an overview of various techniques and systems for centrally querying RDF datasets. Figure 3.1 illustrates the general classification scheme for the centralized RDF storage and querying schemes which we are discussing in this chapter.

3.1 RDF Statement Table

One straightforward way to persist RDF triples is to store triple statements using relational database systems directly in a table-like structure [330]. In particular, in this approach, the input RDF data is maintained as a linearized list of triples, storing them as ternary tuples. This approach is called the "generic" approach [10]. The RDF specification states that the objects in the graphs can be either URIs, literals, or blank nodes. Properties (predicates) are always URI references. Subject nodes can only be URIs or blank nodes which enables specifying the underlying data types for storing subject and predicate values. Storing object values gets a little more complex since the data type of the object literal is specified by the XML schema that is referenced by the property. A common way is to store the object values using a common string representation and perform some type conversion whenever necessary. An example table showing the same dataset as in Fig. 3.2 is shown in Fig. 3.3.

© Springer International Publishing AG 2018
S. Sakr et al., *Linked Data*, https://doi.org/10.1007/978-3-319-73515-3_3

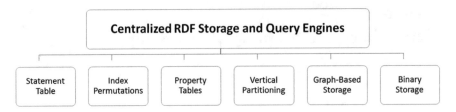

Fig. 3.1 Classification of centralized RDF storage and querying techniques

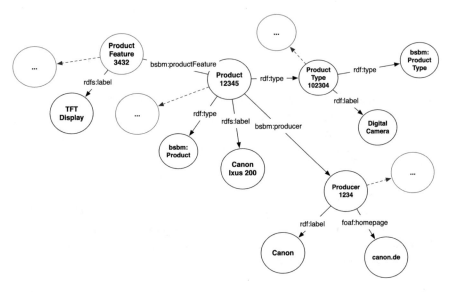

Fig. 3.2 An example of an RDF subgraph using the subject, predicate, and object relations given by the sample data [443]. ©Springer International Publishing AG 2017. Reprinted with permission

An example of *Statement Table* approach is **Jena1** [259]. **Jena1** uses relational databases to store data as a statement table. URIs and Strings are encoded as IDs and two separate dictionaries are maintained for literals and resources/URIs. To distinguish literals from URI in the statement table, there are two columns. In **Jena2** [412], the schema is denormalized and URIs and simple literals are maintained in the statement table. The dictionary tables are used only to store strings whose lengths exceed a threshold. This allows filters operation to be performed directly on the statement table; however, it also results in higher storage consumption, since string values are stored multiple times. **3store** [167] is another system that stores the RDF triples into a single relational table. In addition, this single table stores a hash of the resource URIs and literal values to minimize the storage cost for this table and to ensure that the records in the table are all of the same size. The same hashing function is used for both resources and for literals, so the triples table contains a flag to indicate whether the object of the triple is a literal or a resource (Fig. 3.4).

Subject	Predicate	Object
Product12345	rdf:type	bsbm:Product
Product12345	rdfs:label	Canon Ixus 2010
Product12345	bsbm:producer	bsbm-inst:Producer1234
...	...	...
Producer1234	rdf:label	Canon
Producer1234	foaf:homepage	http://www.canon.com
...	...	...

Fig. 3.3 A simple RDF storage scheme using a linearized triple representation. The illustration uses schema elements from the Berlin SPARQL Benchmark [44]. ©Springer International Publishing AG 2017. Reprinted with permission

model	subject	prediacte	object	literal	inferred
int64	int64	int64	int64	boolean	boolean

hash	model
int64	text

Models

hash	model
int64	text

URIs

hash	model
int64	text

Literals

Fig. 3.4 Logical database design of the triple table in 3store [167]. ©Springer International Publishing AG 2017. Reprinted with permission

In general, the semantic information from the complete RDF graph can be exploited so that additional data can be annotated per triple and stored as a fourth element for each input triple. Harris et al. [168] proposed another system, called **4store**, where RDF triples are maintained as quads of (model, subject, predicate, object), which is somewhat equivalent to RDF Graphs/Databases. In **4store**, triples assigned to the default graph are maintained in a specific model, that is, they are used in query evaluation over the default graph. 4store stores each of the quads in three indexes; in addition, it stores literal values separately. It maintains a hash table of graphs where each entry points to lists of triples in the graph. Literals are indexed through a separate hash table and they are represented as (SPO). **4store** also considers two predicate-based indexes. For each predicate, two radix tries are maintained where the key is either a subject or an object, and respectively object or subject and graph are stored as entries. These indexes are used to filter all quads satisfying a given predicate and their subject/object. They are considered as traditional predicate indexes ($P \rightarrow OS$ and $P \rightarrow SO$).

Virtuoso [112] maintains data as RDF quads that consist of a *graph element id*, *subject*, *predicate*, and *object* where all the quads are maintained in a single table. Each of the attributes can be indexed in different ways. From a high-level perspective, Virtuoso is comparable to a traditional relational database with enhanced RDF support. Virtuoso adds specific types (URIs, language and type-tagged strings) and indexes optimized for RDF. Virtuoso supports two main types of indexes. The default index corresponds to GSPO (graph, subject, predicate, object). In addition, it provides an auxiliary bitmap index (OPGS). As both indexes contain all columns of the original tables, the table is wholly represented by these two indexes and no other persistent data structure needs to be associated with it. In addition, there is no need for a lookup of the main row from an index leaf. The indexes are stored in compressed form and allows the AND of the conditions to be calculated as a merge intersection of two sparse bitmaps. As strings are the most common values in the database, for example, in URIs, Virtuoso compresses these strings by eliminating common prefixes. The system does not precalculate optimization statistics. Instead, it samples data at query execution time. It also does not compute the exact statistics but just estimates a rough number of elements and estimates query cost to pick an optimal execution plan.

RDFMATCH [83] has been presented as an SQL-based table function which is designed to query RDF data. The answers of the RDFMATCH table function can be seamlessly integrated with queries on standard relational tables and also consequently processed by the various SQL's querying constructs. The main implementation of the RDFMATCH function complies to self-join operations on the underlying triple-based RDF table store. The compiled query is evaluated efficiently using B-tree indexes in addition to a set of materialized join views for specialized subject-property. Subject-Property Matrix materialized join views are utilized to reduce the query evaluation overheads that are inherent in the canonical triple-based representation of RDF. A special module is implemented to analyze the triple-based RDF table and estimate the size of the different materialized views, based on which a user can define a subset of materialized views. For a group of subjects, the system defines a set of single-valued properties that occur together. These can be direct properties of these subjects or nested properties. A property p_1 is a direct property of subject x_1 if there is a triple (x_1, p_1, x_2). A property p_m is a nested property of subject x_1 if there is a set of triples such as $(x_1, p_1, x_2), \ldots, (x_m, p_m, x_{m+1})$, where $m > 1$. For example, if there is a set of triples, $(John, address, addr1), (addr1, zip, 03062)$, then the *zip* property is considered as a nested property of *John*.

3.2   Index Permutations for RDF Triples

The approach of index-permuted RDF storage exploits and optimizes traditional indexing techniques for storing RDF data. As most of the identifiers in RDF are URIs strings, one optimization is to replace these strings of arbitrary lengths with unique integers. As the data is sparse and many URIs are repetitive, this technique

Fig. 3.5 Exhaustive indexing [443]. ©Springer International Publishing AG 2017. Reprinted with permission

provides memory saving benefits. To increase the resulting performance, the indexes are built based on shorter encoded values rather than the uncompressed values. In practice, several systems (e.g., [287, 408]) showed that it is possible to use a storage model that applies exhaustive indexing. The foundation for this approach is that any query on the stored data can be answered by a set of indexes on the subjects, predicates, and objects in different orders, namely, all their permutations (Fig. 3.5), so that it allows fast access to all parts of the triples by sorted lists and fast merge joins.

YARS [169] is one of the first approaches to provide exhaustive indexing of RDF datasets. The main idea of exhaustive indexing is based on the fact that this attribute requires a total of 16 indexes. Harth et al. propose to use six indexes covering all major access patterns [*SPOC, POC, OCS, CSP, CP, OS*]. Their indexing approach leverages the property that B+tree indexes can be queried for range and prefix queries. If the key to such index is the full quad of subject, predicate, object, and context, it becomes possible to query only a prefix of the key and use the remaining keys as values. To execute simple queries, YARS [169] evaluates which of the six indexes is the best fit for answering the query. Selecting the index depends on the access pattern; if a subject is specified in the query, the *SPOC* index should be used. If only a predicate is given in the query, the *POC* index should be used instead. More complex queries connected with logical operators require typical relational query optimization like reordering to efficiently execute all kinds of joins.

Janik et al. introduce a system called **BRAHMS** [197], whose storage model evolves around permuted indexes. They store data in three hash tables (S-OP, O-SP, P-SO). The hash tables are organized in a logically contiguous memory block which can be dumped and loaded from disk during startup and shutdown, though the system itself works in-memory. The focus of **BRAHMS** [197] is mainly on the semantic association discovery problem. The problem itself refers to finding a semantic connection between two objects. Tackling this issue, they had to overcome the problem at that time of which SPARQL did not fully support that kind of queries. It supported queries only with a fixed distance, whereas to discover association one was interested in any association that is independent of the distance between objects (arbitrary transitive closures, which were not supported by SPARQL at the time). In BRAHMS, they mainly leveraged two graph algorithms to answer queries: depth-first search and breadth-first search.

Hexastore [408] has mainly focused on generality and scalability in the design of its data storage and query processing mechanisms. Hexastore relies on maintaining the RDF data using a multiple indexing scheme [169]. It does not differentiate against any component of the RDF triples and equally treats the subject, predicate, and object components. In particular, each RDF component has its special index structure. In addition, all possible combinations of the three components are indexed and materialized. Each index structure in a Hexastore is built around one RDF element and determines a prioritization between the other two elements. Two vectors are associated with each RDF element (e.g., subject), one for each of the other two RDF elements (e.g., property and object). In addition, lists of the third RDF element are appended to the elements in these vectors. In total, six distinct indexes are used for indexing the RDF data. These indexes materialize all possible orders of precedence of the three RDF elements. A clear disadvantage of this approach is that Hexastore features a worst-case fivefold storage increase in comparison to a conventional triples table. Figure 3.6 illustrates an example index structure of Hexastore. In this example, the spo index is described. The first level of the index is a sorted list of all subjects where each subject is associated to a list of sorted predicates. Each predicate links to a list of sorted objects. Queries that require many joins and unions in other storage systems can be answered directly by the index. In the case where the query requests a list of subjects that are related to two

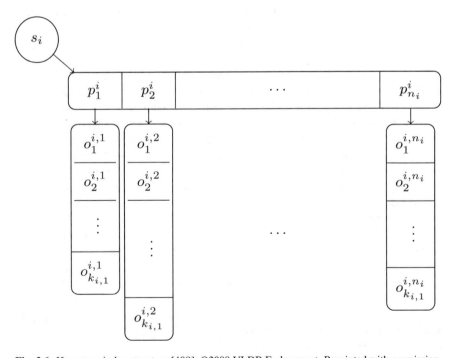

Fig. 3.6 Hexastore index structure [408]. ©2008 VLDB Endowment. Reprinted with permission

particular objects through any property, the answer can be computed by merging the subject lists of the osp index. Since the subject list of this osp index is sorted, this can be done in linear time. In practice, the architectural drawback of this approach is the increase in memory consumption. Since every combination of possible query patterns is indexed, additional space is required due to the duplication of data. Weiss et al. [408] point out that less than a sixfold increase in memory consumption is required; the approach yields a worst-case fivefold increase since for the set of spo, sop, osp, ops, pso, pos indexes, one part can always be reused: the initial sorted list of subjects, objects, and predicates. Due to the replication of the data into the different index structures, updating and inserting into the index can become a second bottleneck.

RDF-3X (RDF Triple eXpress) [287] relies on the same processing scheme of exhaustive indexing but further optimizes the data structures. In RDF-3X, the index data is stored in clustered B+ trees in lexicographic order. Moreover, indexes over count-aggregated variants for all three two-dimensional and all three one-dimensional projections are created [287]. The values inside the B+ tree are delta encoded (computed difference/delta between the ID attributed to the slot in the tree and the ID attributed to the previous slot) to further reduce the required amount of main memory to persist all data. Each triple (in one of the previously defined orders of spo,sop,...) is stored as a block with the maximum of 13 bytes. Since the triples are sorted lexicographically, the expected delta between two values is low, that is, only a few bytes are consumed. Now the header of the value block contains two pieces of information: first, a flag that identifies if $value_1$ and $value_2$ are unchanged and the delta of $value_3$ is small enough to fit in the header block; second, if this flag is not set, it then identifies a case number of how many bytes are needed to decode the delta to the previous block. Figure 3.7 illustrates an example of the RDF-3X compression scheme where the upper part of the illustration shows the general block structure and the lower half shows the explicit case. Here, the flag is set to 0, meaning more than $value_3$ changed. Case 7 identifies that for $value_1$, $value_2$, and $value_3$ exactly one byte had changed. Using this information, the deltas can be extracted and the actual value of the triple can be decoded. The query processor

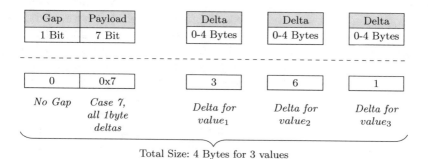

Total Size: 4 Bytes for 3 values

Fig. 3.7 RDF-3X compression example [285]. ©2008 VLDB Endowment. Reprinted with permission

follows the RISC-style design philosophy [74] by exploiting the comprehensive set of indexes on the RDF triples so that it can mostly apply merge-join operations over the ordered index lists. The query optimizer uses its cost model to find the most efficient query execution plan and mostly focuses on reordering the join operations. In practice, selectivity estimation has a significant impact on plan generation. While this is a traditional problem in database systems, the schema-free nature of RDF data makes this issue more challenging. RDF-3X relies on a cost model to perform dynamic programming for plan enumeration. In order to achieve this goal, it uses two types of statistical information: (1) specialized histograms which are generic and can handle any kind of triple patterns and joins and (2) frequent join paths in the data which give more accurate estimation. During query optimization, the query optimizer uses the join-path selectivity information when available and otherwise assumes independence and uses the histograms information. RDF-3X has been extended by introducing a runtime technique for accelerating query executions [286] that uses a lightweight, RDF-specific technique for sideways information passing across different joins and index scans within the query execution plans. This extension enhanced the selectivity estimator of the query optimizer by using fast index lookups on specifically designed aggregation indexes, rather than relying on the usual types of coarse-grained histograms. This provides more accurate estimates at compile time, at a fairly small cost that is easily amortized by providing better directives for the join order optimization.

3.3   Property Tables

Since RDF does not describe any specific schema for the graph, there is no easy way to determine a set of partitioning or clustering criteria to derive a set of tables to store the information. In addition, there is no definite notion of schema stability, meaning that at any time the data schema might change, for example, when adding a new subject-object edge to the overall graph. In general, storing RDF triples in a single large statement table presents a number of disadvantages when it comes to query evaluation. In most cases, for each set of triple patterns which is evaluated in the query, a set of self-joins is necessary to evaluate the graph traversal. Since the single statement table can become very large, this can have a negative effect on query execution. Different approaches [58, 412] have been proposed to alleviate this problem by introducing the concept of property tables. In particular, instead of building one large table for all occurrences of all properties, they proposed two different strategies that can be distinguished into two different concepts: clustered and normalized property tables. In principle, the main goal of clustered property tables is to cluster commonly accessed nodes in the graph together in a single table to avoid expensive joins on the data. Wilkinson [411] proposed the use of

Product Property Table

Subject	Type	Label	NumericProperty1	aaa
Product12345	bsbm:Product	Canon Ixus 2010	NULL	...
...	...	...	...	...

Left-Over Triples

Subject	Predicate	Object
Producer1234	foaf:homepage	http://www.canon.com
...	...	...

Fig. 3.8 An example illustration of clustered property tables. Frequently co-accessed attributes are stored together

clustered property tables for storing data using the Dublin Core schema.[1] In the shown example of Fig. 3.8, one property table for all products and a statement table for all other triples are considered. For efficiency reasons, a product record and all affected triples can only appear in the property table. Property tables were also implemented in **Jena2** [412] together with a statement table. In that context, multiple-value properties are clustered in a separate table. The system also allows to specify the type of the column in the underlying database system for the property value. This can be further leveraged for range queries and filtering. For example, the property *age* can be implemented as an integer, which can then be efficiently filtered.

RStar [251] is a system which is designed to store ontology information and instance data in various relational tables. In particular, ontology information is encoded using tables *Class*, *SubClass*, *Property*, *SubProperty*, and *Property-Class*. In addition, an *InstanceOfClass* table is used to maintain instances of all classes and establish the link between ontology and instance data. In RStar, each literal and each resource is assigned a unique ID and maintained in separate tables to accelerate the data retrieval and reduce the storage cost. In addition, a *Triples* table is used to store all instance triples, without including ontology triples, where each triple contains three columns, namely, *SubID*, *PreID*, and *ObjID*.

DB2RDF [53] introduced a relational encoding scheme for the RDF model which attempts to ideally encode all the predicates for each subject on a single row while efficiently maintaining the inherent variability of the different subjects. DB2RDF uses a *Direct Primary Hash (DPH)* wide relation where each record maintains a subject s in the entry column, with all its associated k predicates and objects stored in the $pred_i$ and val_i columns where $0 \leq i \leq k$. If subject s has more than k predicates, a new tuple is used to store the additional attributes and the process continues until covering and storing all the predicates for s. Since

---

[1] http://dublincore.org/.

multi-valued predicates need special treatment, DB2RDF uses a second relation, *Direct Secondary Hash* (*DS*). Although the encoding scheme of DB2RDF allows one column to store multiple predicates, its hashing mechanism assures that each predicate is always assigned to the same column for the same subjects. In principle, storing all the instances of a predicate in the same column provides all the indexing advantages of traditional relational representations. In addition, storing different predicates in the same column leads to significant space savings where a relatively smaller number of database columns can be used to maintain datasets with a much bigger number of predicates (since otherwise the number of columns will be equal to the number of predicates). In principle, the *DPH* and *DS* relations primarily maintain the outgoing edges of an entity. DB2RDF also encodes the incoming edges of an entity using two additional reverse relations: the *Reverse Primary Hash* (*RPH*) and the *Reverse Secondary Hash* (*RS*). A main advantage of the DB2RDF encoding scheme is that it reduces the number of join operations for star queries (i.e., queries that ask for multiple predicates for the same subject or object).

In general, one of the consequences of this approach is that some information about the schema of the RDF data should be known in advance. If the properties for a materialized type change during runtime, this requires table alternations that are costly and often require explicit table-level locking. In addition, multi-valued attributes cannot be easily represented using a clustered property table. If multi-valued attributes must be considered, a designer has to choose either to not materialize the path of the attribute or, if the sequence of the attribute is bounded, to include all possible occurrences in the materialized clustered property table.

3.4 Vertical Partitioning

SW-Store [2] is an RDF management system that maintains RDF databases by applying a fully decomposed storage model (DSM) [87]. This approach rewrites the triple table into m tables where m is the number of unique properties in the dataset (Fig. 3.9). Each of the m tables consists of two columns. The first column stores the subjects which is described by that property while the second column stores the object values. The subjects which are not described by a particular property are simply omitted from the table for that property. Each of the m tables is indexed by subject so that particular subjects can be retrieved quickly. In addition, fast merge-join operations are exploited to reconstruct information about multiple properties for subsets of subjects. For the case of a multi-valued attribute, each distinct value is listed in a successive row in the table for that property. In practice, a main advantage of this technique is that the algorithm for creating the encoding tables is straightforward and agnostic towards the structure of the RDF dataset. The implementation of SW-Store relied on a column-oriented database system, C-store [368], to maintain the encoding tables as groups of columns instead of maintaining them as groups of rows. In standard row-oriented database systems (e.g., Oracle, DB2, SQLServer, Postgres, etc.), entire tuples are stored consecutively.

<rdf:type>

Subject	Object
Product12345	bsbm:Product

<rdfs:label>

Subject	Object
Product12345	Canon Ixus 2010
Producer1234	Canon

<aaa>

Subject	Object
uuu	xxx
...	...

Fig. 3.9 An example illustration of vertical partitioning. For each existing predicate one subject-object table is created

The problem with this is that if only a few attributes are accessed per query, entire rows need to be read into memory from disk before the projection can occur. By storing data in columns rather than rows, the projection occurs for free, meaning that only the columns that are relevant to a query need to be read.

Peng et al. [309] proposed another method to partition and allocate the RDF partitions by exploring the intrinsic similarities among the structures of queries in the executed workload in order to reduce the number of crossing matches and the communication cost during query processing. In particular, the proposed approach mines and selects some of the frequent access patterns which reflect the characteristics of the workload. Based on the selected frequent access patterns, two fragmentation strategies, vertical and horizontal fragmentation, are used to divide RDF graphs while meeting different kinds of query processing objectives. On the one hand, the design goal of the vertical fragmentation strategy is to achieve better throughput by grouping the homomorphic matches to the same frequent access pattern into the same fragment. This strategy helps to easily filter out the irrelevant fragments during the query evaluation so that only sites that stored relevant fragments need to be accessed to find matches while sites that do not store relevant fragments can be used to evaluate other queries in parallel, which improves the total throughput of the system. In principle, the main focus of the vertical fragmentation strategy is to utilize the locality of SPARQL queries to improve both throughput and query response time. On the other hand, the design goal of the horizontal fragmentation strategy is to achieve better performance by putting matches of one frequent access pattern into the different fragments and distribute them among different sites. As a result, the evaluation of one query may involve many fragments and each fragment has a few matches. In practice, the size of a fragment is often much smaller than the size of the whole data; thus, finding matches of a query over a fragment explores a smaller search space than finding matches over the whole data. Therefore, with horizontal fragmentation, each site finds a few matches over some fragments with the smaller which supports the utilization of the parallelism over the clusters of nodes and reduces the query response time. For fragment allocation, a fragment affinity metric is used to measure the togetherness between the fragments and identify those that are closely related. In particular, if the affinity metric of two fragments is large, it means that these two fragments are often involved by the same query and they should be placed together to reduce the number of cross-site joins.

3.5 Graph-Based Storage

RDF naturally forms graph structures; hence, one way to store and process it is through graph-driven data structures and algorithms. Therefore, some approaches have applied ideas from the graph processing world to efficiently handle RDF data. For example, gStore [444] is a graph-based RDF storage system that models RDF data as a labeled, directed multiedge graph. In this graph, each vertex encodes a subject or an object and each triple is encoded using a directed edge from a subject to its associated object. Given a subject and an object, there may exist more than one property between them which are represented by multiple edges between two vertices. In gStore, the RDF graph is stored as a disk-based adjacency list table. For each class vertex in the RDF graph, gStore assigns a bitstring as its vertex signature. Therefore, the RDF graph is mapped to a data signature graph (Fig. 3.10). In gStore, SPARQL queries are mapped to a subgraph matching query over the RDF graph. During query processing, the vertices of the SPARQL query are encoded into vertex signatures and then the query is encoded into its corresponding query signature graph. Answering the SPARQL query is done by matching the vertex signature of the query graph over vertex signature of the RDF graph. In particular, gStore builds an S-tree for all vertices in their adjacency list table to reduce the search space (Fig. 3.11). The tree leafs correspond to vertices from the initial graph

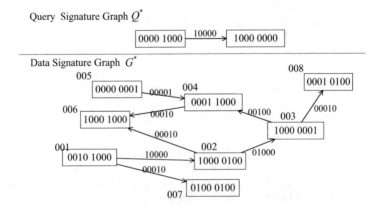

Fig. 3.10 gStore: Signature graphs [444]. ©Springer-Verlag Berlin Heidelberg 2013. Reprinted with permission

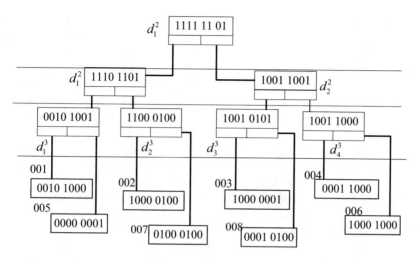

Fig. 3.11 gStore: S-tree [444]. ©Springer-Verlag Berlin Heidelberg 2013. Reprinted with permission

(G*), and each intermediate (parent) node is formed by performing the bitwise OR operation on all children signatures. However, S-trees cannot support multiway join processing. Thus, the authors proposed a VS-tree extension. Given an S-tree, leafs are linked according to the initial graph, and new edges are introduced depending on whether certain leafs are connected in G*. Specifically, two leafs in S-tree (001 and 002 in Fig. 3.11) are linked if there is an edge in G* between vertices corresponding to them. On the upper level in S-tree, super-edges are introduced between nodes if there is at least one connection between the children of those nodes. In other words, if there is a link between two leafs which does not share a parent, a link between their parents is then created. Bitwise "O" operations over connecting edge labels of the children are performed to assign labels to such super-edges.

The **DOGMA** [56] system is based on a balanced binary tree where each node is located on one disk page. Since the page size is fixed, the size of the subgraph located on a page is limited as well. There can be many different indexes built for the same RDF database. DOGMA focuses on minimizing potential cross edges between subgraphs located on different pages. Supposing we have two nodes N1 and N2, the fewer cross edges we have, the more independent the nodes become. When answering a query, we will most probably not have to open/read both of those subgraphs. To partition graphs, **DOGMA** uses the algorithm proposed by Karypis and Kumar [210] which takes as an input a weighted graph and partitions it in the way that the total weight of cross edges (between subgraphs) is minimized and the sum of the weights in each subgraph is approximately equal. They start by assigning a weight of 1 to each vertex and edge in an RDF graph and then coarsen the graph into a subgraph so that the latter contains about half of the vertices from the former, and so on with each of the subgraphs until each of the subgraphs has no more than the predefined number of vertices (i.e., to fit into a disk page). The coarsening algorithm randomly picks one vertex (v), then selects a maximally weighted node (m). It merges the neighbors of the node m and m itself into one node, updates the weights, and removes v. Edges from m to its neighbors are also removed. This process is rerun until the subgraph contains half or less vertices as the initial graph. Then, the index is built for all subgraphs. In **DOGMA**, the storage model itself is an index, though the authors also propose two additional indexes to help in pruning the result of candidates. The DOGMA internal partition distance (IPD) index stores, for each vertex v in node N, the distance to the edge of the subgraph corresponding to N. During query execution, for two vertices (v, u), the algorithm looks for nodes to which the vertices belong ($N! = M$). N and M are at the same level of the tree and closest to the root. If such nodes do not exist, because the vertices are in the same leaf node of the tree, then the distance between them is set to 0; otherwise, it is set to the maximal distance from each of them to the border of the subgraph the vertex belongs to (formally $d(u, v) = max(ipd(v, N), ipd(u, M))$). The idea behind the DOGMA external partition distance (EPD) index is to maintain distances to other subgraphs. For each lowest-level subgraph, a color is assigned. For each vertex and color, the shortest distance from v to a subgraph colored with c is stored. To answer a query, DOGMA first retrieves for all variable vertices in $Q*$ a set of result candidates w.r.t. the vertices. The sets are initialized with vertices that are connected to a defined vertex with a defined predicate. Then, for the vertex with the lowest cardinality of result candidates, each candidate is set as a value of the vertex, such that there is a new constant vertex. The algorithm can be rerun to prune result candidates for other vertices, and so on until the final result is found. The basic algorithm presented above is efficient enough for simple queries on neighboring vertices. Considering vertices located in different nodes, additional indexes to help prune the result candidates would be needed. The authors propose a second algorithm, which verifies if two vertices are "in range." Let v be a variable vertex with a set of result candidates, and c a constant vertex with a long range dependency on v. Then any result candidate of v must not be further away from c than the distance between c and v in the query (more formally $d(v, c) >= d(T(v), s)$). Any other candidate can be pruned. While the result candidates are initialized, the algorithm ensures that each element satisfies this constraint. To efficiently look up for a $d(v, c)$, a distance index is introduced through two lower-bound distance indexes.

Turbo$_{HOM++}$ [220] is another graph-based approach that transforms RDF graphs into labeled graphs and applies subgraph homomorphism methods to RDF query processing. In order to improve its query evaluation performance, it applies type-aware transformation and tailored optimization techniques. For the type-aware transformation, it embeds the types of an entity (i.e., a subject or an object) into the vertex label set so that it can eliminate corresponding query vertices/edges from the query graph. Using this approach, the query graph size decreases, its topology becomes simpler than the original query, and thus, this transformation improves performance accordingly by reducing the amount of graph exploration. Turbo$_{HOM++}$ tackles the matching order problem by using the *candidate region exploration* technique which attempts to accurately estimate the number of candidate vertices for a given query path then explores each region by performing a depth-first search. In order to speed up query performance further, Turbo$_{HOM++}$ applies a series of performance optimizations as well as Non-Uniform Memory Access (NUMA)-aware parallelism for fast RDF query processing.

AMbER (Attributed Multigraph Based Engine for RDF querying) [193] is a graph-based RDF engine that represents the RDF data into multigraph where subjects/objects constitute vertices and multiple edges (predicates) can appear between the same pair of vertices. During query evaluation, SPARQL queries are also represented as multigraphs and the query answering task is transformed to the problem of subgraph homomorphism. In addition, AMbER employs an approach that exploits structural properties of the multigraph query to efficiently access RDF multigraph information and return the results.

In TripleT [120], Fletcher et al. introduce the term of atom around which triples are co-located. A key k, regardless of its role in the triples, is selected and then all triples where k occurs are co-located together to improve data locality. For example, for k three buckets are created: one containing pairs (p, o) where k is the subject, one containing pairs (s, o) where k is the predicate, and one containing pairs (s, p) where k is the object. All those pairs are sorted. The storage model itself has an index with keys corresponding to subjects and objects. Thanks to this indexing scheme, TripleT can perform a join as a single lookup on a common join variable (same value for subject and object) and then merge values related to the subjects and the objects.

The RIQ system (RDF Indexing on Quads) introduced a *decrease-and-conquer* strategy for fast SPARQL query processing [360]. Instead of indexing the entire RDF dataset, RIQ identifies groups of similar RDF graphs and creates indexes on each group separately. RIQ employs a new vector representation for RDF graphs. This representation captures the properties of the triples in an RDF graph and triple patterns in a query. It facilitates grouping similar RDF graphs using locality sensitive hashing. It relies on filtering index on the groups and compactly represents the index as a combination of Bloom and Counting Bloom Filters. During query processing, RIQ employs a streamlined approach where it constructs a query plan for a SPARQL query (containing one or more graph patterns), searches the filtering index to quickly identify candidate groups that may contain matches for the query, and rewrites the original query to produce an optimized query for each candidate. The optimized queries are then executed using an existing SPARQL processor that supports quads to produce the final results. Figure 3.12 illustrates the architecture of the RIQ system. The indexing engine of RIQ transforms an RDF graph into its vector representation, constructs a filtering index based on the vector representation by creating groups of similar RDF graphs, and builds a separate index on each group. The filtering engine generates a query plan for a SPARQL query, constructs the vector representation of each BGP in the query, and identifies, using the filtering index, candidate groups that may contain a match for the query. The Execution Engine rewrites the query methodically to generate an optimized query for each candidate group. It executes the optimized queries using an existing SPARQL processor that supports quads to produce the final output.

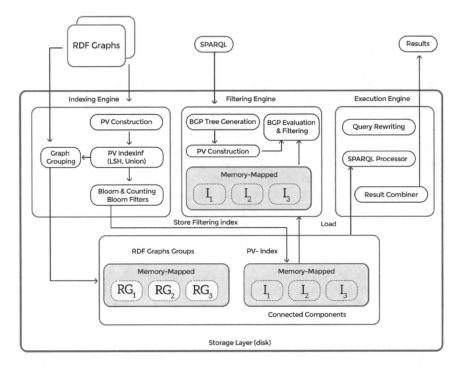

Fig. 3.12 The architecture of RIQ system [360]

3.6 Binary Encoding for RDF Databases

BitMat [25] is a three-dimensional (subject, predicate, object) bit matrix which
is flattened to two dimensions for representing RDF triples. In this matrix, each
element of the matrix is a bit encoding the absence or presence of that triple.
Therefore, very large RDF triple-sets can be represented compactly in memory
as BitMats. Figure 3.13 shows some sample RDF data and a corresponding bit
matrix. The data is then compressed using D-gap compression[2] on each row
level. Bitwise AND/OR operators are used to process join queries expressed as
conjunctive triple patterns. In particular, BitMat creates three auxiliary tables to
maintain mappings of distinct subjects, predicates, and objects to the sequence-
based identifiers. Then, it groups the RDF triples by predicates and builds a subject
BitMat for each predicate group and concatenates (S,O) matrices together to get the
two-dimensional BitMat. To make the matrix size more compact, BitMat applies
RLE on each subject row in the concatenated BitMat. During query processing, the
BitMat representation allows fast identification of candidate result triples in addition
to providing a compact representation of the intermediate results for multi-joins. The
join procedure of BitMat relies on three main primitives: (1) *filter*, which returns

---

[2]http://bmagic.sourceforge.net/dGap.html.

Subject	Predicate	Object
:the_matrix	:released_in	"1999"
:the_thirteenth_floor	:released_in	"1999"
:the_thirteenth_floor	:similar_plot_as	:the_matrix
:the_matrix	:is_a	:movie
:the_thirteenth_floor	:is_a	:movie

Distinct subjects: [:the_matrix, :the_thirteenth_floor]
Distinct predicates: [:released_in, :similar_plot_as, :is_a]
Distinct objects: [:the_matrix, "1999", :movie]

	:released_in			:similar_plot_as			:is_a		
:the_matrix	0	1	0	0	0	0	0	0	1
:the_thirteenth_floor	0	1	0	1	0	0	0	0	1

Note: Each bit sequence represents sequence of objects (:the_matrix, "1999", :movie)

Fig. 3.13 BitMat: sample bit matrix [25]

BitMat by identifying a subset of triples that satisfy the triple pattern, and clears the bits of all other triples; (2) *fold*, which returns a bit-array by applying a bitwise OR on the two dimensions; and (3) *unfold*, which returns BitMat for the bit set to 0 in the mask. In principle, the main goal of the BitMat multi-join algorithm is to ensure that the intermediate result set remains small across any number of join operations.

TripleBit system [428] has been designed as a storage structure that can directly and efficiently query the compressed data. It uses a bit matrix storage structure and the encoding-based compression method for storing huge RDF graphs more efficiently. Such storage structure enables TripleBit to use merge joins extensively for join processing. In particular, TripleBit uses the Triple Matrix model where RDF triples are represented as a two-dimensional bit matrix. In this matrix, each column of the matrix corresponds to an RDF triple, with only two entries of bit value associated with the subject entity and object entity of the triple. Each row is defined by a distinct entity value, with the presence in a subset of entries, representing a collection of the triples having the same entity. TripleBit sorts the columns by predicates in lexicographic order and vertically partitions the matrix into multiple disjoint buckets, one per predicate. In addition, TripleBit uses two auxiliary indexing structures: (1) ID-Chunk bit matrix, which supports a fast search of the relevant chunks matching to a given subject or object, and (2) ID-Predicate bit matrix, which provides a mapping of a subject (S) or an object (O) to the list of predicates to which it relates. These indexing structures are effectively used to improve the speedup for scan and merge-join performance. TripleBit employs a dynamic query plan generation algorithm to generate an optimal execution plan for a join query with the aim of minimizing the size of intermediate results as early as possible. TripleBit utilizes unique IDs for the same entities to further improve the query processing efficiency as the query processor does not need to distinguish whether IDs represent subject or object entities when processing joins.

Chapter 4
Distributed RDF Query Processing

Check for
updates

With increasing sizes of RDF datasets, executing complex queries on a single node
has turned to be impractical especially when the node's main memory is dwarfed
by the volume of the dataset. Therefore, there was a crucial need for distributed
systems with a high degree of parallelism that can satisfy the performance demands
of complex SPARQL queries. Several distributed RDF processing systems have
been introduced where the storage and query processing of linked data is managed
on *multiple* nodes. In contrast to centralized systems, distributed RDF systems are
characterized by larger aggregate memory sizes and higher processing capacity.
On the other hand, they might incur significant intermediate data shuffling when
answering complex SPARQL queries that span multiple disjoint partitions. The
previous chapter presented an overview of the various *centralized* storage and
query processing techniques for RDF datasets. In this chapter, we give an overview
of various techniques and systems for efficiently querying large RDF datasets in
distributed environments. Figure 4.1 illustrates the general classification scheme for
the distributed RDF storage and querying schemes which we are discussing in this
chapter.

4.1 NoSQL-Based RDF Systems

Section 2.7.1 introduced the NoSQL big data storage systems. Several approaches
have been exploiting the new wave of NoSQL database systems for building
scalable RDF management systems. Figure 4.2 gives an overview of RDF systems
classified according to their underlying NoSQL database design. For example,
JenaHBase [212] uses HBase, a NoSQL column family store, to provide various
custom-built RDF data storage layouts which cover various trade-offs in terms of
query performance and physical storage (Fig. 4.3). In particular, JenaHBase designs
several HBase tables with different schemas to store RDF triples. The simple layout
uses three tables each indexed by subjects, predicates, and objects. For every unique

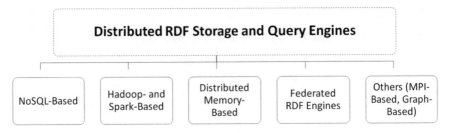

Fig. 4.1 Classification of distributed RDF storage and querying techniques

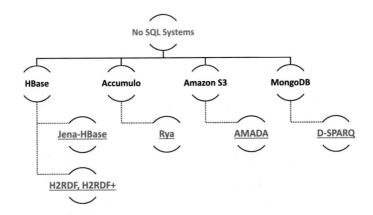

Fig. 4.2 NoSQL-based RDF systems

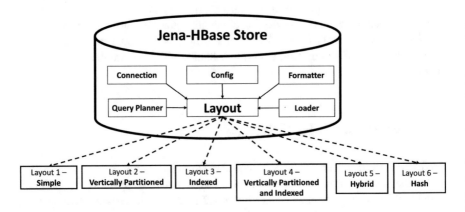

Fig. 4.3 The architecture of JenaHBase system [212]

predicate, the vertically partitioned layout (see Sect. 3.4) creates two tables where each of them is indexed by subjects and objects. The indexed layout uses six tables representing the six possible combinations of indexing RDF triples. The hybrid layout combines both the simple and VP layouts. The hash layout combines the hybrid layout with hash values for nodes and a separate table maintaining hash-to-node encodings. For each of these layouts, JenaHBase processes all operations (e.g., loading triples, deleting triples, querying) on an RDF graph by implicitly converting them into operations on the underlying storage layout.

The Rya system [316] has been implemented on top of Accumulo, a distributed key-value and column-oriented NoSQL store that supports the ordering of keys in a lexicographic ascending order. Accumulo orders and partitions all key-value pairs according to the Row ID part of the key. Rows with similar IDs are grouped into the same node for efficient and faster access. Rya stores the RDF triple (subject, predicate, and object) in the Row ID part of the Accumulo tables. In addition, it indexes the triples across three separate tables (SPO, POS, and OSP) that support all the permutations of the triple pattern. These tables store the triple in the Accumulo Row ID and order the subject, predicate, and object differently for each table. This approach exploits the row-sorting mechanism of Accumulo to efficiently store and query triples across multiple Accumulo tablets. SPARQL queries are evaluated using indexed nested loop join operations. Rya counts all the distinct subjects, predicates, and objects stored and uses this information for query optimization and join reordering. The statistics only need to be updated if the distribution of the data changes significantly because the query planner will reorder the query based on which triple pattern has the highest selectivity. If the data distribution does not change much over time, the query planner will not produce a different ordering of the triple patterns. While Rya is built on top of Accumulo and takes advantage of some of the Accumulo specific features, Rya is designed to work on top of any NoSQL columnar database. To achieve this goal, Rya provides a Data Access Object (RyaDAO), a simple abstraction of the persistence and query layer. Therefore, instead of having to implement the full interface for every persistence layer, users can utilize the RyaDAO interface.

H2RDF [304] is a distributed RDF storage system that combines a multiple-indexing scheme over HBase, a horizontally scalable NoSQL store, and the Hadoop framework. H2RDF creates three RDF indexes (SPO, POS, and OSP) over the HBase store. During the data loading, H2RDF collects all the statistical information which is utilized by the join planner algorithm during query processing. During query processing, the Join Planner navigates through the query graph and greedily selects the joins that need to be executed based on the selectivity information and the execution cost of all alternative join operations. H2RDF uses a join executor module which, for any join operation, chooses the most advantageous join scenario by selecting among centralized and fully distributed executions, via the Hadoop platform. Particularly, centralized joins are evaluated in a single cluster node, while distributed join operations are evaluated by launching MapReduce jobs to process them. H2RDF+ [305, 306] extended the approach of H2RDF by storing all permutations of RDF indexes. Using this indexing scheme, all SPARQL queries can be efficiently processed by a single index scan on the associated index. In addition, it guarantees that each join operation between triple patterns can be evaluated via merge joins that can effectively utilize the precomputed orderings.

AMADA [21] has been presented as a platform for RDF data management which is implemented on top of the Amazon Web Services (AWS) cloud platform. It is designed as a Software-as-a-Service (SaaS) which allows users to upload, index, store, and query RDF data. In particular, RDF data is stored using Amazon Simple Storage Service (S3), the AWS store for large objects. AMADA builds its own data indexes using SimpleDB, a simple database system supporting SQL-style queries based on a key-value model that supports single-relation queries, that is, no joins. In AMADA, the query execution is performed using virtual machines within the Amazon Elastic Compute Cloud (EC2). In practice, once a query is submitted to the system, it gets sent to a query processor module running on an EC2 instance, which performs a lookup to the indexes in SimpleDB in order to find out the relevant indexes for answering the query, and evaluates the query against them. Results are written in a file stored in S3, whose URI is sent back to the user to retrieve the query answers.

CumulusRDF [227] implements two RDF storage schemes on top of the Apache Cassandra NoSQL system. The first scheme covers the six combinations of RDF triple pattern with indexes to support evaluating single triple patterns in a straightforward manner using the index. The second scheme employs prefix lookups where one index covers multiple patterns and minimizes the number of indexes and thus index maintenance time and space. In particular, CumulusRDF uses two storage layouts: hierarchical layout and flat layout. The Hierarchical Layout builds on Cassandra's supercolumns. The first index is constructed by inserting *SPO* triples directly into a supercolumn three-way index, with each RDF term occupying key, supercolumn, and column positions, respectively, and an empty value. For each unique s as row key, there are multiple supercolumns, one for each unique p. For each unique p as supercolumn key, there are multiple columns, one for each o as column key. The column value is left empty. Given that layout, CumulusRDF can perform (hash-based) lookups on the search items. The Flat Layout is based on the standard key-value data model. As columns are stored in a sorted fashion, CumulusRDF can perform range scans and therefore prefix lookups on column keys.

D-SPARQ [279] has been presented as a distributed RDF query engine on top of **MongoDB**, a NoSQL document database.[1] D-SPARQ constructs a graph from the input RDF triples, which is then partitioned across the machines in the cluster. After partitioning, all the triples whose subject matches a vertex are placed in the same partition as the vertex. In addition, a partial data replication is then applied where some of the triples are replicated across different partitions to enable the parallelization of query execution. Grouping the triples with the same subject enables D-SPARQ to efficiently retrieve triples which satisfy subject-based star patterns in one read call for a single document. D-SPARQ also uses indexes involving subject-predicate and predicate-object. The selectivity of each triple pattern plays an important role in reducing the query runtime during query execution by reordering the individual triple patterns within a star pattern. Thus,

---

[1] https://www.mongodb.com/.

for each predicate, D-SPARQ keeps a count of the number of triples involving that particular predicate.

4.2 Hadoop-Based RDF Systems

In Sect. 2.7.2, we introduced Hadoop as one of the most popular big data processing systems. In particular, for about a decade, Hadoop has been the shining big star in the big data sky. Several systems have been exploiting the Hadoop framework for building scalable RDF processing engines.

SHARD [324] is one of the first Hadoop-based approaches that used a clause-iteration technique to evaluate SPARQL queries against RDF datasets. It is designed to exploit the MapReduce-style jobs for high parallelization of SPARQL queries. Even though the authors do not introduce any novel storage model, they nevertheless expect data to be stored in a specific format (not ordinary triples). In the datafile, they expect each line to correspond to a star-like shape centering around a subject and all edges from this node. The files containing all the data are stored directly on HDFS without any specific partitioning scheme, by exploiting the replication factor of the underlying distributed file system.

```
Kurt  owns  car0  livesIn  Cambridge
car0  a  car  madeBy  Ford  madeIn  Detroit
Detroit  a  city
Cambridge  a  city
```

The example above represents the following triples:

```
Kurt  owns  car0
Kurt  livesIn  Cambridge
car0  a  car
car0  madeBy  Ford
car0  madeIn  Detroit
Detroit  a  city
Cambridge  a  city
```

Rohloff et al. [324, 325] introduce, in their SHARD system, a clause iteration algorithm, the main idea of which is to iterate over all clauses and incrementally bind variables and satisfy constraints. During the first iteration, the *Map* step filters each of the bindings and the *Reduce* step removes duplicates where the key values for both *Map* and *Reduce* are the bound variables in the *SELECT* clause. The output collection consists of keys (which are variable bindings from the *SELECT* clause) and NULL values. The intermediate MapReduce jobs continue to construct query responses by iteratively binding graph data to variables in later clauses as new variables are introduced and then joining these new bindings to the previous bound variables such that the joined bound variables align with iteratively increasing subsets of the query clauses. The intermediate steps execute MapReduce operations simultaneously over both the graph data and the previously bound variables which were saved to disk to perform this operation. This iteration of map-reduce-join

---

Algorithm 3 SHARD: iteration algorithm [324]

Require: triples, query
 1: *mrOutput ⟵ NULL*
 2: *mrInput ⟵ triples*
 3: firstClauseMapReduce(mrInput, mrOutput, query.clause(0))
 4: *boundVars ⟵ query.clause(0).getVars()*
 5: **for** *i ⟵* 1 **to** *query.numClauses −* 1 **do**
 6:     *mrInput ⟵ union(triples, mrOutput)*
 7:     *curVars ⟵ query.clause(i).getVars()*
 8:     *comVars ⟵ intersection(boundVars, curVars)*
 9:     intermediateClauseMapReduce(mrInput,mrOutput, query.clause(i), comVars)
10: **end for**
11: *mrInput ⟵ mrOutput*
12: selectMapReduce(mrInput, mrOutput, query.select())
13: **return** *mrOutput*

---

continues until all clauses are processed and variables are assigned which satisfy
the query clauses. A final MapReduce step consists of filtering bound variable
assignments to obtain just the variable bindings requested in the *SELECT* clause
of the original SPARQL query. Algorithm 3 runs a `firstClauseMapReduce`
MapReduce job to perform the first step. As an output, it returns sets of possible
assignments to the variables of the first clause. `boundVars` tracks variables that
were bound during this step. For the following example query:

```
SELECT  ?person  WHERE  {
              ?person  :owns  ?car  .
              ?car  :a  :car  .
              ?car  :madeIn  :Detroit  .}
```

for example, variables `?person` and `?car` are bound and set to `boundVars`.
The iterating step runs the `intermediateClauseMapReduce` MapReduce
job to perform the second step. It identifies triples matching to each clause (one
by one) and then performs joins over intermediate results of this step and all
previous steps. For instance, after the very first step, the system gets a set of
bound variables `<(?car car0), null>`; after the first iteration, it gets a map of
variables bound during the second and first steps `<(?car car0), (?person,
Kurt)>`. The reduce phase combines those two and returns `<(?car car0
?person, Kurt)>`.

Huang et al. [191] propose a hybrid solution combining a single node RDF store
(RDF-3X; see Sect. 3) and Hadoop MapReduce to provide horizontal scalability. To
distribute triples across nodes, they leverage the METIS graph partitioning system.[2]
Hence, they co-locate triples forming a subgraph (star-like structure) on a particular
node. This enables to maximize the number of operations performed in parallel on
separate processing nodes avoiding expensive centralized cross-node joins. All this

---

[2]http://glaros.dtc.umn.edu/gkhome/views/metis.

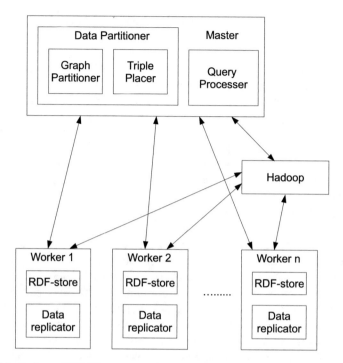

Fig. 4.4 MapReduce + RDF-3X: system architecture [191]. ©2011 VLDB Endowment. Reprinted with permission

reduces the amount of data that is transferred over the network for intermediate results. Figure 4.4 shows the architecture of the system.

Data is loaded and partitioned on the master node while triples are distributed among workers. On each node in the Hadoop cluster, there is an installation of the native RDF store which receives and loads subsets of triples. The authors partition graph vertices so that each worker receives a subset of those vertices that are close to each other in the graph. Having all vertices partitioned, the system assigns triples to the worker in the way that the triple is placed on the machine if its subject is among vertices owned by the worker. The process consists of two steps. First, the system divides vertices into disjoint subsets. Then, it assigns triples to workers. Before partitioning vertices, the system removes all triples where the predicate is `rdf:type`. Following this step, the system prepares an input list of edges and vertices (an undirected graph) for METIS. As an output from METIS, the system receives partitions of vertices that are disjoint. Having all vertices partitioned, the system starts placing triples on nodes in a cluster. The basic idea is to place a triple on a partition if its subject is among the vertices assigned to the partition; this forms 1-hop star-like subgraph. This can be extended to further hops so that objects of triples are extended with triples considering them as subjects. The triple placement can also be performed on an undirected graph such that triples containing the vertex assigned to a partition as an object are also placed in it. Both of these extensions are trade-offs between duplicating data on worker nodes and query execution performance (the more extended the subgraphs are, the less joins have to be performed in the final step). Huang et al. [191] took advantage of their partitioning scheme and of their backend triple store. Queries are decomposed into chunks executed in parallel and then reconstructed with MapReduce. They push as much of query processing as possible to the triple store while the remaining part is consolidated by Hadoop. The system divides queries into two kinds: first, those that can be executed on a node, meaning that each node has sufficient data to generate complete result tuples, and second, those that have to be decomposed into sub-queries executed on nodes, whose results are finally collected and joined at the master node.

Hose and Schenkel [189] building on the work by Huang et al. [191] propose a workload-aware replication of RDF triples. Their rationale is that in many applications queries have a very similar structure including the same predicates. These regularities can be leveraged to replicate triples to further reduce the network communication, thus increasing its performance. Their contributions are (1) replication method which takes into account the workload patterns and (2) query optimization technique leveraging their replication method. First, the authors prepare a representative workload. They remove constant strings and URIs at the subject and object positions and filter expressions. For optional clauses, the authors include all possible combinations of the non-optional patterns. The triple patterns that are optional are then added to the workload set as separate workload queries to guarantee that all needed triples are replicated. Following this step, for all workload queries exceeding n-hop data partitioning [191], the authors determine what data should be replicated to avoid cross-node joins. A complex workload query that needs to be decomposed is split into all possible combinations of simple queries (queries executed entirely on one node). For each of these combinations, the authors compute the number of triples that have to be replicated in order to allow the execution of a complex query on a single node. In other words, the goal is to convert a complex query into a simple query with the replication of triples. The authors choose the combination of simple triples which involves the minimum number of triples to be replicated, and they replicate these triples. The query execution can then be performed entirely in parallel without expensive cross-node joins, similarly to the system proposed by Huang et al. [191].

The PigSPARQL [339] system compiles SPARQL queries into the Pig query language [300], a data analysis platform over the Hadoop framework. Pig uses a fully nested data model and provides relational-style operators (e.g., filters and joins). As illustrated in Fig. 4.5, in PigSPARQL, a SPARQL query is parsed to generate an abstract syntax tree which is subsequently compiled into a SPARQL algebra tree. Using this tree, PigSPARQL applies various optimizations on the algebra level such as the early evaluation of filters and using the selectivity information for reordering the triple patterns. Finally, PigSPARQL traverses the optimized algebra tree in a bottom-up manner and generates an equivalent sequence of Pig Latin expressions for every SPARQL algebra operator. For query execution,

Fig. 4.5 The architecture of PigSPARQL system [339]

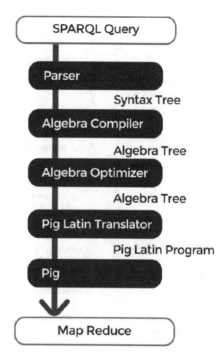

Pig automatically maps the resulting Pig Latin script onto a sequence of Hadoop jobs. An advantage of taking PigSPARQL as an intermediate layer that uses Pig between SPARQL and Hadoop is that it allows SPARQL to be independent of the actual Hadoop version or implementation details.

RAPID+ [321] is another Pig-based system that uses an algebraic approach for optimizing and evaluating SPARQL queries on top of the Hadoop framework. Ravindra et al. proposed an intermediate algebra called Nested Triple Group Algebra (NTGA) [218, 219, 321] to optimize their query execution process. This approach minimizes the number of MapReduce cycles to answer the query. It also introduces algorithms to postpone the decompression of intermediate results so they can be kept in compact form, thus reducing the number of I/O operations. The fundamental concept of NTGA is a TripleGroup [320], which is a group of triples sharing the same subject or object (star-like structure). Within one MapReduce operation, they precompute all possible star substructures, thus materializing all possible first-hop joins. Having computed all star-like structures, the system filters out those stars that do not fulfill query constraints. In the next step, if necessary, the system joins the stars. Figure 4.6 shows an example query and its execution plan. The first step (LOLoad) loads all data and at the same time also applies value-based filters on the data to avoid processing irrelevant triples. Then, during one Reduce operation, the LOCogroup operator groups triples and applies constraints on the groups, such that all irrelevant "stars" are filtered out. The last step in the flow is

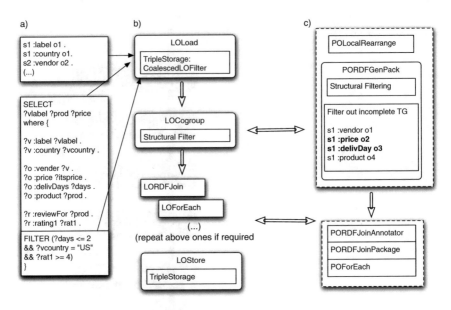

Fig. 4.6 RAPID+: query execution schema [321]. ©Springer-Verlag Berlin Heidelberg 2011. Reprinted with permission. (**a**) SPARQL query. (**b**) Logical plan. (**c**) Physical/MapReduce plan

joining stars based on subjects or objects, which is achieved with the LORDFJoin operator.

CliqueSquare [103, 139] is another Hadoop-based RDF data management platform for storing and processing big RDF datasets. With the central goal of minimizing the number of MapReduce jobs and the data transfer between nodes during query evaluation, CliqueSquare exploits the built-in data replication mechanism of the Hadoop Distributed File System (HDFS). Each of its partitions has three replicas by default, to partition the RDF dataset in different ways. In particular, for the first replica, CliqueSquare partitions triples based on their subject, property, and object values. For the second replica, CliqueSquare stores all subject, property, and object partitions of the same value within the same node. Finally, for the third replica, CliqueSquare groups all the subject partitions within a node by the value of the property in their triples. Similarly, it groups all object partitions based on their property values. In addition, CliqueSquare implements a special treatment for triples whose property is *rdf:type* by translating them into an unwieldy large property partition. CliqueSquare then splits the property partition of *rdf:type* into several smaller partitions according to their object value. For SPARQL query processing, CliqueSquare relies on a clique-based algorithm which produces query plans that minimize the number of MapReduce stages. The algorithm is based on the variable graph of a query and its decomposition into clique subgraphs. The algorithm works in an iterative way to identify cliques and to collapse them by evaluating the joins on the common variables of each clique. The process ends when the variable graph consists of only one node. During physical query execution, CliqueSquare exploits the different RDF partitions to perform the most common types of RDF queries locally on each node and reduce the data transfer through the network. In particular, it allows most incoming queries to be processed in a single MapReduce job, which enables a significant performance competitive advantage.

MapSQ [117] has been presented as a MapReduce-based framework for SPARQL Queries on GPU. It uses a MapReduce-based join algorithm to handle SPARQL queries in a parallel way and applies a co-processing strategy to manage the process of evaluating queries where the CPU is used to assign sub-queries and the GPU is used to compute the join of sub-queries.

4.3 Spark-Based RDF Systems

In Sect. 2.7.3, we introduced the Spark project as one of the popular and currently expanding big data processing frameworks. Several systems have been designed to exploit the Spark framework for building scalable RDF processing engines. For example, S2RDF[3] (*S*PARQL on *S*park for *RDF*) [340] introduced a relational partitioning schema for encoding RDF data called ExtVP (the *Ext*ended *V*ertical *P*artitioning) that extends the Vertical Partitioning (VP) schema introduced by Abadi et al. [2] (see Sect. 3.4) and uses a semi-join-based pre-processing to efficiently minimize query input size by taking into account the possible join correlations between the underlying encoding tables of the RDF data, join indexes [395]. In particular, ExtVP precomputes the possible join relations between partitions (i.e., tables) of VP. The main goal of ExtVP is to reduce the unnecessary I/O, comparisons, and memory consumption during executing join operations by avoiding the dangling tuples in the input tables of the join operations, that is, tuples that do not find a join partner. Clearly, ExtVP comes at the cost of some additional storage overhead in comparison to the basic VP encoding. Therefore, ExtVP does not use exhaustive precomputations for all the possible join operations. Instead, an optional selectivity threshold for ExtVP can be specified to materialize only the tables where reduction of the original VP tables is large enough. This mechanism facilitates the ability to control and reduce the size overhead while preserving most of its performance benefit. Therefore, during query execution, S2RDF can use the precomputed semi-join tables, if they exist, or alternatively uses the base encoding tables. S2RDF is designed on top of Spark[4] and executes SPARQL queries by compiling them into SQL queries which are evaluated using Spark SQL [24], an SQL query processor based on Spark, over ExtVP encoding. S2RDF uses the Parquet[5] columnar storage format for storing the RDF data on the Hadoop Distributed File System (HDFS).

---

[3]http://dbis.informatik.uni-freiburg.de/S2RDF.

[4]http://spark.apache.org/.

[5]https://parquet.apache.org/.

SparkRDF [78, 79] is another Spark-based RDF engine which partitions the RDF graph into MESGs (Multi-layer Elastic SubGraphs) according to relations (R) and classes (C) by building five kinds of indexes (C,R,CR,RC,CRC) with different granularities to support efficient evaluation for the different query triple patterns (TPs). These indexes are modeled as RDSGs (Resilient Discreted SubGraphs), a collection of in-memory subgraphs partitioned across nodes. SPARQL queries are evaluated over these indexes using a series of basic operators (e.g., filter, join). All intermediate results are represented as RDSGs and maintained in distributed memory to support faster join operations. SparkRDF uses a selectivity-based greedy algorithm to build a query plan with an optimal execution order of query triple patterns (TPs) that aims to effectively reduce the size of intermediate results. In addition, it uses a location-free prepartitioning strategy that avoids the expensive shuffling cost for the distributed join operations. In particular, it ignores the partitioning information of the indexes while repartitioning the data with the same join key to the same node.

The S2X (SPARQL on Spark with GraphX) [341] RDF engine has been implemented on top of GraphX [141], an abstraction for graph-parallel computation that has been augmented to Spark [429]. It defines a property graph representation of RDF for GraphX and uses a vertex-centric algorithm to match basic graph patterns (BGP). S2X combines graph-parallel abstractions of GraphX to implement the graph pattern matching constructs of SPARQL with data-parallel computation of Spark to build the results of other SPARQL operators. BGP matching in S2X is realized in a graph-parallel manner using the GraphX API and the other operators and modifiers (e.g., Optional, Filter, Order By, Projection, Limit, and Offset) are realized in a more data-parallel manner using the API of Spark. Relying on Spark as the backend of S2X, graph-parallel and data-parallel computation can be combined smoothly without the need for data movement or duplication. A similar approach has been followed by Goodman and Grunwald [142] for implementing an RDF engine on top of the GraphLab framework [249], another graph-parallel computation platform.

SPARQLGX [147] relies on SPARQL query translation to translate the queries into Scala code which is then directly executed by Spark [429]. SPARQLGX leverages the Vertical Partitioning (VP) schema proposed by Abadi et al. [2] (see Sect. 3.4). RDF triples are vertically partitioned by predicates and stored on the Hadoop file system (HDFS) in files corresponding to predicates' name. Each file contains only subject and object since the predicate is indicated by the file name. The query execution starts with translating every triple pattern to a Scala call that retrieves corresponding files from HDFS. If, in the triple pattern, the predicate is bound, SPARQLGX retrieves a file with its name, whereas in the opposite case, the system has to open all predicate files. Then, to find corresponding entities in the file, SPARQLGX uses the *filter* method from Scala. When it comes to queries involving multiple triple patterns, the query execution requires join operations; SPARQLGX simply indexes the triples by the join variable in-memory, that is, the variable that is in common for a given set of triple patterns, and uses *join* from Scala. In order to optimize the performance, SPARQLGX computes the statistics on the data. The statistics are used to order the join operations and hence to minimize the intermediate results involved in joins. SPARQLGX also allows ad hoc triples to be queried without any pre-processing and expensive vertical partitioning (e.g., from streams). To achieve that, the system implements the second translation schema called direct evaluator. Instead of searching in the vertically partitioned predicate files, the direct evaluator performs direct searches on the input files containing raw triples; the remaining query execution process is the same. Naacke et al. [282] conducted a study to compare five different query processing approaches of SPARQL queries based on different join execution models on top of Apache Spark. The results of the study showed that hybrid query plans that combine partitioned join and broadcast joins help to improve query performance in almost all cases. Although SPARQL Hybrid RDD is slightly more efficient than the hybrid Data Frames solution due to the absence of a data compression/decompression overload, it becomes interesting to switch to the Data Frames representation when the size of RDDs almost saturates the main memory of the cluster.

TripleRush [370] is based on the graph processing framework Signal/Collect [369], a parallel graph processing system written in Scala, and applies similar concepts to that of GraphX [141]. TripleRush evaluates queries by routing partially matched copies of the query through an index graph. By routing queries to data, the system eliminates joins in the traditional sense. TripleRush implements three kinds of Signal/Collect vertices:

1. *Triple Vertices* that represent RDF triples: each vertex contains a subject, a predicate, and an object.
2. *Index Vertices* for triple patterns that route to triples: each vertex contains a triple pattern (with one or more positions as wild cards); these vertices build a graph from a match-it-all triple pattern to actual triples.
3. *Query Vertices* to coordinate the query execution process: such vertices are created for each query executed in the system; a vertex then initiates a query traversal process through the index graph before returning the results.

The most distinguished feature of TripleRush is the ability to inherently divide a query among many processing units.

4.4 Main Memory-Based Distributed Systems

Trinity.RDF [432] has been presented as a distributed in-memory RDF system. Trinity.RDF is built on top of Trinity [350], a distributed main memory-based key-value storage system and a custom communication protocol using the Message Passing Interface (MPI) standard. In particular, Trinity.RDF provides a graph interface on top of the key-value store by randomly partitioning the RDF dataset across a cluster of machines by hashing on the graph nodes. Therefore, each machine maintains a disjoint part of the graph. For any SPARQL query, a user submits his query to a proxy. Trinity.RDF performs parallel search on each machine

by decomposing the input query into a set of triple patterns and conducting a
sequence of graph traversal to produce bindings for each of the triple patterns. The
proxy generates a query plan and submits the plan to all the machines that maintain
the RDF dataset where each machine evaluates its part of the query plan under the
coordination of the proxy node. Once the bindings for all the variables are resolved,
all machines return the evaluated bindings to the proxy where the final result is
computed and delivered to the end user.

AdHash [12, 166] is another distributed in-memory RDF engine which initially
applies lightweight hash partitioning that distributes triples of the RDF triples by
hashing on their subjects. AdHash attempts to improve the query execution times by
increasing the number of join operations that can be executed in parallel without data
communication through utilizing hash-based locality. In particular, the join patterns
on subjects included in a query can be processed in parallel. The locality-aware
query optimizer exploits this property to build a query evaluation plan that reduces
the size of intermediate results transferred among the worker nodes. In addition,
AdHash continuously monitors the data access patterns of the executed workload
and dynamically adapts to the query workload by incrementally redistributing and
replicating the frequent partitions of the graphs. The main goal for the adaptive
dynamic strategy of AdHash is to effectively minimize or eliminate the data
communication cost for future queries. Therefore, hot patterns are redistributed and
potentially replicated to allow future workloads which contain them to be evaluated
in parallel by all worker nodes without any data transfer. To efficiently manage
the replication process, AdHash specifies a budget constraint and uses an eviction
policy for the redistributed patterns. As a result, AdHash attempts to overcome the
disadvantages of static partitioning schemes and dynamically reacts with changing
workloads. Figure 4.7 illustrates the architecture of the AdHash RDF engine. In this
architecture, the master starts by partitioning the data across the worker nodes and
gathering global statistical information. In addition, the master node is responsible

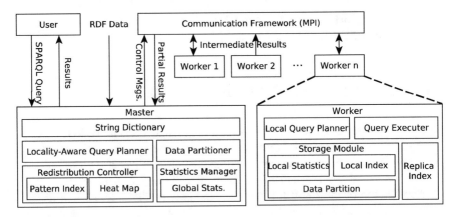

Fig. 4.7 The architecture of AdHash system [166]. ©2015 VLDB Endowment. Reprinted with
permission

for receiving queries from users, generating execution plans, coordinating worker nodes, collecting the final results, and returning the results to users. The statistics manager maintains statistics about the RDF graph that are exploited during the global query planning and adaptive repartitioning purposes. These statistics are distributedly gathered during the bootstrapping phase. The redistribution controller monitors the executed query workload in the form of heat maps and starts an adaptive Incremental ReDistribution (IRD) process for hot patterns. In this process, only data which is retrieved by the hot patterns is redistributed and potentially replicated across the worker nodes. In principle, a redistributed hot pattern can be answered by all workers in parallel without communication. The locality-aware query planner uses the global statistics and the pattern index from the redistribution controller to decide if a query, in whole or partially, can be processed without communication. Queries that can be fully answered without communication are planned and executed by each worker independently. On the other hand, for queries that require communication, the planner exploits the hash-based data locality and the query structure to find a plan that minimizes communication and the number of distributed joins.

Potter et al. [312] propose a distributed algorithm to answer queries over a partitioned RDF graph. The algorithm dynamically decides when and how to exchange data between the machines, that is, it exchanges data only when it is needed. The algorithm adapts the index nested loop join and at each stage it decides if the next stage should be further executed on the same machine or if it should be moved/forked to another server. Specifically, after reordering the triple patterns from the query, each server tries to recursively find RDF triples which match the pattern. Each stage of the nested join loop, which corresponds to a triple pattern, takes as an input a triple pattern and the partial answers of the previous stages. Before evaluating a triple pattern with bindings from previous partial answers, the server verifies if there is another server in the cluster that has RDF triples which can contribute to the query execution. If there is a machine that can contribute to the query evaluation, it receives a message with the current partial answer, that is, the answer including all previous stages of the query execution. The new machine can then continue the forked query evaluation with data located on this machine. The presented variant of the index nested loop join algorithm dynamically jumps to the relevant servers when it is required by the query execution process based on the query itself and the data partitioning. The servers exchange the messages asynchronously without static synchronization in the query plan. A similar approach of graph exploration was also proposed in the Trinity.RDF system [432]. However, even as Trinity.RDF transfers the raw data between servers, there is another system presented by Potter et al. [312] that transfers the partial answers instead, which can decrease the amount of transferred data, hence increasing its performance.

4.5 Other Distributed RDF Systems

Partout [127] is a distributed engine that relies on a workload-aware partitioning strategy for the RDF data by allowing queries to be executed over a minimum number of machines. Partout exploits a representative query load to collect information about frequently co-occurring sub-queries and for achieving optimized data partitioning and allocation of the data to multiple nodes. As shown in Fig. 4.8, the architecture of Partout consists of a coordinator node and a cluster of n hosts that store the actual data. The coordinator node is responsible for distributing the RDF data among the host nodes, designing an efficient distributed query plan for a SPARQL query, and initiating query evaluation. The coordinator does not have direct access to the actual data but instead utilizes global statistics of the RDF data, generated at partitioning time, for query planning. Each of the host nodes runs a triple store, RDF-3X (see Chap. 3). Queries are issued at the coordinator, which is responsible for generating a suitable query plan for the distributed query execution. The data is located at the hosts which are hosting the data partitions. Each host executes its part of the query over its local data and sends the results to the coordinator, which finally generates the query result. The global query optimization algorithm avoids the need for a two-step approach by starting with a plan optimized with respect to the selectivities of the query predicates and then applying heuristics to obtain an efficient plan for the distributed setup. Each host relies on the RDF-3X optimizer for optimizing its local query plan.

TriAD (Triple-Asynchronous-Distributed) [161] uses a main-memory and shared-nothing architecture which is based on an asynchronous Message Passing protocol. TriAD applies a classical master-slave architecture in which the slave nodes autonomously and asynchronously exchange messages among them to evaluate multiple join operations in parallel. Relying on asynchronous communication allows the sibling execution paths of a query plan to be processed

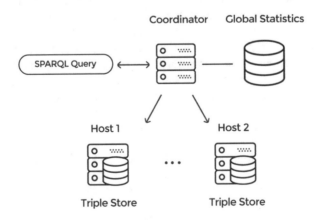

Fig. 4.8 The architecture of Partout system [127]

in a freely multithreaded fashion and only get merged (i.e., get synchronized) when the intermediate results of the entire execution paths are joined. Similar to the index permutation approaches described in Sect. 3.2, TriAD employs six comprehensive combinations of indexing over the RDF elements. The indexes are maintained in a distributed main-memory data structure where each index is first hash-partitioned according to its join key and then locally sorted in lexicographic order. Therefore, TriAD can perform efficient, distributed merge joins over the hash-partitioned permutation lists. In addition, TriAD uses join-ahead pruning using an additional RDF summary graph. The join-ahead pruning is executed at the master node, in order to prune entire partitions of triples from the SPO lists that cannot contribute to the results of a given SPARQL query. TriAD uses a bottom-up dynamic programming mechanism for join order enumeration and considers the locality of the index structures at the slave nodes, the data exchange cost of the intermediate results, and the option to execute sibling paths of the query plan in a multithreaded fashion, in order to estimate the query execution plan with the cheapest cost.

The **DREAM** (*D*istributed *R*DF *E*ngine with *A*daptive Query Planner and *M*inimal Communication) system [165, 174] has been designed with the aim of avoiding partitioning RDF graphs and partitions SPARQL queries only, thus attempting to combine the advantages of the centralized and distributed RDF systems. DREAM stores a dataset intact at each cluster machine and employs a query planner that effectively partitions any SPARQL query, Q. Specifically, the query planner transforms Q into a graph, G, decomposes G into sets of subgraphs, each with a basic two-level tree structure, and maps each set to a separate machine. Afterwards, all machines process their sets of subgraphs in parallel and coordinate with each other to return the final result. No intermediate data is shuffled and only minimal control messages and metadata are exchanged. To decide upon the number of sets (which dictates the number of machines) and their constituent subgraphs (i.e., G's *graph plan*), the query planner enumerates various possibilities and selects a plan that will expectedly result in the lowest network and disk costs for G. This is achieved through utilizing a cost model that relies on RDF graph statistics. Using the above approach, DREAM is able to select different numbers of machines for different query types, hence rendering it adaptive.

Wukong [354] has been presented as a distributed graph-based RDF store that leverages remote direct memory access (RDMA)-based graph exploration to provide highly concurrent and low-latency queries over large datasets. Wukong provides an RDMA-friendly distributed key/value store that provides differentiated encoding and fine-grained partitioning of graph data to reduce RDMA transfers. To support efficient scale-out, Wukong follows a graph-based design by storing RDF triples as a native graph and leverages graph exploration to handle queries. Wukong leverages full-history pruning to avoid the cost of expensive final join operations. For countering conventional wisdom of preferring migration of execution over data, Wukong seamlessly combines data migration for low latency and execution distribution for high throughput by leveraging the low latency and high throughput of one-sided RDMA operations. Consequently, Wukong can avoid the costly centralized final join on the results aggregated from multiple machines. Wukong extends an RDF graph by introducing index vertices so that indexes are naturally parts of the graph. To partition and distribute data among multiple machines, Wukong applies a differentiated partition schema to embrace both locality (for normal vertices) and parallelism (for index vertices) during query processing. Based on the observation that RDF queries only touch a small subset of graph data, Wukong further incorporates predicate-based finer-grained vertex decomposition and stores the decomposed graph data into a refined, RDMA-friendly distributed hash table to reduce RDMA transfers. Depending on the selectivity and complexity of queries, Wukong decomposes a query into a sequence of sub-queries and handles multiple independent sub-queries simultaneously. For each sub-query, Wukong adopts an RDMA communication-aware mechanism. For selective queries, it uses in-place execution that leverages one-sided RDMA read to fetch necessary data so that there is no need to move intermediate results. For nonselective queries, it uses one-sided RDMA WRITE to distribute the query processing to all related machines. To prevent large queries from blocking small queries when handling concurrent queries, Wukong provides a latency-centric work stealing schema to dynamically oblige queries in straggling workers.

Cheng et al. [82] presented a hybrid method for processing RDF that combines similar-size and graph-based partitioning strategies. In this approach, similar-size partitioning is used for fast loading data while graph-based partitioning is used to achieve efficient query processing. A two-tier index architecture is adopted. The first tier is a lightweight *primary index* which is used to maintain low loading times. The second tier is a series of dynamic, multilevel secondary indexes, evaluated during query execution, which is utilized for decreasing or removing the inter-machine data transfer for subsequent operations which maintain similar graph patterns. Additionally, this approach relies on a set of parallel mechanisms which combine the loading speed of similar-size partitioning with the execution speed of graph-based partitioning. For example, it uses fixed-length integer encoding for RDF terms and indexes that are based on hash tables to increase access speed. The indexing process does not use network communication in order to increase the loading speed. The local lightweight primary index is used to support very fast retrieval and avoid costly scans while the secondary indexes are used to support nontrivial access patterns that are built dynamically, as a by-product of query execution, to amortize costs for common access patterns.

The DiploCloud system [422, 423] has been designed to use a hybrid storage structure co-locating semantically related data to minimize inter-node operations. The co-located data patterns are mined from both instance and schema levels. DiploCloud uses three main data structures: molecule clusters, template lists, and a molecule index. *Molecule clusters* extend property tables to form RDF subgraphs that group sets of related URIs in nested hash tables and to co-locate data corresponding to a given resource. *Template lists* are used to store literals in lists, like in a columnar database system. Template lists allow to process long lists of literals efficiently; therefore, they are employed mainly for analytics and aggregate queries. The molecule index serves to index URIs based on the molecule cluster to which they belong. In the architecture of DiploCloud, the Master node is composed of three main subcomponents: a key index encoding URIs into IDs, a partition manager, and a distributed query executor. The Worker nodes of the system hold the partitioned data and its corresponding local indexes. The workers store three main data structures: a type index (grouping keys based on their types), local molecule clusters, and a molecule index. The worker nodes run sub-queries and send results to the Master node. The data partitioner of DiploCloud relies on three molecule-based data partitioning techniques: (1) *Scope-k Molecules* manually defines the size for all molecules, (2) *Manual Partitioning* where the system takes an input manually that defines the shapes of molecules, and (3) *Adaptive Partitioning* starts with a default shape of molecules and adaptively increases or decreases the size of molecules based on the workload. Star-like queries are executed in parallel without any central coordination. For queries requiring distributed joins, DiploCloud picks one of two execution strategies: (1) if the intermediate result set is small, DiploCloud ships everything to the Master node that performs the join, and (2) if the intermediate result set is large, DiploCloud performs a distributed hash join.

The **EAGRE** [434] system has been presented as an Entity Aware Graph compREssion technique to encode RDF datasets using key-value storage structures that preserves the structure and semantic information of RDF graphs. The main idea of this technique is to extract entities and entity classes from the original RDF in order to build a compressed RDF entity graph. Based on the EAGRE model, EAGRE adopts a graph partition mechanism that distributes RDF data across the worker nodes and designs an in-memory index structure to efficiently accelerate the evaluation of range and order-sensitive queries. In particular, the entity classes are partitioned on the computing nodes in a way that they preserve the structure locality of the original RDF graph. The evaluation process of a SPARQL query starts by identifying the entity classes using an in-memory index for the compressed RDF entity graph on a query engine. Then, the query is submitted to the worker nodes which maintain the RDF data where the query coordinator on each worker participates in a voting process that decides the scheduling function of distributed I/Os. EAGRE uses a distributed I/O scheduling mechanism to reduce the cost of the disk scans and the total time for the query evaluation process. In practice, whenever some workers complete their local I/O operation, they exploit the scheduler to feed other workers with the gathered statistical information of the processed data.

Figure 4.9 illustrates the architecture of the **SemStore** system [421] for distributed processing of RDF queries. SemStore consists of the following main components: a data partitioner, a master node, and a number of computing nodes. The SemStore partitioner adopts a partitioning mechanism, Rooted Sub-Graph (RSG), that is designed to effectively localize all the queries in the shapes of a star, a chain, a tree, or a cycle that captures the most frequent SPARQL queries. After partitioning the RDF graph, the data partitioner assigns each partition to one of the underlying computing nodes. The SemStore partitioner uses a k-means partitioning algorithm for assigning the highly correlated RSGs into the same node. Each computing node builds local data indexes and statistics for its assigned subgraph and utilizes this information during local join processing and optimizations. In

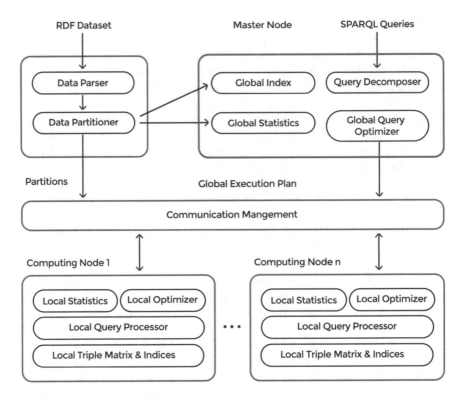

Fig. 4.9 The architecture of SemStore system

addition, the data partitioner builds a global bitmap index over the vertices of the RDF graph and collects the global statistics. In SemStore, each computing node uses a centralized RDF processor, TripleBit (see Chap. 3), for local query evaluation. The master node is the SemStore component that receives the user query, builds the distributed query plan, and coordinates distributed data transfer between the computing nodes.

Blazegraph[6] is an open-source triple store written in Java which is designed to scale horizontally by distributing data with dynamic key-range partitions. It also supports transactions with multiversion concurrency control relying on timestamps to detect conflicts. It maintains three RDF indexes (SPA, POS, OSP) and leverages a B+Tree implementation. These indexes are dynamically partitioned into key-range shards that can be distributed between nodes in a cluster. Its scale-out architecture is based on multiple services (see Fig. 4.10). The shard locator service maps each key-range partition to a metadata record that allows to locate the partition. A transaction service coordinates locks to provide the isolation. A client service allows to execute

---

[6]https://www.blazegraph.com.

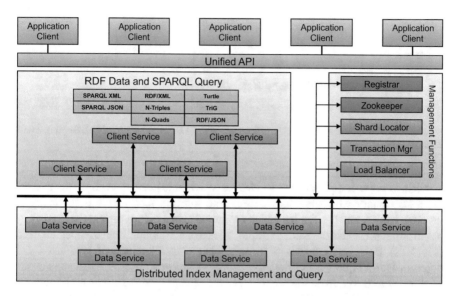

Fig. 4.10 Blazegraph services architecture [381]. ©2017 Blazegraph by SYSTAP, LLC

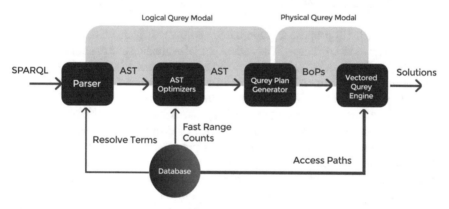

Fig. 4.11 Blazegraph query execution [381]. ©2017 Blazegraph by SYSTAP, LLC

distributed tasks. The query execution process is depicted in Fig. 4.11. It starts with the translation of a SPARQL query to an Abstract Syntax Tree (AST). Then, the tree is rewritten to optimize the execution. Finally, it is translated to a physical query plan, vectorized, and submitted for execution.

HDT[7] (Header, Dictionary, Triples) has been presented as a data structure and binary serialization format. However, the framework includes querying tools and enables distributed query processing in conjunction with Hadoop. The data format

---

[7]http://www.rdfhdt.org/.

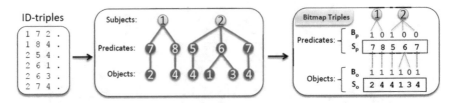

Fig. 4.12 HDT triples encoding [257]. ©Springer-Verlag Berlin Heidelberg 2012. Reprinted with permission

consists of three components: (1) a Header which holds metadata about the dataset, (2) a Dictionary which encodes strings into integers that are used internally to describe triples, and (3) Triples which are encoded in a binary format that transform the RDF representation into multiple trees (one tree for one distinct subject) (Fig. 4.12). Each tree consists of three levels (root/subject, list of predicates, and objects). During query execution, the patterns starting with a specified subject can be directly retrieved from the binary tree corresponding to the subject. To facilitate the evaluation of triple patterns that specify a predicate or an object, HDT introduces additional indexes. SPARQL queries containing multiple triple patterns are resolved by using merge and index joins.

Peng et al. [310] propose a graph-based approach to evaluate SPARQL queries over a distributed RDF dataset. They adopt partial evaluation and assembly approach described by Jones et al. [206]. The method assumes that RDF data is partitioned among multiple machines in a cluster and it divides the query execution into two steps. First, each node partially evaluates the query with the data that it owns and builds a collection of intermediate results, that is, partial matches. Second, the partial matches are joined either in centralized or distributed manner. To compute the partial matches, the authors employ their previous work, gStore (see Chap. 3). The algorithm matching subgraphs first finds a graph vertex u that matches to a query vertex v. Then, among the neighbors of the vertex u, it searches for a vertex u' that can match one of the neighbors of v from the query, v'. As a result, the edge uu' satisfies the query vv'. This process extends the results step-by-step until no more matches can be found or the entire query is satisfied. Since the data is fragmented among many machines, the algorithm terminates when the query is satisfied up to the limits of the local data, that is, it generates a partial match. In order to combine the partial matches, the authors first propose a centralized algorithm where all intermediate results are sent to one machine that performs an iterative join process. On every iteration the intermediate results from one machine are joined with the output of the previous iteration. To optimize this algorithm, the authors divide all local partition matches from a single machine into multiple sets, such that two local partition matches from one set cannot be joined. As a consequence, joins are performed only between partition matches from different sets; hence, it limits the data space considered in iterations. The second algorithm proposed by Peng et al. combines the partial matches in a distributed manner by using Bulk

Synchronous Parallel model [396]. First, all machines receive partial matches that contain some crossing edges, that is, edges that belong partially to one partition, partially to the other. Second, the machines perform local joins with their local partial matches. Each node performs joins up to the limit of the data it has, so it produces intermediate results. Finally, the intermediate results are then sent to nodes that contain some crossing edges with these intermediate results and another iteration is performed on the local joins. To avoid duplicates, the transition of local partial matches is only allowed to machines with a higher identifier.

In general, the way the RDF graph is partitioned can significantly impact the performance of any distributed RDF query engine. chameleon-db [13] has been proposed as a workload-aware RDF data management system that automatically and periodically adjusts its layout of the RDF database with the aim of optimizing the query execution time and auto-tuning its performance. Such adjustment is done in a way that enables partitions to be concurrently updated without the need of stopping the query processing. Similar to gStore [444], in chameleon-db, RDF data and SPARQL queries are represented as graphs, and queries are evaluated using a subgraph matching algorithm. However, in contrast with gStore which evaluates the queries over the entire RDF graph, chameleon-db partitions the RDF graph and prunes out the irrelevant partitions during query evaluation by using partition indexes. In practice, during the distributed execution of RDF queries, it is natural that some intermediate *dormant* tuples are returned as part of the results of sub-queries; however, these tuples do not contribute to the final result because, for instance, they may not join with intermediate results of another sub-query. The main goal of the chameleon-db partitioning strategy, called as partition-restricted evaluation (PRE), is to carefully identify the graph partitions that truly contribute to the final results in order to minimize the number of dormant triples which is required to be processed during query evaluation and hence improve the system performance for that workload. To prune the irrelevant partitions, chameleon-db uses an incremental indexing technique that uses a decision tree to keep track of which segments are relevant to which queries. In addition, it uses a *vertex-index* which is a hash table that maps URIs to the subset of partitions that contain vertices of that URI and a *range-index* that keeps track of the minimum and maximum literal values within each partition for each distinct predicate.

Wang et al. [405] have been building on the system described by Peng et al. [310] and proposed a distributed method to evaluate regular path queries,[8] that is, queries over an RDF graph that retrieve resources connected by a sequence of predicates matching a regular expression. The authors use partial evaluation to parallelize the execution within multiple nodes containing partitioned RDF triples. First, every node finds the property paths within its local data. Second, every node finds the possible connection with the previously computed paths and triples distributed among other machines. In order to compute the possible connections, the presented system maintains two special indexes that point to directly connected resources on

---

[8]https://www.w3.org/TR/sparql11-property-paths/.

other machines. Then, all partial answers are grouped in parallel based on three types of partial answer:

- Prefix partial answer: *object has an outgoing edge* to a different graph partition.
- Infix partial answer: *subject has an incoming edge* from and *object has an outgoing edge* to a different graph partition.
- Suffix partial answer: *subject has an incoming edge* from a different graph partition.
- Complete answer: the path is complete and there are no incoming and outgoing edges to different graph partitions.

Finally, all grouped partial answers are sent to a coordinating node that performs joins to generate the final results.

4.6 Federated RDF Query Processing

The proliferation of datasets in the Lined Open Data cloud[9] (9960 datasets as of June 2017) makes answering RDF queries over multiple SPARQL endpoints an important feature. Such queries, referred to as federated queries, in fact perform ad hoc data integration and complex graph operations over heterogeneous distributed data collections. In this section, we discuss a selection of systems that have been designed to support federated RDF query processing.

Saleem et al. [335] provide an extensive fine-grained evaluation of existing federated query engines. They show that factors like the number of sources selected, total number of SPARQL ASK requests used, and source selection time have a significant impact on the query execution time. The authors conclude that the method used to select sources (index-based or index-free) greatly affects the query performance. Moreover, using SPARQL ASK to select sources without any caching is very expensive (two orders of magnitude difference in the query execution time). Saleem et al. conducted a survey[10] among the domain experts and based on the results they categorized the federated systems into three categories:

1. *Query federation over multiple endpoints*: These systems execute queries on specified endpoints.
2. *Query federation over Linked Data*: These systems rely on the Linked Data principles by dereferencing URIs during the query execution.
3. *Query federation on top of a Distributed Hash Table*: These systems store RDF data on top of a Distributed Hash Table; however, this method requires all endpoints to use the DHT approach.

---

[9]http://stats.lod2.eu/.

[10]http://goo.gl/.

The most challenging part of executing a federated query is the source selection [298, 318]. Executing all triple patterns of a query on all data sources and joining the results is the most naive technique; however, such a system would have very slow performance. The amount of data transferred via the network and the computation overhead needed for joining all the intermediate results and eliminating possible duplicates would make such a system unusable. There are several techniques to select relevant sources for sub-queries:

- *SPARQL ASK*: It provides a simple boolean answer whether an endpoint has data to answer the query.
- *Catalog-assisted*: These systems use external data catalogs to retrieve statistics about datasets on distributed endpoints of which the statistics are used to optimize query execution.
- *Index-assisted*: These systems collect their own statistics before or during query execution; such statistics can include results of ASK queries, description of instances, schema, prefixes, ontology, classes, and predicates, that is, metadata that can be used to facilitate the source selection.

To minimize the number of sub-queries, most of the systems group triple patterns into sub-queries that can be entirely executed on one endpoint. The results of such sub-queries are post-processed to combine them and deliver the final results. After executing queries on multiple endpoints, the intermediate results have to be joined. The federated engines adopted various join strategies from the relational databases:

- *Nested Loop Join*: It iterates over the triples matching the first triple pattern (outer) and for every binding iterates over the triples matching the second triple pattern (inner); the bindings that provide joins are included in the results.
- *Hash Join*: It builds a hash table of a triple pattern that gives a smaller number of results; then, it iterates only over the bigger result set and probes the hash table for each binding.
- *Bind Join*: It passes the bindings of one triple pattern to the second triple pattern, and uses them during the second triple pattern evaluation to filter the results; hence, only relevant entities, which are capable to produce joins, are retrieved.
- *Symmetric Join*: It builds a hash table for results of two triple patterns, for every new result tuple for one triple pattern the algorithm probes if it is present in the hash table corresponding to the other triple pattern; if it is present the algorithm outputs a join result; this method allows for non-blocking execution of joins and it produces the final results as early as possible without waiting for a complete execution of all triple patterns.

Quilitz and Leser built their system DARQ[11] as a mediator-based information system [410] (Fig. 4.13). The federated query engine acts as a mediator between

---

[11]DARQ is a distributed extension of Jena ARQ https://jena.apache.org/documentation/query/index.html.

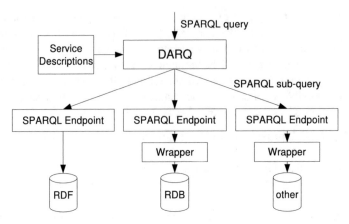

Fig. 4.13 The mediator-based architecture of DARQ [317]. ©Springer-Verlag Berlin Heidelberg 2008. Reprinted with permission

clients executing SPARQL queries and data sources, that is, SPARQL endpoints. DARQ provides transparent access to multiple distributed data sources. DARQ requires from a user to provide a list of available data sources along capabilities, limitations, and statistics of the data sources (service). Such a service description contains the following information:

- Data description describes what predicates appear in a data source in relation with what subjects or objects; this gives information about what triple patterns can be evaluated on the endpoint.
- Limitations describe certain restrictions imposed by the underlying data, for example, an LDAP service behind a SPARQL endpoint is required to provide a name or an email of a user to execute a search.
- Statistical information allows the system to compute the cost of a query; statistics consist of a total number of triples, number of triples for each couple (P,R), where P is a predicate and R is a subject or an object, number of triples for each predicate.

DARQ uses the information provided in service descriptions to select relevant data sources that can contribute to results. The system searches for data sources that can provide data with respect to predicates from triple patterns. If a triple pattern has specified a subject or an object, it is also used to narrow the set of endpoints. Following this step, triple patterns that have the same set of sources are grouped in a sub-query which is sent to the endpoints. To combine the results of sub-queries, the system uses either a nested loop join or a bind join, depending on the cost estimation. The goal is to minimize the amount of data transferred and to reduce the number of transitions. The cost function uses statistics provided within the service description and is based on the expected result size of a sub-query.

Schwarte et al. [348] recognized that the number of remote requests has a significant impact on the query execution time. To minimize the number of such

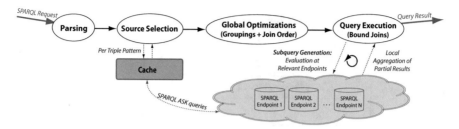

Fig. 4.14 FedX query processing model [348]. ©Springer-Verlag Berlin Heidelberg 2011. Reprinted with permission

remote requests, they implemented a new join processing and grouping techniques in the FedX system. To assure completeness of results, FedX assumes that the list of data sources is known at the query time. As depicted in Fig. 4.14, the query processing starts with a query parsing, then the system selects relevant sources for every triple pattern. Next, the system applies query optimization techniques, that is, join ordering and grouping of triple patterns. The groups of triple patterns are then executed on relevant endpoints. The partial results are joined with the modified nested loop join strategy to further minimize network traffic. To select a relevant source for a triple pattern, FedX sends a SPARQL ASK query to all known endpoints. The results of ASK queries are cached for later use. The join order optimization is based on a variable counting technique [366]. This technique estimates the cost of execution by counting free variables, which are not bound through previous joins. In order to further minimize the cost of joins executed locally, FedX, similarly to DARQ, groups triple patterns that have the same set of sources on which they can be executed. This allows these triple patterns to be sent to the endpoints as a conjunctive query and minimize the cost of local joins, as well as network traffic. A set of triple patterns can be also grouped together with SPARQL UNION and sent to a remote data source instead of sending each triple pattern separately. This technique requires to keep track of the original mappings. Moreover, it requires local post-processing to return the final results. The advantage of this method is that the number of remote requests can be reduced by the factor determined by the number of grouped triple patterns. FedX is implemented in Java on top of Sesame[12] as a Storage Layer Interface (SAIL).[13] Nikolov et al. [292] built on top of FedX a query engine that is optimized for full-text search and top-k queries.

SPLENDID [144] uses statistics obtained from VoID [11] (Vocabulary of Interlinked Datasets) descriptions to optimize the execution of federated queries. The main components of this system are the Index Manager and the Query Optimizer (Fig. 4.15). The Index Manager maintains the local copy of collected and aggregated

---

[12]http://rdf4j.org/.

[13]http://docs.rdf4j.org/sail/.

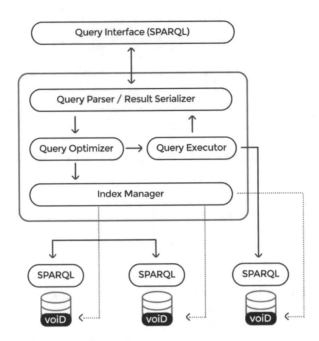

Fig. 4.15 The architecture of SPLENDID

statistics. The statistics for each endpoint provide information like triple count, number of distinct predicates, subjects, and objects. Moreover, SPLENDID keeps inverted indexes for each predicate and type. These indexes map predicates and types to corresponding data sources where they can be found and the number of their occurrence within a particular data source. The Query Optimizer transforms the query into a syntax tree, selects a data source to federate the execution, and optimizes the order of joins. To select a data source for a triple pattern, SPLENDID uses two inverted indexes for bound predicates and types; it gives, however, the priority to types. In case a triple pattern has neither bound predicate nor type, then all the available data sources are preselected. To refine the data source selection, the system sends SPARQL ASK queries with a triple pattern to all preselected data sources. In case one source is exclusively selected for a group of triple patterns, SPLENDID, similarly to FedX and DARQ, groups them and sends to this source as a single sub-query. To join the sub-results, SPLENDID implements two strategies: (1) for small result sets, the tuples are requested in parallel and a hash join is performed locally, and (2) for large result sets and high selectivity of join variables, one sub-query is executed and the join variable in the second one is repeatedly replaced with the results of the first sub-query (bind join [163]).

The WoDQA system [8] also used the VoID statistics to discover datasets relevant for a query. Their focus is on minimizing the number of datasets used to execute a query. WoDQA consists of three main modules: DataAnalyzer, QueryReorganizer, and Jena ARQ (a query executor). DataAnalyzer discovers relevant data sources and eliminates irrelevant ones. DataAnalyzer is a rule-based approach; it follows 12 rules to decide whether a data source is relevant. The rules are divided into three groups:

- IRI-based rules analyze namespace of IRIs and vocabularies in the VoID document.
- Linked-based rules verify whether a triple links two resources from the same or different datasets.
- Shared-variable-based rules analyze whether the variables span among many data sources or they are unique to only one data source.

The query is transformed to a set of sub-queries which are executed on relevant endpoints. Triple patterns that are designated for the same data source are grouped together to avoid unnecessary network traffic.

The ANAPSID system [5] leveraged the concept of a non-blocking join operator, Xjoin [394], which is optimized to quickly produce results even in the presence of slow endpoints, and the Symmetric Hash Join [99]. ANAPSID has four main components:

- *Catalog* to store list of available endpoints along with the ontology they use and execution timeouts indicating the capabilities of the endpoint.
- *Query Decomposer* to decompose queries into sub-queries and choose endpoints to execute each of them.
- *Query Optimizer* to determine the exact execution plan of sub-queries based on the collected statistics.
- *Adaptive Query Engine* that gathers partial results and performs final joins; this module produces final results incrementally as the data arrives from remote endpoints; it can detect whether an endpoint is blocked and modify the execution plan to prioritize sub-queries executed on available endpoints.

To join the results from the remote endpoints, ANAPSID implements the Adaptive Group Join operator, *agjoin*, which is based on Xjoin and Symmetric Hash Join. These operators maintain a separate hash table for results of each sub-query and as a consequence for each endpoint. Sub-queries are executed in parallel on each endpoint. When a tuple arrives from one endpoint, it is inserted to the corresponding hash table. The hash table indexes tuples by instantiations of join variables. Then, the operator immediately probes the other hash tables for a possible join operation. The join is performed and final results are produced as soon as possible, without waiting for all sub-queries to complete. ANAPSID implements a three-stage policy in order to manage flushing the hash table items to a secondary memory. On the first stage, operates in the main memory, and when the main memory is full, the system moves the least recently used items to the secondary memory. When both sources are blocked, that is, there is no item in the main memory to perform a join, then the operator starts checking items in the secondary memory. Finally, the third stage is fired when all data from all sources have arrived. In this case, all remaining data in the main and secondary memory are consumed to produce the remaining results.

The **LHD** (Large scale High speed Distributed engine) system [404] also leveraged the concept of Xjoin [394] with a main focus on a highly parallel infrastructure. In addition, the system leveraged Double-Pipelined Hash Join [319]. The system maintains multiple hash tables in order to join many sub-queries simultaneously. As results for sub-queries are arriving, they are stored in parallel in the hash tables and at the same time probed against other hash tables to check whether a join can be produced. To minimize the amount of data transferred via the network, LHD uses VoID statistics in order to estimate the cardinality of each sub-query. Based on the cardinality, it estimates the cost of a sub-query. The cardinality estimation is based on the number of triples and the number of distinct subjects and objects in a data source. Moreover, the system takes into account the number distinct subjects and objects corresponding to specified query predicates. To generate the query plan, the system chooses the cheapest possible join order for a query. Then, it executes triple patterns that have specified subject or object. Finally, LHD uses dynamic programming to find optimal plan and join order to execute triple patterns with unbound subject and object. LHD is built on top of Jena.

The **ADERIS** system [250] made an assumption that in many cases SPARQL endpoints do not provide any statistics about their data. Therefore, ADERIS does not rely on statistical data; it executes queries in an adaptable manner. The system joins data as it becomes available and modifies the join order based on the selectivity at runtime. First, ADERIS fetches triples that can contribute to execute the query. Then, the system builds a set of predicate tables (see property tables in Sect. 3.3) for the fetched triples. It creates one table for each predicate from the fetched triples. To facilitate joins, ADERIS creates indexes on these predicate tables. Finally, the system uses nested loop joins and adaptive join reordering [243] to join data from the generated property tables and to obtain final results.

The **Avalanche** system [37] has been designed to query Web of Data without assumption about the data location or distribution. The authors of the system claimed that one cannot make any assumptions about data distribution, schema-alignment, availability, and content stability; hence, they propose an approach that embraces the uncertainties of the Web of Data. Avalanche does not guarantee that the results are complete or that we will always receive the same results for the same query. The system, however, can execute queries over the highly distributed and heterogeneous infrastructure of the web. Avalanche can provide up-to-date results of queries executed in an adaptive manner without detailed statistics about data. The system has six main components that are combined in an asynchronous pipeline:

- The Source Selector retrieves prospective sources of data from online catalogs or search engines, for example, VoID.[14]
- The Statistic Requester retrieves, from the selected data sources, cardinalities for all triple patterns from the query; cardinalities can be retrieved either with the VoID vocabulary or aggregated with a SPARQL COUNT query.

---

[14]http://void.rkbexplorer.com/.

- The Plan Generator builds a two-dimensional matrix containing cardinalities of all triple patterns within data sources; plans are generated by exploring all possible triple-pattern/data source pairs for the query.
- The Plan Executors start executing the query plans as soon the first plan is generated; the executors run in parallel and place the results in a Results Queue.
- The Results Queue keeps the results of executed query plans.
- The Query Execution Monitor monitors the Results Queue and decides whether to stop the query execution.

Avalanche relaxes the need to generate exact query execution plans and cost estimation. It executes the plans in parallel; hence, the optimal plan should be highly ranked but does not have to be the fastest. Query plans are generated in an iterative way, so the executors do not wait for the generator to accomplish its work. As Avalanche does not need the exact cost model, it can significantly simplify the used metrics. The system considers network latency and bandwidth to be uniformly distributed between data sources. Avalanche does not compute the exact join selectivity as it is next to impossible for a highly distributed infrastructure such as the Web of Data. The system only estimates the selectivity; hence, it does not have to maintain complex statistics about data and it does not involve any computations and network cost. Due to the repeated nature of the plan generation strategy (repeated Greedy Depth First Search) and the partial cost estimation, the query execution plans are generated in a partially sorted order. Avalanche keeps track of executed sub-queries and their results for all plans in order to avoid executing the same sub-query, from different execution plans, multiple times, that is, it caches partial results and reuses a local copy instead of re-executing the same sub-query. The authors of this system assume that they have no control over the distribution and availability of data on the web; hence, they cannot provide the complete answer for a query. As a result of this, they implemented three stopping conditions for the query execution process:

- A timeout for the execution
- Top-K unique results
- A relative result-saturation, that is, a metric based on the number of results received within a sliding window of time

Charalambidis et al. [73] implemented their federated query execution system, SemaGrow, within the Sesame framework[15] SemaGrow uses the same source selection technique as SPLENDID and combined it with heuristics to group triple patterns that can be executed on the same data source. The authors recognize that grouping triple patterns can also have a negative effect on the query performance; hence, they introduce a configurable option that allows the system to consider all combinations of triple patterns to find the optimal query execution plan. In other words, the requirement of grouping triple patterns to be executed at the same source

---

[15]http://rdf4j.org/.

can be changed from hard to soft. To choose the optimal query execution plan, the authors use a recursive cost estimation based on statistics. The statistics are either provided by source metadata or are estimated from the cardinality of sub-queries. The plan generation in SemaGrow uses a standard technique for optimizing join order, namely, the dynamic programming. To execute a selected query plan, the system leverages a reactive asynchronous non-blocking strategy. It means that operators subscribe to data streams and are notified when data becomes available. The authors implemented a similar join technique as in that of FedX, that is, a bind join with grouping multiple bindings into a single query with the UNION expression.

Günter Ladwig and Thanh Tran tackled the problem of querying both remote and local data sources simultaneously [228]. They propose a Symmetric Index Hash Join (SIHJoin) which takes advantage of fast access to local data in order to optimize query execution. The proposed solution is based on a symmetric hash join, which is a push-based join processing strategy which starts the query execution from the root of a query plan and pushed data to higher levels of the query plan. Essentially, when only remote data sources are involved, the SIHJ performs joins in the same way as a symmetric hash join. However, when a query execution involves local data, the proposed join operator combines the push and pull strategies. The remote joins are executed by pushing data, but the local data is pulled by the operator when it is needed. The bindings that arrive to a join operator are used to instantiate triple patterns. Then, the operator performs a lookup of the local data to decide whether a particular binding can contribute to the join results. The access to local data is asynchronous so the query plans can continue independently.

Saleem et al. [333] recognized that in a highly decentralized infrastructure of Linked Data datasets can contain duplicated data; hence, they propose a duplicate-aware approach for federated queries. The main idea behind this approach is to avoid querying endpoints that produce duplicates in the results. The system, called DAW, combines the min-wise independent permutations (MIP) [57] and triple selectivity to detect data overlapping between endpoints that are involved in the query execution. DAW is implemented as an extension of three federated query processing engines described above, that is, DARQ, SPLENDID, and FedX. To execute a query, DAW would first use the underlying federated engine to identify data sources containing data for every triple pattern. Then, the sources are ranked based on their contribution to final results. Finally, some sources are dropped if they do not provide new tuples or they contribute very little to the output, that is, below a predefined threshold. This selected set of sources together with the query is sent to the federated query engine which divides the query into sub-queries and executes on the endpoints. To rank the sources, DAW estimates the overlapping data between data sources for a triple pattern, that is, how similar results can be provided from the sources for a given triple pattern. This estimation is done in two ways: (1) if the triple pattern has a bound subject or object, DAW uses selectivity information of the patterns to estimate the overlaps, and (2) in case only the predicate is bound, DAW uses MIP vectors since MIP vectors group triples by predicates. The idea behind the min-wise independent permutations (MIP) is to represent large sets as vectors of significantly smaller size and to enable operations on sets, for example, overlap, without comparing all elements of the sets. DAW creates a MIP vector for all distinct predicates within a data source, that is, MIP vectors are produced for sets of triples containing the predicate within the dataset.

Montoya et al. [265] extended the idea of DAW by proposing a system named FEDRA with the attempt to minimize the amount of data transferred by taking advantage of duplicated data. FEDRA takes into account that some data sources can contain replicated data; thus, they can be preferred as they can give a better overall performance. FERDA is integrated with FedX and ANAPSID. First, the system finds relevant fragments of data for every triple pattern and determines endpoints on which these data fragments are stored and replicated. Then, for triple patterns with multiple fragments, it reduces the number of endpoints by finding the minimal common set of data sources. Finally, for triples with one fragment, the system groups the triple patterns with the same fragments to execute possible joins directly on the endpoints.

Hassain et al. [175, 176] tackled the problem of heterogeneous vocabularies that are used among various data providers in a federated environment. This problem makes it difficult to execute queries for integrating data from many SPARQL endpoints. The proposed solution creates a Roadmap that describes all possible links between entities using various vocabularies. The Roadmap is exposed as a SPARQL endpoint which is used by their query engine (Domain-Specific Query Engine built on top of Jena) which is capable to automatically transform expressions from one vocabulary to another. Based on the mapping vocabulary (Roadmap), this engine translates terms from a query into terms that are appropriate for the endpoint where the query is to be executed. Such translated triple patterns are executed in a federated manner on multiple endpoints and the results are combined.

Some other approaches leverage federated query processing to develop search platforms summarizing data [86], to address the scalability issue and to develop distributed data processing platforms with a single point of access [334], or to develop systems that support access control in a decentralized environment [213].

Chapter 5
Processing of RDF Stream Data

We are witnessing a paradigm shift, where real-time, time-dependent data is becoming ubiquitous. For example, services like Twitter, Facebook, and blogs deliver massive streams of (typically unstructured) real-time data on various topics. Integrating these new information sources not only among themselves but also with other existing sources would enable a vast range of new, real-time applications in the areas of smart cities, green IT, and e-health, just to name a few. However, due to the heterogeneous nature of such diverse streams, harvesting data is still a difficult and labor-intensive task, which currently requires a lot of "hand-crafting". As Linked Data facilitates the data integration process among heterogeneous data sources, RDF Stream Data has the same goal with respect to data streams. It bridges the gap between stream and more static data sources. To support the processing on RDF stream data, there is a need on investigating how to extend RDF to model and represent stream data. Then, from the RDF-based data representation, the query model processing models need to be defined to build the stream processing engine that is tailored for streaming data. This chapter provides an overview on how such requirements are addressed in the current state of the art of RDF Stream Data processing.

5.1 RDF Streaming Data in A Nutshell

Recently, there have been efforts to lift stream data to a semantic level, for example, by the Graph of Things [238] or publishing stream data web streams, for example, by TripleWave [258]. The goal is to make stream data available according to the Linked Data principles that extend the RDF data model to represent stream data, called RDF Stream Data. To give an idea of how RDF Stream Data is generated under the RDF-based representation, Fig. 5.1 shows a data layout driven by SSN

© Springer International Publishing AG 2018
S. Sakr et al., *Linked Data*, https://doi.org/10.1007/978-3-319-73515-3_5

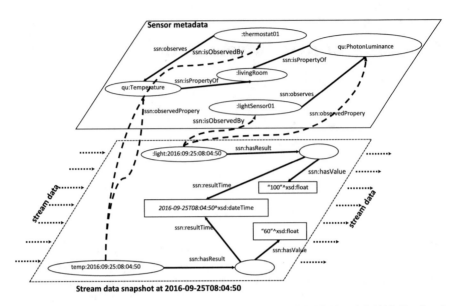

Fig. 5.1 Example of RDF data stream. ©Springer International Publishing AG 2018. Reprinted with permission

ontology.[1] The figure gives a visual view of how stream data of sensor observations of a light sensor and a temperature sensor in a living room are connected into metadata of these sensors and the living room (static or slowly changed data). The upper layer is the sensor metadata shown from the sensor perspective and system perspective, that is, temperature sensor and light sensor observe temperature property and photon luminance of the living room perspective (the serialized form of this subgraph is presented in Fig. 5.2). The metadata in the upper layer provides the context for the stream data elements in the lower layer via the links such as *ssn:observedProperty* or *ssn:isObservedBy*. The appealing nature of the stream data represented in this form is that the processing engine does not to need to know the schema of the incoming stream sources upfront to be able to correlate or aggregate them.

In a nutshell, the processing flow of RDF data stream is illustrated in Fig. 5.3. The processing engine can accept two types of data sources, that is, traditional RDF datasets and stream data sources represented in RDF format. The query is usually described in declarative form, commonly as an extension of the SPARQL query language. However, the processing requirements on the stream data are different than that of traditional SPARQL which is only executed once. The query over stream data is the long-standing query over stream which is continuously executed over data, called continuous query. For example, a continuous query on

---

[1] https://www.w3.org/TR/vocab-ssn/.

```
:phillipHue01   cf:AimbientLightSensor;
   ssn:madeObservation  :light:2016:09:25:08:04:50,
:light:2016:09:25:08:04:51,  :light:2016:09:25:08:04:52.
:light:2016:09:25:08:04:50  :observedProperty
                                    qu:photonLuminance;
   :hasResult [:hasValue 100^xsd:float;
         :resultTime 2016-09-25T08:04:50^xsd:dateTime];
:thermostat01   cf:TemperatureSensor;
   ssn:madeObservation  :temp:2016:09:25:08:04:50,
      :temp:2016:09:25:08:04:51,:temp:2016:09:25:08:04:52.
:temp:2016:09:25:08:04:50  :observedProperty
                                    qu:Temperature;
   :hasResult [:hasValue 25^xsd:float;
         :resultTime 2016-09-25T08:04:50^xsd:dateTime]
```

Fig. 5.2 Stream of sensor observations in turtle

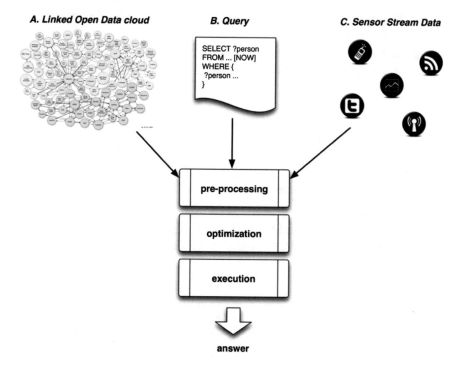

Fig. 5.3 Abstract RDF stream processing flow. ©Springer-Verlag Berlin Heidelberg 2012. Reprinted with permission

the data stream in Fig. 5.1 can repeatedly "report average temperature in the last 30 s" (the query language and operators will be introduced in later sections of this chapter).

5.2 Data Representation of RDF Streams

A *data stream* is an unbounded, continuously arriving sequence of time-stamped *stream elements*. The stream elements may arrive in some order [384] or out of order with explicit timestamps [244]. The stream elements are continuously pushed by external stream sources, and their arrival might be unpredictable. As a result, the system processing data streams has no control over the order of the stream elements and the streaming rate. Therefore, it is only able to access stream elements sequentially in the order in which they arrive. RDF Stream Data is modeled by extending the definitions of RDF nodes and RDF triples presented in Chap. 2. Stream elements of RDF Stream Data are represented as RDF triples or graphs (set of triples) with temporal annotations. A temporal annotation of an RDF triple can be an interval-based [248] or point-based label [162] or a mixture of both [270]. There have been several formal definitions of RDF stream, but in this book chapter, we will use the latest definitions from Dell'Aglio et al.[98] which is the most general definition so far.

Definition 1 (RDF Stream) A *time-stamped RDF graph* is a pair (G, t), where G is an RDF graph and $t \in T$ is a time instant. An *RDF stream* S is a (potentially) unbounded sequence of time-stamped RDF graphs in a non-decreasing time order:

$$S = (G_1, t_1), (G_2, t_2), (G_3, t_3), (G_4, t_4), \ldots$$

where, for every $i > 0$, (G_i, t_i) is a time-stamped RDF graph and $t_i \leq t_{i+1}$.

Example 5.1 Figure 5.4 illustrates a stream $S = (G_1, 2), (G_2, 4), (G_3, 6), (G_4, 8)$, $(G_5, 10), \ldots$, where each G_i contains the depicted RDF triples.

Time-Varying Graphs As the nature of the continuous query over RDF Stream Data associated with traditional RDF graphs as metadata is continuously changing over time, these RDF graphs are likely to be changed during the lifetime of

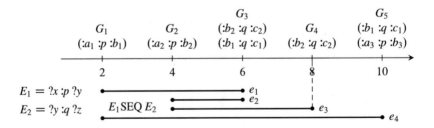

Fig. 5.4 Illustration of the arriving and processing order of a stream. The stream, shown on the top left is composed of five items $(G_1, 2) \ldots (G_5, 10)$. Events that matched the pattern E_1 SEQ E_2 are depicted below the timeline. The bold lines denote the intervals that justify the events. ©Springer International Publishing AG 2016. Reprinted with permission

the query. Hence, we introduce the notion of time-varying graphs to capture the evolution of the graph over time (similar to time-varying relations in [22]).

Definition 2 (Time-Varying Graph) A *time-varying graph* $\overline{G}$ is a function that relates time instants $t \in T$ to RDF graphs:

$$\overline{G}: T \rightarrow \{G \mid G \text{ is an RDF graph}\}.$$

An *instantaneous RDF graph* $\overline{G}(t)$ is the RDF graph identified by the time-varying graph $\overline{G}$ at a given time instant t.

RDF streams and time-varying graphs differ on the time information: while in the former, time annotations are accessible and processable by the stream processing engine, in the latter there are no explicit time annotations. In this sense, t in Definition 2 can be viewed as a timestamp denoting the access time of the engine to the graph content.

Let us revisit two types of time labels for representing the time information of RDF stream elements. An interval-based label is a pair of timestamps, commonly natural numbers representing logical time. A pair of timestamps, [start, end], is used to specify the interval in which the RDF triple is valid. For instance, *:John :at :livingroom, [7, 9]* means that John was at the "living room" from 7 to 9. A point-based label is a single natural number representing the point in time that the triple was recorded or received. In the previous example, the triple :John :at :office might be continuously recorded by a tracking system, so three temporal triples could be generated *:John :at :livingroom, 7, :John :at ::livingroom,8 , :John :at ::livingroom,9*. Point-based labels might look redundant and less efficient in comparison to interval-based labels. Furthermore, interval-based labels are more expressive than point-based because the later is a special case of the former, that is, when start = end. Streaming SPARQL [49] uses interval-based labels for representing its physical data stream items and EP-SPARQL [19] uses them for representing triple-based events. However, point-based labels are more practical for streaming data sources because they allow triples to be generated unexpectedly and instantaneously. For example, a tracking system detecting people at an office can generate a triple with a timestamp whenever it receives a reading from a sensor. Otherwise, the system has to buffer the readings and do further processing in order to generate the interval in which a triple is valid. Moreover, the instantaneous nature of point-based labels is vital for some applications that need to process the data as soon as it arrives in the system. For instance, an application that notifies where John is should be triggered at time point 7 and not wait until time 9 to report that he was in the office from 7 to 9. Point-based labels are supported in C-SPARQL [34], SPARQLstream [63], and CQELS [235].

When processing RDF stream elements, there are typically three types of time information that we would take into consideration: *Event time* is the time at which events actually occurred. *Processing time* is the time at which events are observed in the system. If the stream elements are sent from a remote source, then, there might be "received time" or "arrival time" which is somewhere between Event time and Processing time. We now focus only on Event time and Processing time as they directly dictate the output of the processing operations on the stream data. In an ideal world, Event time and Processing time would always be equal, with events being processed immediately as they occur. In reality, this is highly unlikely, however, and the skew between Event time and Processing time is not only nonzero, but often a highly variable function of the characteristics of the underlying input sources, execution engine, and hardware. Things that can affect the level of skew include shared resource limitations, such as network congestion, network partitions, or shared CPU in a non-dedicated environment, and in addition, software causes, such as distributed system logic, contention, etc. Features of the data themselves, including key distribution, variance in throughput, or variance in disorder (e.g., a plane full of people taking their phones out of airplane mode after having used them offline for the entire flight), can also affect the skew level.

5.3   RDF Streaming Query Model

To build a query model, most of the current systems are based on existing defined algebras, for example, relational algebras. Intuitively, a continuous query provides answers at any point in time by taking into account all the data that have arrived so far. This data is commonly in the form of relations used as inputs of relational algebras. Therefore, two types of continuous query algebras based on relational counterparts have been proposed. The first one is the *stream-to-stream* algebra that was employed in defining the semantics of Streaming SPARQL [49]. In a stream-to-stream algebra, each operator consumes one or more streams (and zero or more relations) and incrementally produces an output stream [88, 225].

The second type is the *mixed algebra* [22, 134]. Mixed algebra includes three sets of operators: *stream-to-relation operators* which produce a relation from a stream (e.g., sliding windows), *relation-to-relation operators* which produce a relation from one or more input relations (i.e., the standard relational algebraic operators), and *relation-to-stream operators* which produce a stream from a relation. Conceptually, at every time tick, an operator converts its input to relations, computes any new results, and converts the results back as a stream that can be consumed by the next operator. Since the converted relations change over time, a natural way of switching back to a stream is to report the difference between the current result and the result computed one time tick ago. This is similar to computing a set of changes (insertions and/or deletions) required to update a materialized view. The mixed algebra is used in formalizing the semantics of C-SPARQL [34], SPARQL$_{stream}$ [63], [446], and CQELS [235]. There are also logical algebras for CEP [59, 109] that have been inspired by relational algebra and logic programming.

5.3.1   Stream-to-Stream Operator

A Stream-to-Stream operator continuously calls one-time queries in native SQL over physical or logical streams to produce results to a derived stream. These operators are specified by common SQL constructions such as SELECT, FROM, WHERE, and GROUP BY. Kramer and Seeger [225] defined the window specification by extending the FROM clause. Other logical standard operators are defined similar to relational algebras.

5.3.2   Stream-to-Relation Operator

A stream-to-relation operator takes a stream S as input and produces a relation R as output with the same schema as S. For example, CQL [22] introduced three operators: time-based, tuple-based, and partitioned windows.

1. *Time-based sliding windows.* A time-based sliding window on a stream S takes a time-interval T as a parameter and is specified by following the reference to S with [Range T]. Intuitively, a time-based window defines its output relation over time by sliding an interval of size T time units capturing the latest portion of an ordered stream. More formally, the output relation R of "S [*Range T*]" is defined as:

$$R(t) \;=\; \{s \mid \langle s, t' \rangle \in S \wedge (t' \leq t) \wedge (t' \geq max\{t - T + 1, 0\})\} \qquad (5.1)$$

when $T = 0$, $R(t)$ consists of tuples obtained from elements with timestamp t, denoted with syntax "S [NOW]". And when $T = \infty$, $R(t)$ consists of tuples obtained from elements with timestamps up to t, given with the SQL-99 syntax "S [Range Unbounded]".

Example 5.2 "RFIDstream [Range 60 s]" represents a time-based sliding window of 60 s over a stream of RFID readings. At any time instant t, $R(t)$ will contain a bag of RFID readings from the previous 60 s.

2. *Tuple-based windows.* A tuple-based sliding window on a stream S takes a positive integer N as a parameter and is specified by following the reference to S in the query with [Rows N]. At any given point in time, the window contains the last N tuples of S. More formally, let $s_1, s_2, \ldots$ denote the tuples of S in increasing order of their timestamps, breaking ties arbitrarily. The output relation R of "S [Rows N]" is defined as:

$$R(t) \;=\; \{s_i \mid max\{1, n(t) - N + 1\} \leq i \leq n(t)\} \qquad (5.2)$$

where $n(t)$ denotes the size of S at time t, that is, the number of elements of S with timestamps $\leq t$.

Example 5.3 Similar to Example 5.2, "RFIDstream [ROWS 1]" returns the last RFID reading from the stream at any time instant.

3. *Partitioned windows.* A partitioned sliding window is applied to a stream S with two parameters: a positive number N for number of rows and a subset of attributes of S, $\{A_1, \ldots, A_k\}$. The CQL syntax for partitioned windows is [Partition S By $A_1, \ldots, A_k$ Rows N]. Similar to SQL Group By, this window operator logically partitions stream S into sub-streams based on equality of attributes $A_1, \ldots, A_k$. The parameter N is used to compute the tuple-based windows from those sub-streams.

Example 5.4 "RFIDstream [Partition By *tagid* ROWS 1]" partitions the RFID-stream into a collection of sub-streams based on *tagid* and gets the latest readings from each sub-stream. This query can be used to find where the last locations of all the RFID tags were detected.

The windows might have a *slide* parameter for specifying the granularity at which window slides. The formal definition has been presented by Sullivan and Heybey [22]. Additionally, fixed windows and value-based windows were proposed in [372].

5.3.3 *Relation-to-Relation Operator*

The relation-to-relation operators are introduced to employ relational operators. Therefore, they have the same semantics as their counterparts. However, CQL introduces the *instantaneous relations* that are relations that are computable at a specific time instant t, for example, outputs from stream-to-relation operators.

The semantics of a continuous query on RDF streams are defined as a composition of the query operators. In Streaming SPARQL and C-SPARQL, a query is composed as an operator graph. The definition of the operator graph is based on the SPARQL query graph model [172]. The continuous semantics defines how the output stream is generated when the time progresses. For example, in CQL [22], the continuous semantics are defined by three streaming operators, namely, ISTREAM, DSTREAM, and RSTREAM. The ISTREAM and DSTREAM operators are used for generating the stream of new results or expired results, respectively. The RSTREAM operator generates the stream of the latest results of the query. Therefore, ISTREAM and DSTREAM only stream new outputs or expired outputs instead of streaming all the outputs of each query shot regardless of the previous query shot like RSTREAM. These streaming operators are accompanied by definitions that show the relationship between their two consecutive outputs. Such definitions provide the foundation for building the incremental computation algorithms of continuous query processing in CQELS [233].

For defining the semantics of continuous query languages, current state-of-the-art approaches extend the query operators of SPARQL such as join, union, and

Table 5.1 Algebraic operators used in RDF stream processing engines

	Data transformation	Algebraic operators	Underlying systems
Streaming SPARQL	Physical RDF stream→ logical RDF stream	Stream-to-stream	Modified SPARQL engine
C-SPARQL	RDF↔relation	Stream-to-relation, relation-to-relation, relation-to-stream	SPARQL engine and STREAM or ESPER
SPARQL$_{stream}$	Relation→RDF	Stream-to-relation, relation-to-relation	SNEE engine
EP-SPARQL	RDF→logic facts	Stream-to-stream under logic rules	Prolog engines
CQELS	Native RDF	Stream-to-relation, relation-to-relation, relation-to-stream	Native physical operators

filter [311]. As such operators consume and output mappings, these approaches also introduce operators on RDF streams to output mappings. For instance, in C-SPARQL, the stream operator is defined to access an RDF stream identified by its IRI, and the window operator is defined to extract an RDF graph from an RDF stream based on a certain window. The definitions of window operators on RDF streams are adopted from window operators on relational streams of CQL [22]. Table 5.1 shows how above operators are used in corresponding engines.

Commonly, the only difference to SPARQL in terms of query operator is the windowing operators. The windowing operators [241] slice up a dataset into finite chunks for processing as a group. When dealing with unbounded data, windowing is required for some operations (to delineate finite boundaries in most forms of grouping: aggregation, outer joins, time-bounded operations, etc.), and unnecessary for others (filtering, mapping, inner joins, etc.). For bounded data, windowing is essentially optional, though still a semantically useful concept in many situations (e.g., back-filling large-scale updates to portions of a previously computed unbounded data source). Windowing is effectively always time based; while many systems support tuple-based windowing, this is essentially time-based windowing over a logical time domain where elements that in order have successively increasing logical timestamps. Windows may be either aligned, that is, applied across all the data for the window of time in question, or unaligned, that is, applied across only specific subsets of the data (e.g., per key) for the given window of time. Figure 5.5 highlights three of the major types of windows encountered when dealing with unbounded data [9]. Fixed windows (sometimes called tumbling windows) are defined by a static window size, for example, hourly windows or daily windows. They are generally aligned, that is, every window applies across all of the data for the corresponding period of time. For the sake of spreading window completion load evenly across time, they are sometimes unaligned by phase shifting the windows for each key by some random value. Sliding windows are defined by a window size and slide period, for example, hourly windows starting every minute. The period may be less than the size, which means the windows may overlap. Sliding windows are

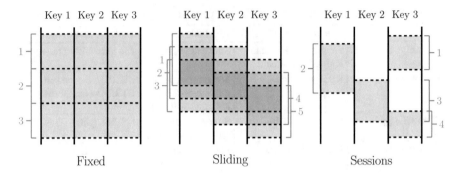

Fig. 5.5 Three typical windowing patterns

also typically aligned; even though the diagram is drawn to give a sense of sliding motion, all five windows would be applied to all three keys in the diagram, not just to Window 3 alone. Fixed windows are really a special case of sliding windows where size equals the period. Sessions are windows that capture some period of activity over a subset of the data, in this case per key. Typically they are defined by a timeout gap. Any events that occur within a span of time less than the timeout are grouped together as a session. Sessions are unaligned windows. For example, Window 2 applies to Key 1 only, Window 3 to Key 2 only, and Windows 1 and 4 to Key 3 only.

5.4 RDF Streaming Query Languages and Syntax

To define a declarative query language for RDF Stream Data, first the basic query patterns need to be introduced to express the primitive operators. These basic patterns are triple matching, window matching, and sequential operators. Then, the composition of basic query patterns can be expressed by the AND, OPT, UNION, and FILTER patterns of SPARQL. These patterns correspond to the operators of SPARQL [311]. To support aggregation operators, Barbieri et al. [34] defined their semantics with the query pattern AGG. The query pattern AGG is defined to be compatible with other query patterns of SPARQL. Thereby, the evaluation of query pattern AGG is defined as $[[P\ AGG\ A]] = [[P]] \bowtie [[A]]$ where A is an aggregate function that consumes the output of a SPARQL query pattern P to return a set of mappings.

The above query pattern construction rules enable the SPARQL grammar to be extended for continuous queries. Figure 5.6 illustrates EBNF grammar of the **Streaming SPARQL** language that extends the SPARQL 1.0 grammar by adding the *DatastreamClause* and a clause for defining windows. Similarly, the

$$
\begin{aligned}
\textit{SelectQuery} &::= \text{`SELECT' (`DISTINCT' | `REDUCED'`)?} (\textit{Var} | \text{`*'})(\textit{DatasetClause*} | \\
&\quad \textbf{DatastreamClause}*)\textit{WhereClause SolutionModifier} \\
\textit{DatastreamClause} &::= \text{`FROM'} (\textit{DefaultStreamClause} | \textit{NamedStreamClause}) \\
\textit{DefaultStreamClause} &::= \text{`STREAM'} \textit{SourceSelector Window} \\
\textit{NamedStreamClause} &::= \text{`NAMED' `STREAM'} \textit{SourceSelector Window} \\
\textit{GroupGraphPattern} &::= \{ \textit{TriplesBlock?} ((\textit{GraphPatternNotTriples} | \textit{Filter }) \text{`.'?} \\
&\quad \textit{TriplesBlock?})*(\textbf{Window})?) \text{'}\}\text{'} \\
\textbf{Window} &::= (\textit{SlidingDeltaWindow} | \textit{SlidingTupleWindow} | \textit{FixedWindow}) \\
\textit{SlidingDeltaWindow} &:= \text{`WINDOW' `RANGE'} \textit{ValSpec} \text{`SLIDE'} \textit{ValSpec?} \\
\textit{FixedWindow} &:= \text{`WINDOW' `RANGE'} \textit{ValSpec} \text{`FIXED'} \\
\textit{SlidingTupleWindow} &::= \text{`WINDOW' `ELEMS' INTEGER} \\
\textit{ValSpec} &::= \text{INTEGER} | \textit{Timeunit?} \\
\textit{Timeunit} &:= (\text{`MS' | `S' | `MINUTE' | `HOUR' | `DAY' | `WEEK'})
\end{aligned}
$$

Fig. 5.6 EBNF grammar of streaming SPARQL

$$
\begin{aligned}
\textit{FromStrClause} &\rightarrow \text{`FROM' [`NAMED'] `STREAM'} \textit{StreamIRI} \text{[`RANGE'} \textit{Window} \text{']}' \\
\textit{Window} &\rightarrow \textit{LogicalWindow} | \textit{PhysicalWindow} \\
\textit{LogicalWindow} &\rightarrow \textit{Number TimeUnit WindowOverlap} \\
\textit{TimeUnit} &\rightarrow \text{`d' | `h' | `m' | `s' | `ms'} \\
\textit{WindowOverlap} &\rightarrow \text{`STEP'} \textit{Number TimeUnit} | \text{`TUMBLING'}
\end{aligned}
$$

Fig. 5.7 EBNF grammar of C-SPARQL

C-SPARQL language extends the SPARQL 1.1 grammar[2] by adding the *FromStr-Clause* and a clause for windows (Fig. 5.7). In principle, the grammars of *Streaming SPARQL* and *C-SPARQL* are similar. The URI of the stream is defined after the keywords *FROM STREAM*, and the triple patterns are placed in the *WHERE* clause. In Streaming SPARQL [49], using an RDF dataset is not clearly described; therefore queries with traditional RDF dataset cannot be expressed in its language. In these two query languages, the *FROM* clause for representing a window on a RDF stream creates a limitation when two windows are defined on one single RDF stream in a query. However, using a stream window clause after the *FROM* keyword only allows one window in each stream URI. In C-SPARQL, it is possible to get around this issue by creating two separate logical streams from the same stream. These new streams will then be used to apply the two windows needed. For example, we can clone a new stream from the original stream. However, cloning a stream to get the URI is impractical not only for representing a query but also in terms of processing efficiency. In a recent C-SPARQL implementation, multiple windows on one stream URI is introduced. However, this new option leads to an ambiguity. In particular, the windows are not accompanied by the triple patterns. Thus, the compiler would not be able to identify which triple patterns are specified for which windows.

---

[2]http://www.w3.org/TR/sparql11-query/#grammar.

GraphPatternNotTriples ::= *GroupOrUnionGraphPattern* | *OptionalGraphPattern*
                                      | *MinusGraphPattern* | *GraphGraphPattern*
                                      | **StreamGraphPattern** | *ServiceGraphPattern*
                                      | *Filter* | *Bind*

Fig. 5.8 EBNF grammar of CQELS-QL

To address the above issues, **CQELS-QL** [235] defines its grammar based on the SPARQL 1.1 grammar[3] (Fig. 5.8). It adds a query pattern to represent window operators on RDF Stream, called **StreamGraphPattern**, into the *GraphPatternNotTriples* pattern of SPARQL 1.1. Assuming that each stream has an IRI as the identifier, the **StreamGraphPattern** pattern is defined as follows:

StreamGraphPattern ::= 'STREAM' '[' *Window* ']' *VarOrIRIref* '{' *TriplesTemplate* '}'

       Window ::= *Rangle* | *Triple* | 'NOW' | 'ALL'

       Range ::= 'RANGE' *Duration* ('SLIDE' *Duration*)?

       Triple ::= 'TRIPLES' INTEGER

    Duration ::= (INTEGER 'd' | 'h' | 'm' | 's' | 'ms' | 'ns')$^{+}$

where *VarOrIRIRef* and *TripleTemplate* are patterns for the *variable/IRI* and *triple template* from SPARQL 1.1. *Range* corresponds to a time-based window, while *Triple* corresponds to a triple-based window. The keyword *SLIDE* is used for specifying the sliding parameter of a time-based window, whose time interval is given by *Duration*.

For generating an RDF stream from the query output, the CONSTRUCT language construct is introduced in C-SPARQL and CQEL-QL. The triple patterns of the CONTRUCT grammar define the template of the output RDF stream. As the relational operators are defined based on their corresponding operators in SPARQL, the grammar of SPARQL1.1 is reused. For relational streaming operators, CQELS-QL modifies the SELECT grammar with the new modifiers STREAM, DSTREAM, and RSTREAM corresponding to its abstract syntax [232]. If the modifier of the SELECT keyword is omitted, it implicitly means SELECT ISTREAM. Similarly, we extend the CONSTRUCT grammar for being able to represent the RDF streaming operator.

5.5 System Design and Implementation

5.5.1 Design

In addition to the existing work on scalable querying of linked data (see Chaps. 3 and 4), designing a processing engine for RDF Stream Data also benefits from the

---

[3]http://www.w3.org/TR/sparql11-query/#grammar.

research in the area of Data Streams Management Systems (DSMS). However, there are particular aspects of RDF Stream Data that prevent existing work in these two areas to be directly applied. One distinguishing aspect of streams that the Linked Data principles do not consider is their temporal nature. Usually, Linked Data is considered to be changing infrequently. Data is first crawled and stored in a centralized repository before further processing. Updates on a dataset are usually limited to a small fraction of the dataset and occur infrequently, or the whole dataset is replaced by a new version entirely. Query processing in Linked Data databases, as in traditional relational databases, is pull based and one-time, that is, the data is read from the disk, the query is executed against it once, and the output is a set of results for that point in time. In contrast, in Linked Stream Data, new data items are produced continuously, the data is often valid only during a time window, and it is continually pushed to the query processor. Queries are continuous, that is, they are registered once and then are evaluated continuously over time against the changing dataset. The results of a continuous query are updated as new data appears. Therefore, current Linked Data query processing engines are not suitable for handling RDF Stream Data.

Data Streams Management Systems, on the other hand, are designed to handle and scale with fast changing, temporal data, such as Linked Stream Data. However RDF Stream Data is usually represented as an extension of RDF, the most popular standard for Linked Data representation. This contrasts with the relational storage model used in DSMS. It has been shown that in order to efficiently process RDF data using the relational model, the data needs to be heavily replicated (cf. Chap. 3). Replication of fast changing RDF streams is prohibitive; therefore DSMS cannot be directly used for storage and processing of RDF Stream Data.

The most popular data model used for stream data is the relational model [1, 22, 71]. In the relational model, stream elements are relational tuples with a fixed schema. Stream elements can be modeled in an object-based model to classify the stream contents according to a type hierarchy. For example, Tribica [372] proposes hierarchical data types for representing Internet protocol layers for its network monitoring system. Another example of modeling data sources by objects is the COUGAR system for managing sensor data [52]. In COUGAR, each type of sensor is modeled as an abstract data type, whose interface consists of the supported signal processing methods. This model is also used in complex event processing (CEP) engines such as SASE [6, 420], ZStream [261], and ESPER.[4] CEP is closely related to stream processing, but its focus is more on making sense of events by deriving high-level knowledge or complex events from lower level events [108], rather than modeling and processing time-dependent information. On top of that, many dynamic applications are built upon large network infrastructures, such as social networks, communication networks, biological networks, and the web. Such applications create data that can be naturally modeled as graph streams, in which

---

[4]http://esper.codehaus.org/.

edges of the underlying graph are received and updated sequentially in a form of a stream [36, 42, 93, 437].

The architectural design of the current systems that support continuous query processing over RDF Stream Data can be classified into two categories. The first category follows a "whitebox" architecture and needs to implement the physical operators such as sliding windows, join, and triple pattern matching. Such operators can be implemented using techniques and algorithms proposed in the literature mentioned above. To consume data, these operators use access methods which may employ data structures such as B+Trees+, hash tables, or triple-based indexes for fast random data access to RDF datasets or RDF streams. To execute a declarative query in an SPARQL-like language, the optimizer has to translate it to a logical query plan and then find an optimal execution plan based on the corresponding operator implementations. This execution plan is then executed by the executor. As the continuous query is executed continuously, the optimizer must re-optimize it to find a new execution plan to adapt to the changes in the data and the computing environment, if a processing cost threshold is exceeded. In the whitebox architecture, the query engine needs to implement all the components of a DSMS. Streaming SPARQL and CQELS follow a whitebox approach.

To avoid implementing most of these components, an alternative is the "blackbox" architecture. The blackbox architecture uses existing systems as subcomponents for the processing needed. Usually, the chosen subcomponents are accessed with different query languages and different input data formats. Hence, the blackbox approach needs a Query Rewriter, an Orchestrator, and a Data Transformer. The Query Rewriter rewrites a SPARQL-like query to sub-queries that the underlying systems can understand. The Orchestrator is used to orchestrate the execution process by externalizing the processing to subsystems with the rewritten sub-queries. In some cases, the Orchestrator also includes some components for correlating and aggregating partial results returned from the blackbox systems if they support this. The Data Transformer is responsible for converting input data to compatible formats of the Access methods used in the subcomponents. The Data Transformer also has to transform the output of the underlying systems to the format that the Orchestrator requires. By delegating the processing to available systems, building a system following the blackbox architecture takes less effort than using the whitebox approach. However, such systems do not have full control over the subcomponents, for example, for optimization purposes, and they suffer from performance costs and lower throughputs.

5.5.2 Implementation Aspects

5.5.2.1 Time Management

The described semantics for continuous queries in a data stream system typically assume the presence of timestamps on data stream elements. Thus, a consistent semantics for multiple streams and updatable relations relies on timestamps. To achieve semantic correctness, the DSMS query processor usually needs to process tuples in an increasing order of timestamps. That is, the query processor should never receive a stream element with a lower timestamp than any previously received ones. According to Srivastava and Widom [363], there are two common types of timestamps: *system timestamp* and *application timestamp*.

A system timestamp is assigned to a stream element when entering the DSMS using the DSMS system time. An application timestamp is given by the data sources before sending the stream elements to the DSMS. As an example of application timestamps, consider monitoring sensor readings to correlate changes in temperature and pressure. Each tuple consists of a sensor reading and an application timestamp affixed by the sensor, denoting the time at which that reading was taken. In general, there may not be any relationship between the time at which the reading is taken (the application timestamp) and the time at which the corresponding stream tuple reaches the DSMS (the system timestamp).

An exemplar of architecture for time management is shown in Fig. 5.9 [363]. As stream tuples may not arrive at the DSMS in an increasing timestamp order, there is an *input manager* that buffers tuples until they can be moved to the query processor in proper order. Continuous queries registered to the query processor consume ordered stream tuples, for example, with windowing operators. The decision when a tuple can be moved to the query processor is based on *heartbeats*. A heartbeat for a set of streams S^1, S^2, and S^3 at wall-clock time c is defined as the maximum application timestamp τ such that all tuples arriving on S^1, S^2, and S^3 after time c must have timestamp $> \tau$.

Along with the proposal for generating heartbeats by the same authors [363], there are also other proposals for time management from other data stream management projects, such as Aurora [1], Niagara [77], TelegraphCQ [71], and

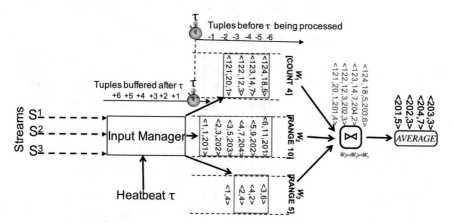

Fig. 5.9 Example architecture for time management

Gigascope [88]. The operators of Aurora have a slack parameter to deal with out-of-order streams. Essentially, the slack parameter instructs its operator to wait a certain period of time before closing each window. In Niagara, the proposed solution is based on punctuations [384]. Punctuations define arbitrary predicates over streams. Thus, heartbeats can be thought of as special types of punctuations. A more detailed comparison of heartbeat solutions has been provided by Srivatava and Widom [363].

5.5.2.2   Scheduling and Handling Memory

After the query optimizer chooses a physical query plan, the query engine starts to execute it. In contrast to pull-based operators of DBMSs, DSMS operators consume data pushed into the plan by the sources. At any point during an execution, there may be many tuples in the input and interoperator queues. Queues allow sources to push data into the query plan and operators to retrieve data as needed [1, 22, 29, 252, 253]. Jiang and Chakravarthy [200] discussed the details of calculating queue sizes of streaming relational operators using classical queueing theory.

In general, each operator consumes data from its input queue(s) to return outputs to the upper queues. The DSMS scheduler must determine which data item in which queue to process next. A round-robin strategy can be used to execute each operator until it has processed all the data items in its queue(s). Another simple technique, first-in-first-out, is to process one data item at a time in order of arrival, such that each item is processed to completion by all the operators in the plan. This execution strategy ensures good response times; however, scheduling one tuple at a time may incur too much overhead.

Another scheduling strategy is to allocate a time slice to each operator, during which the operator extracts tuples from its input queue(s), processes them in timestamp order, and deposits output tuples into the next operator's input queue. The time slice may be fixed or dynamically calculated based upon the size of an operator's input queue and/or processing speed. A possible improvement could be to schedule one or more tuples to be processed by multiple operators at once. In general, there are several possible conflicting criteria involved in choosing a scheduling strategy, among them queue sizes in the presence of bursty stream arrival patterns [33], average or maximum latency of output tuples [65, 201, 303], and average or maximum delay in reporting the answer relative to the arrival of new data [352]. More strategies [65, 353, 398] have been proposed for scheduling operators to achieve low latency by producing high output rates.

To handle memory overflow, the secondary storage must be used in the query operators. The XJoin operator [394] was introduced to address memory overflow in binary window joins by spilling some partitions of inputs to disk. XJoin extends the Symmetric Hash Join (SHJ) [188, 413] to use less memory by allowing parts of the hash tables to be moved to a secondary storage. The MJoin operator [399] generalizes the XJoin operator to deal with multiway stream joins. MJoin maximizes the output rate of the multi-join operator by efficiently coordinating the spilling processes instead of spilling the inputs to disk randomly without considering the values in their join attributes.

If the secondary storage is used for storing the sliding window, then an index might be used to improve the performance. However, the index introduces maintenance costs especially in the context of frequent updates. In order to reduce the index maintenance costs, it is desirable to avoid bringing the entire window into memory during every update. This can be done by partitioning the data to localize updates (i.e., insertions of newly arrived data and deletion of tuples that have expired from the window) to a small number of disk pages. For example, if an index over a sliding window is partitioned chronologically [124, 355], then only the youngest partition incurs insertions, while only the oldest partition needs to be checked for expirations (the remaining partitions in the "middle" are not accessed). A similar idea of grouping objects by expiration time appears in [105] in the context of clustering large file systems, where every file has an associated lifetime. However, the disadvantage of chronological clustering is that records with the same search key may be scattered across a very large number of disk pages, causing index probes to incur prohibitively many disk I/Os. One way to reduce index access costs is to store a reduced (summarized) version of the data that fit in fewer disk pages [70], but this does not necessarily improve index update times. In order to balance the access and update times, a wave index has been proposed that chronologically divides a sliding window into n equal partitions, each of which is separately indexed and clustered by a search key for efficient data retrieval [355]. However, the access time of this approach is slower because multiple subindexes are probed to obtain the answer.

5.5.3 Systems

This section will discuss the RDF Stream processing engines listed in Table 5.2. This table categorizes the systems by architecture, re-execution strategy, how the

Table 5.2 Summary of typical RDF stream processing engines

	Architecture	Re-execution	Scheduling	Optimization
Streaming SPARQL	Whitebox	Periodical	Logical plan	Algebraic and static
C-SPARQL	Blackbox	Periodical	Logical plan	Algebraic and static
EP-SPARQL	Blackbox	Eager	Logic program	Externalized
SPARQL$_{stream}$	Blackbox	Periodical	External call	Externalized
CQELS	Whitebox	Eager	Adaptive physical plans	Physical and adaptive

engine schedules the execution, and what type of optimization is supported. Since Streaming SPARQL and C-SPARQL schedule the execution at the logical level, the optimization can only be done at the algebraic level and statically. On the contrary, CQELS is able to choose the alternative execution plans composed from available physical implementations of operators; thus, the optimizer can adaptively optimize the execution at the physical level. EP-SPARQL and SPARQL$_{stream}$ schedule the execution via a declarative query or a logic program; so it completely externalizes the optimization to other systems.

5.5.3.1 Streaming SPARQL

Streaming SPARQL [49] is the first attempt to build an RDF processing engine by extending SPARQL and a SPARQL query processor. Even though it extends the ARQ[5] query compiler to transform the continuous query to a logical query plan, it does not use a stream data management system to translate SPARQL-like continuous query to stream-based primitives. Its logical query plan is then compiled to a physical execution plan that is composed of physical query operators which are composed of two groups of physical operators. Stateless operators do not need any information about the stream history or stream future. Each stream element can be processed directly. Operators of this group are triple pattern matching, filter, union, project, construct, and our time-based window operators. The other group contains stateful operators. These operators need further information to process an element, for example, a sort operator needs to know all elements before it can sort the set. Join, left join, basic graph pattern matching, duplicate elimination reduction, orderBy, slice, ask, and element-based windows are stateful operators. For dealing with the stream nature of incoming and outgoing data of such operators, Streaming SPARQL uses a special data structure, called sweep area [225], which provides an abstract datatype with methods to insert, replace, or query elements. With this design and implementation approach, it can be counted as a whitebox engine.

Streaming SPARQL extends SPARQL 1.0 for representing continuous queries on RDF streams. For implementing the physical operators, Streaming SPARQL heavily uses Jena ARQ libraries to add stream algebras which are proposed in [225]. However, to the best of our knowledge, the implementation of the system is not publicly available. For optimization, Streaming SPARQL suggests that algebraic optimization be applied after translating a declarative query to a logical query plan. To illustrate how the process of compiling a query in Streaming SPARQL is done, Fig. 5.10 shows the physical query plan translated from the query in Listing 5.1.

---

[5]https://jena.apache.org/documentation/query/.

Fig. 5.10 A physical query
plan for Streaming SPARQL.
©Springer-Verlag Berlin
Heidelberg 2008. Reprinted
with permission

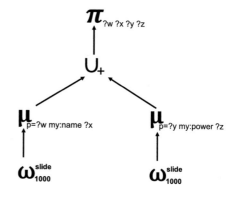

Listing 5.1 Example of Streaming SPARQL query

```
SELECT ?w ? x ?y ? z
FROM STREAM <http://src.net/graph.rdf>
WINDOW RANGE 1000 SLIDE
WHERE
{?w my:name ?x}  UNION {?y my:power ?z}
```

5.5.3.2 C-SPARQL

C-SPARQL implements the blackbox architecture. The C-SPARQL engine uses a
SPARQL plug-in to connect to a SPARQL query engine to evaluate the static part
of the query, that is, the sub-queries involving the RDF datasets. For evaluating
the parts of the query relevant to streams and aggregates, the engine delegates the
processing to an existing relational data stream management system. One limitation
of this architecture is that aggregations can only be performed by the DSMS using
CQL. A C-SPARQL query is first parsed and sent to the orchestrator (Fig. 5.11).
The orchestrator is the central component of C-SPARQL engine and it translates the
query into a static and a dynamic part. The static sub-queries are used to extract the
static results from the SPARQL engine, while the dynamic sub-queries are registered
in the DSMS. The query initialization is executed only once when a C-SPARQL
query is registered as the continuous evaluation is handled subsequently by the
DSMS. Therefore, C-SPARQL does not support updates in the non-stream data.
The evaluation process of the C-SPARQL engine is illustrated in Fig. 5.12.

The results returned from the SPARQL engine for the static part of the query are
loaded into materialized relations as inputs for the DSMS. These relations together
with RDF streams are computed via cascading views created as CQL queries [22],
driven by the C-SPARQL query. The first views in the query pipeline are sliding
window views over RDF streams. They are then correlated with the static relations
via join views. As C-SPARQL employs algebraic optimization, it tries to filter the
data as early as possible. Hence, it pushes the filters to the bottom of the query

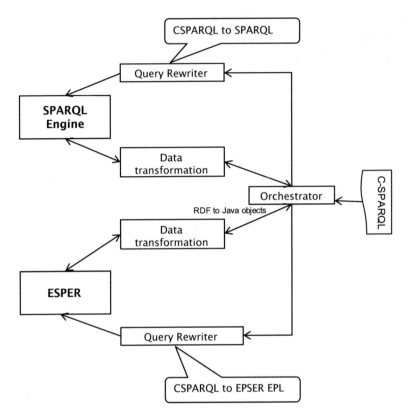

Fig. 5.11 Architecture of C-SPARQL

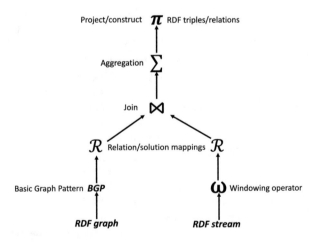

Fig. 5.12 Evaluation process of C-SPARQL

pipeline by rewriting rules [361]. The order of the evaluation process illustrates how views are created on top of each other. At the time of this writing, a version of C-SPARQL based on Jena[6] and ESPER[7] C-SPARQL is open sourced at https://github.com/streamreasoning/CSPARQL-engine.

5.5.3.3 EP-SPARQL

EP-SPARQL uses the blackbox approach backed by a logic engine. It translates queries into logic programs which are then executed by a Prolog engine. The execution mechanism of EP-SPARQL is based on event-driven backward chaining (EDBC) rules, introduced by Anicic et al. [18]. EP-SPARQL queries are compiled into EDBC rules, which enable timely, event-driven, and incremental detection of complex events (i.e., answers to EP-SPARQL queries). EDBC rules are logic rules, and hence can be mixed with other background knowledge (domain knowledge that is used for stream reasoning). Therefore, it provides a unified execution mechanism for event processing and stream reasoning which is grounded in logic programming.

For the encoding, EP-SPARQL uses a simple correspondence between RDF triples of the form $\langle s, p, o \rangle$ and Prolog predicates of the form $triple(s', p', o')$ so that s', p', and o' correspond to the RDF symbols s, p, and o, respectively. This means that whenever a triple $\langle s, p, o \rangle$ is satisfied, the corresponding predicate $triple(s', p', o')$ is satisfied too, and vice versa. Consequently, a time-stamped RDF triple $\langle \langle s, p, o \rangle, t_\alpha, t_\omega \rangle$ corresponds to a predicate $triple(s', p', o', T'_\alpha, T'_\omega)$ where T'_α and T'_ω denote timestamps. Timestamps are assigned to triples either by a triple source (e.g., a sensor or an application that generates triple updates) or by an EP-SPARQL engine. They facilitate time-related processing and do not necessarily need to be kept once the stream has been processed (e.g., the pure RDF part could be persisted in a RDF triple store without timestamps). From RDF triples and time-stamped RDF encoded as logic predicates, query operators like $SeqJoin, EqJoin,$ and $Filters$ for the EP-SPARQL query language are rewritten as rule patterns.

To enable the detection of more complex events, EP-SPARQL combines streams with background knowledge. This knowledge describes the context (domain) in which complex events are detected. As such, it enables the detection of real-time situations that are identified based on explicit data (e.g., events) as well as on implicit knowledge (derived from the background knowledge). The background knowledge may be specified as a Prolog knowledge base or as an RDFS[8] ontology. This enables EP-SPARQL's execution model to have all relevant parts expressible in a unified (logic rule) formalism, and ultimately to reason over a unified space. At the time of writing, an implementation of EP-SPARQL is available at https://github.com/sspider/etalis.

---

[6]http://jena.apache.org/.

[7]http://esper.codehaus.org/.

[8]http://www.w3.org/TR/rdf-schema/.

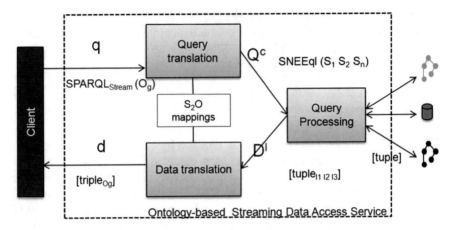

Fig. 5.13 Architecture of SPARQL$_{stream}$. ©Springer-Verlag Berlin Heidelberg 2010. Reprinted with permission

5.5.3.4   SPARQL$_{stream}$

SPARQL$_{stream}$ is designed for supporting the integration of heterogeneous relational stream data sources. The SPARQL$_{stream}$ engine rewrites the SPARQL$_{stream}$ query language to a relational continuous query language, for example, SNEEql [128]. Figure 5.13 illustrates the architecture of the system. In order to transform the SPARQL$_{stream}$ query, expressed in terms of the ontology, into queries in terms of the data sources, a set of mappings must be specified. These mappings are expressed in the S$_2$O mapping language, an extension of the R$_2$O mapping language [63]. It supports streaming queries and data, most notably window and stream operators. After the continuous query has been generated, the query processing phase starts. The evaluator uses distributed query processing techniques [222] to extract the relevant data from the sources and to perform the required query processing, that is, selection, projection, and joins. Query execution in sources such as sensor networks may include in-network query processing, pull- or push-based delivery of data between sources, and other data-source-specific settings. The result of the query processing is a set of tuples that the data translation process transforms into ontology instances. At the time of writing, a version of SPARQL$_{stream}$ is available at https://github.com/jpcik/morph-streams.

5.5.3.5   CQELS

CQELS was built under a *whitebox* architecture which is based on its generic execution framework illustrated in Fig. 5.14. This architecture accepts RDF streams and RDF datasets as inputs and returns RDF streams or relational streams in the

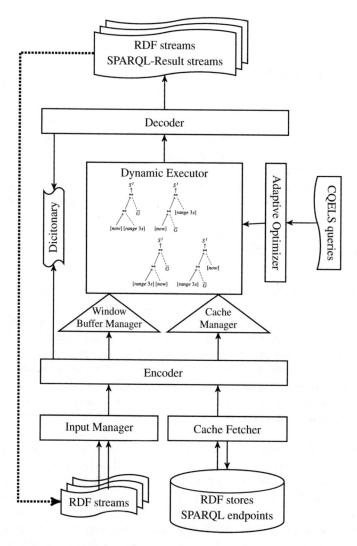

Fig. 5.14 Architecture of CQELS execution framework

SPARQL Result format[9] as output. The output RDF streams can be fed into any CQELS engine, and the relational streams can be used by other relational stream processing systems. CQELS Framework provides a platform-independent infrastructure to implement RSP engines for computing continuous queries expressed as an extension of SPARQL 1.1, called CQELS-QL. The CQELS execution

---

[9]http://www.w3.org/TR/rdf-sparql-XMLres/.

framework[10] is composed of native and adaptive components organized in the processing flow as follows:

- The stream data is pushed to the Input Manager and is then encoded by the Encoder into a normalized representation. RDF datasets, which can be hosted in a local RDF store or remote RDF stores with SPARQL endpoints, are retrieved by the Cache Fetcher. The Cache Fetcher also encodes the data using the Encoder.
- The Window Buffer Manager and Cache Manager are responsible for managing the input data from the RDF streams and RDF datasets, respectively, and for feeding them into the Dynamic Executor.
- The Dynamic Executor enables a dynamic execution strategy where the query plan can be changed during the lifetime of a continuous query. The most efficient query plan is continuously advised by the Adaptive Optimizer based on data statistics and operator costs.
- The outputs of the Dynamic Executor have to be decoded by the Decoder before being streamed out. The Encoder and Decoder share a Dictionary for encoding and decoding.

To be a platform-agnostic execution framework, the design of the aforementioned components of the CQELS Framework is abstract enough to be realized by various hosting platforms which can provide different library/software stacks as well as different hardware architectures. The first version of the CQELS engine [235] was implemented as a stand-alone version for PCs. It uses popular libraries like Apache Jena, a high performance computing framework for implementing new data structures for Window Buffer Manager associated with in-memory incremental evaluation algorithms for sliding window operators [233]. This version is accompanied by several adaptive optimization algorithms to boost the processing throughput of the CQELS engine.

To build CQELS engines for resource-constrained environments like embedded devices such as mobile phones, the embedded CQELS engine is created by reducing code footprint. It uses lightweight data structures for Window Buffer as well as reuse RDF On The Go (RDF-OTG) [237] code based on the compact versions of Encoder/Decoder, Dictionary, and Cache Manager/Fetcher. Additionally, the CQELS embedded engine extends SPARQL physical query operators of RDF-OTG to sliding windows operators. For scalability, CQELS uses Apache Storm[11] and Apache HBase[12] as underlying software stacks for coordinating parallel execution processes to build an RSP engine on the cloud computing infrastructure, called CQELS Cloud [236]. We adapt highly efficient algorithms of CQELS engine on stand-alone PCs to the distributed share-nothing architecture; thus, CQELS Cloud can scale up to million inputs per second with 100,000 concurrent queries on a cluster of 32 EC2 computing nodes.

---

[10]http://cqels.org.

[11]http://storm.apache.org/.

[12]https://hbase.apache.org/.

Chapter 6
Distributed Reasoning of RDF Data

Large RDF interconnected datasets, especially in the form of open as well as enterprise knowledge graphs, are constructed and consumed in several domains. Reasoning over such large knowledge graphs poses several performance challenges. Chapter 4 provided an overview for several distributed RDF querying engines. In this chapter, we provide an overview of distributed RDF reasoning systems. In practice, although there has been some prior work on scalable approaches to RDF reasoning, the interest in this field started gathering momentum with the rising popularity of modern big data processing systems (e.g., Hadoop, Spark). In particular, in this chapter, we cover five main categories of distributed RDF reasoning systems: (1) Peer-to-Peer RDF reasoning systems, (2) NoSQL-based RDF reasoning systems, (3) Hadoop-based RDF reasoning systems, (4) Spark-based RDF reasoning systems, and (5) shared memory RDF reasoning systems.

6.1 The Process of RDF Reasoning

Increasing amounts of structured data, especially in the form of RDF (Resource Description Framework), are getting generated and consumed. This type of structured data along with its model and provenance information is often referred to as a *knowledge base* or a *knowledge graph*. Linked Data, which is an initiative to interconnect related datasets, has around 10,000 interlinked RDF datasets and 150 billion triples.[1] Automated construction of knowledge bases is an active area of research where techniques from natural language processing, machine learning, information extraction, etc., are used to build knowledge bases [294]. Several popular and large knowledge bases such as DBpedia [230], YAGO [254], NELL [264], Wikidata [401], Biperpedia [160], and Knowledge Vault [104] were constructed

---

[1] http://stats.lod2.eu/.

© Springer International Publishing AG 2018
S. Sakr et al., *Linked Data*, https://doi.org/10.1007/978-3-319-73515-3_6

automatically. Knowledge is extracted from text [104, 264] and streaming data [229]. These knowledge bases have kept evolving and increasing in size over time. NELL has already accumulated over 80 million facts (as of 2015) in its knowledge base and Google's Knowledge Vault has around 1.6 billion facts (as of 2014). DBpedia has around three billion triples in 2014[2] and Wikidata currently has around one billion triples.[3]

There are several web pages that are marked up to add structure to the text. Mechanisms such as Microformats,[4] Microdata,[5] and Schema.org[6] can be used for marking up the HTML content. Among them, Schema.org, an initiative started by Bing, Google, Yahoo, and Yandex, is very popular. There are around 12 million websites [156] that use the Schema.org markup. The marked up structured content can be easily converted to RDF, which is a W3C standard, using libraries such as Apache Any23.[7] This would result in billions of RDF triples. Two important operations that can be performed over RDF triples are querying and reasoning. Various RDF querying approaches have already been discussed in earlier chapters. We will look at RDF reasoning in this chapter. Reasoning is required to infer logical consequences and check the consistency of the knowledge base. The inferred logical consequences can be used to generate answers to the questions posed against the knowledge base which would not have been possible otherwise. For example, consider a knowledge base with the following facts

```
<LinkedDataBook>     <rdf:type>     <Book>
<LinkedDataStory>    <rdf:type>     <Article>
<Book>     <rdfs:subClassOf>     <Publication>
<Article>     <rdfs:subClassOf>     <Publication>
```

Given these facts, a simple query asking for the list of all publications would give an empty result. But it is easy to see at least for a human that `<LinkedDataBook>` and `<LinkedDataStory>` are also publications. A reasoner allows a machine to derive all such logical conclusions from the given knowledge correctly and at scale. In this chapter, we describe different RDF reasoning systems that use forward chaining (fixed point iterative approach) and backward chaining (see Sect. 2.5).

In fixed point iterative approach and backward chaining, entailment rules have to be applied in the facts in the RDF knowledge graph. These entailment rules can be categorized into four as given in the RDF 1.0 Semantics [178]: (1) Simple Entailment Rules, (2) RDF Entailment Rules, (3) RDFS Entailment Rules, and (4) Datatype Entailment Rules. These rules are given in the RDF 1.0 Semantics document and have been repeated here in Tables 6.1, 6.2, 6.3, and 6.4 for the sake

---

[2]http://wiki.dbpedia.org/about/facts-figures.

[3]http://tools.wmflabs.org/wikidata-exports/rdf/.

[4]http://microformats.org/.

[5]https://www.w3.org/TR/microdata/.

[6]http://schema.org/.

[7]https://any23.apache.org/.

Table 6.1 RDF simple entailment rules

Rule name	If RDF graph contains pattern	Then add
se1	uuu aaa xxx	uuu aaa _:nnn where _:nnn identifies a blank node allocated to xxx by rule se1 and se2
se2	uuu aaa xxx	_:nnn aaa xxx where _:nnn identifies a blank node allocated to uuu by rule se1 and se2

Table 6.2 RDF literal generalization rule (lg) and literal instantiation rule (gl)

Rule name	If RDF graph contains pattern	Then add
lg	uuu aaa lll	uuu aaa _:nnn where _:nnn identifies a blank node allocated to the literal lll by this rule
gl	uuu aaa _:nnn where _:nnn identifies a blank node allocated to the literal lll by rule lg	uuu aaa lll

Table 6.3 RDF entailment rules

Rule name	If RDF graph contains pattern	Then add
rdf1	uuu aaa yyy	aaa rdf:type rdf:Property
rdf2	uuu aaa lll where lll is a well-typed XML literal	_:nnn rdf:type rdf:XMLLiteral where _:nnn identifies a blank node allocated to lll by rule lg

of completeness. All the entailment rules use the following conventions: aaa, bbb, etc., stand for any URI reference, that is, any possible predicate of a triple; uuu, vvv, etc., for any URI reference or blank node identifier, that is, any possible subject of a triple; xxx, yyy, etc., for any URI reference, blank node identifier or literal, that is, any possible subject or object of a triple; lll for any literal; and _:nnn, etc., for blank node identifiers. Of the four categories of entailment rules, almost all the approaches discussed in this chapter use only RDFS Entailment Rules (Table 6.4) or part of them since other rules generate blank nodes and are considered trivial.

Existing reasoners cannot handle RDF knowledge bases that have billions of triples. They are constrained by the resources available on a single machine. Reasoning over large knowledge bases needs a scalable approach because it is not possible for a single machine to keep up with the growth rate of data. In this chapter we describe several scalable approaches to RDFS reasoning.

Table 6.4 RDFS entailment rules

Rule name	If RDF graph contains pattern	Then add
rdfs1	uuu aaa lll	_:nnn rdf:type rdfs:Literal
	where _:nnn identifies a blank node	where lll is a plain literal
	allocated to lll by rule rule lg	(with or without a language tag)
rdfs2	aaa rdfs:domain xxx	uuu rdf:type xxx
	uuu aaa yyy	
rdfs3	aaa rdfs:range xxx	vvv rdf:type xxx
	uuu aaa vvv	
rdfs4a	uuu aaa xxx	uuu rdf:type rdfs:Resource
rdfs4b	uuu aaa vvv	vvv rdf:type rdfs:Resource
rdfs5	uuu rdfs:subPropertyOf vvv	uuu rdfs:subPropertyOf xxx
	vvv rdfs:subPropertyOf xxx	
rdfs6	uuu rdf:type rdf:Property	uuu rdfs:subPropertyOf uuu
rdfs7	aaa rdfs:subPropertyOf bbb	uuu bbb yyy
	uuu aaa yyy	
rdfs8	uuu rdf:type rdfs:Class	uuu rdfs:subClassOf rdfs:Resource
rdfs9	uuu rdfs:subClassOf xxx	vvv rdf:type xxx
	vvv rdf:type uuu	
rdfs10	uuu rdf:type rdfs:Class	uuu rdfs:subClassOf uuu
rdfs11	uuu rdfs:subClassOf vvv	uuu rdfs:subClassOf xxx
	vvv rdfs:subClassOf xxx	
rdfs12	uuu rdf:type	
	rdfs:ContainerMembershipProperty	uuu rdfs:subPropertyOf rdfs:member
rdfs13	uuu rdf:type rdfs:Datatype	uuu rdfs:subClassOf rdfs:Literal

6.2 Peer-to-Peer RDF Reasoning Systems

In a Peer-to-Peer (P2P) system, resources such as computing, storage, etc., are decentralized and each node in the system can act as both a server and a client [347]. All the nodes in the network collaborate to accomplish a common goal, which in this case is RDF reasoning. We describe several P2P-based RDF reasoning systems in this section.

A generic architecture for a Peer-to-Peer RDF reasoning system is shown in Fig. 6.1. Each node in the network has an RDF reasoner, input pool, and output pool. The input data from the database is distributed across various input pools of the nodes. The reasoner on each node works only on the data in the input pool. After generating inferred axioms, they are sent to the router which determines whether the inferred axiom needs to go either to the input pool or output pool. Note that the router can in theory send the inferred axiom(s) to the input/output pool of other nodes as well. This is specific to the particular algorithm of the RDF reasoning system. Another point to note is that the router can be part of the node as well

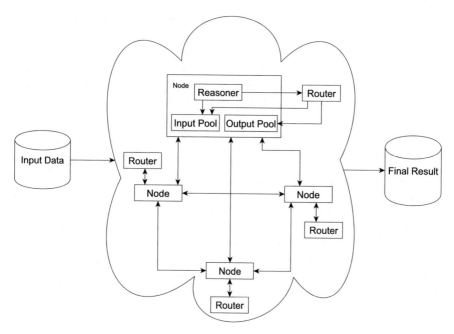

Fig. 6.1 Generic architecture of peer-to-peer RDF reasoning systems

or it can be part of a pool of generic routers, that is, routers not connected to any particular node.

MaRVIN (MAssive RDF Versatile Inference Network) [301] is a parallel and distributed platform for massive processing of RDF data, based on a peer-to-peer model. Marvin implements the *divide-conquer-swap* strategy, which partitions the given dataset into subsets (divide), computes the closure (conquer), and repartitions data by exchanging triples among neighboring nodes (swap). Eventual completeness of the inference is guaranteed, since triples that may emit new knowledge are gradually collocated on the same node. Kotoulas et al. [223] extended this work with a technique to improve the problem of load balancing which affect a fixed term-based partitioning criterion. This technique creates elastic regions in case the frequency of some terms is significantly higher than others. Duplicate detection and removal is supported in order to minimize memory and bandwidth overheads. The approach of randomly exchanging triples among nodes provides good load balancing properties, but is highly inefficient since triples appear on random nodes, thus postponing derivation. On the other hand, the deterministic approach (triples are redirected to a specific node according to their key) is efficient as triples that will lead to derivations are located on the same node, but at the cost of highly unbalanced workloads for skewed dataset distributions. MaRVIN achieves a balance between random and deterministic approach, combining load balancing with efficient derivation. The implemented SpeedDate algorithm swaps triples within a neighborhood of nodes, thus popular keys are distributed over several nodes, and provides a certain degree of determinism as triples are constantly located within a restricted subset of nodes.

Kotoulas et al. [223] studied various metrics by providing simulated results. Simulations deal with the number of nodes, number of items in the system, various data distributions, node availability during the reasoning process, recall, load balancing, and scalability. The system is more efficient when compared to the random approach, showing similar load balancing properties, and is more scalable compared to the deterministic approach, thus being able to utilize a higher degree of parallelization. Considering scalability, the average throughput per node follows a square root curve with respect to the number of items. Subsequently, authors provide experiments on real RDF data. Despite the platform's overhead, the system reached a throughput of 2.3 million triples per second on 32 nodes, when no reasoning was applied. However, when the reasoning process is included, the system is shown to scale to up to 64 nodes for processing datasets of up to 14.9M triples. In addition, MaRVIN shows sublinear speedups (reaching a speedup of 12.94 on 64 nodes), while performing better when low tolerance to duplicates is allowed. Kotoulas et al. [223] extended the evaluation to 64 computing nodes and datasets with up to 200 million triples and resulted in an overall throughput of 450 thousand triples per second.

Weaver and Hendler [406] identified a property of RDFS reasoning called *ABox Partition Safe* that facilitates embarrassingly parallel reasoning over RDFS datasets. The triples in an RDFS ontology can be categorized into two parts:*schema (or ontological) triples* and *instance (or assertion) triples*. All RDFS rules contain at most one instance of triple pattern in the rule body. On the other hand, the assumption that schema triples tend to be a fixed part in ontologies is always reasonable. Thus, the main algorithm replicates the schema triples to all processors and partitions the assertion triples into fairly even parts and distributes them to different processors. The authors further prove that the partition schema (called ABox Partition Schema) is correct in each iteration of materialization. This approach is implemented in MPI and evaluated on a cluster with 128 cores using LUBM benchmark. The results indicate that materialization time increases linearly on the processors: materializing a version of LUMB ontology containing about 650 million triples takes 8 min. For ensuring that parallelism is maintained, the system does not eliminate the duplicate triples globally. The authors also showed that such duplicates tend to halve when the dataset doubles in size.

Kaoudi et al. [207] proposed a method for scalable RDFS reasoning using distributed hash tables (DHTs), a popular instantiation of P2P networks. The proposed algorithm allows uniform handling of instance data and schema knowledge. No additional global information about the schema is required in this approach. The authors rewrote the RDFS entailment rules into datalog rules, thus allowing some optimization techniques of datalog reasoning to be utilized for RDFS reasoning. The authors also proposed two distributed algorithms for forward chaining and backward chaining reasoning. The proposed backward chaining algorithm is the first top-down algorithm designed for RDFS reasoning in a distributed environment. The RDF triples are stored as tuples in relational tables. The proposed algorithms are then implemented to adapt to the DHT platform. The experiments are carried out on a distributed cluster with 123 available nodes. A dataset with binary-tree-shaped RDFS class hierarchies is produced using the RBench generator. The experimental results show that the bandwidth of forward chaining algorithm increases exponentially with the tree depth while it remains constant in backward chaining algorithm. To evaluate the backward chaining algorithm, inserting 10^3 and 10^4 triples into the network takes about 8 and 50 s respectively. However, in the forward chaining algorithm, the time needed for inserting 10^3 and 10^4 triples varies dramatically from about 100 to 10,000 s. Experiments show that a simple forward chaining implementation cannot scale well. The main issues are caused by redundant computation and communication overhead.

Hoeksema and Kotoulas [185] studied stream reasoning over RDF data and C-SPARQL [35] query answering using Yahoo S4.[8] The reasoning process feeds triples to C-SPARQL query processing, where a number of components dealing with different aspects of a C-SPARQL query is defined. In particular, the authors described the components that provide variable bindings for matched query patterns, perform joins on variables in the query, filter incoming bindings, and emit the final results in the required format. The authors also discussed the two types of windows supported by C-SPARQL, namely, a window that comprises of either a fixed number of triples or a fixed period of time during which triples are entering the stream. The latter approach is chosen as it is more appropriate given a distributed setting. Triples that enter the system are assigned a timestamp and an expiration time, while triples that are derived again after their expiration are reassigned their corresponding timestamps. Moreover, the authors described several components that support aggregates such as SUM, AVG, COUNT, MIN, and MAX. The system is evaluated based on two metrics, namely, maximum throughput in terms of triples per second (with maximum supported throughput of 160,000 triples per second) and the number of processing nodes. When no reasoning is performed and the applied query passes through any given triple (pass-through query), high throughput is achieved even with three nodes showing linear performance. However, when RDFS reasoning is performed over the pass-through query, the system has shown the ability to scale up to 8 nodes, but it is unclear why linear performance is not retained for 16 and 32 nodes. In addition, two queries are considered where no RDFS reasoning is applied. For both queries linear performance is reported for up to eight compute nodes.

Salvadores et al. [336] presented a backward chaining system to perform minimal RDFS reasoning on top of 4Store [168], a distributed RDF storage engine. In 4Store, data is distributed in nonoverlapping segments which are evenly distributed across the peers, while terminological knowledge is replicated on all nodes. This allows the system to perform reasoning without any internode communication. Whenever a query must be processed, each node rewrites it in multiple queries exploiting the terminological knowledge that is available locally. Since the rules

---

[8]http://incubator.apache.org/s4/.

in the minimal RDFS segment are rather simple, this process can be carried out efficiently by chaining the sub-queries. The method is implemented inside the Java engine 4Store. The development of the system seems have been discontinued. An experimental evaluation was carried out using the **LUBM** [157] dataset and up to five machines. As inputs, the authors used a number of datasets with a number of triples between 13 and 138 million triples and five atomic queries. The system produced derivations between 150 and 300 thousands triples per second, but unfortunately no comparison with other systems was performed. Hogan et al. [187] discussed optimizations of rule-based materialization approaches for reasoning over large static RDFS datasets. The authors generalized and formalized the notion of partial indexing techniques which are optimized for application of linear rules and which rely on a separation of terminological data. Due to their focus on the linear rules in RDFS, pD*, and OWL 2 RL rule set, many of the rule executions can be perfectly parallelized. A reasoner called SAOR is implemented based on a distributed platform. In their evaluation, they showed that the time consumption for most expensive tasks such as TBox extraction and ABox reasoning decreased by half when the number of machines is doubled.

6.3 NoSQL-Based RDF Reasoning Systems

Several RDF reasoning systems used NoSQL databases in order to improve their scalability. **VLog** [393] is a reasoner which was designed to perform Datalog evaluation on large knowledge graphs. The principal characteristic of VLog is that is uses relatively fewer resources than the other engines to compute the derivation. This allows its usage on machines that are equipped with commodity hardware. For instance, the authors showed that it is possible to compute the materialization of 0.5B LUBM triples using a normal laptop. Since VLog implements standard Datalog reasoning, it can execute rules in the RDFS fragment or OWL RL. The main novelty of VLog is that it adopts a columnar storage strategy to store the inferenced tuples. With such approach, the tuples are stored column by column rather than row by row. This strategy is good for compression since the system can apply well-known database techniques like run-length encoding (RLE) or standard delta encoding. Furthermore, in some cases columns can be reused for different predicates. These optimizations effectively reduce the space required to store the inference. One major problem of this approach is that columnar stores perform poorly with updates. To overcome this limitation, VLog avoids the insertion of new elements in existing tables and creates new tables instead. This causes a problem during the rules execution since multiple tables must be merged: To reduce the number of merges, the system performs a sort of backtracking reasoning to infer whether a table can lead to new inference. The merge is avoided whenever the system determines this is not the case. VLog is implemented in C++. The system is neither parallel nor distributed. It can interface to several backend to retrieve the input for the Datalog computation. So far, it can interface with Trident (an in-house

graph engine) and MySQL and MonetDB—two popular DBMS. VLog is superior
to the other competitors in terms of main memory consumption. Urbani et al. [393]
compared the performance with RDFox on fairly large KBs (up to 0.5B triples)
and showed how the system uses much less main memory. In its current version,
VLog has two limitations: First, reasoning is sequential and hence the scalability
is limited only to the speed of the CPU, while parallel approaches can scale on
two dimensions—CPU *and* number of CPUs. Second, the system performs only a
limited indexing on the materialized inference, which means that data might need
further processing before it can be efficiently queried.

Rya [315] is a scalable RDF data management system built on top of Accumulo,[9]
a key-value store that is based on Google's Bigtable [72]. Although Rya is primarily
a RDF storage and querying system, it does have support for basic inference. Rya
makes use of OpenRDF Sesame, now superseded by Eclipse RDF4J,[10] for parsing,
storing, and querying RDF data. Rya's querying engine makes changes to the query
execution plan of RDF4J to implement some optimizations such as reordering joins
and expanding triple patterns to implement inferencing. Rya supports inference
on the following properties: rdf:type, subPropertyOf, and equivalentProperty. It
expands any SPARQL query involving these relations to also return the inferred
triples. Experiments were conducted on an 11 node cluster with each node having
an 8 core 2.33 GHz process with 16 GB RAM. LUBM was used as the dataset with
triples ranging from 1.3 million (LUBM-10 for 10 universities) to 2.1 billion triples
(LUBM-15000 for 15,000 universities). Although the performance and scalability
are good, they do not in particular address how their basic inferencing impacts the
performance.

6.4   Hadoop-Based RDF Reasoning Systems

Several RDF reasoning systems have been implemented on top of the Hadoop
framework [409]. A generic architecture for both Hadoop- and Spark-based RDF
reasoning systems is represented in Fig. 6.2. In this architecture, schema triples
are replicated across all the nodes since they are relatively less in number when
compared to the instance triples. Instance triples are distributed across the cluster.
The distribution mechanism is dependent on the specific algorithm used by the
reasoner. This schema and instance triple distribution approach is followed by many
of the Hadoop- and Spark-based RDF reasoning systems. The idea behind this is to
make the joins local.

WebPIE [387, 389] is a distributed forward chaining reasoner that relies on the
MapReduce primitives to distribute and parallelize the computation. The system is
implemented on top of the Hadoop framework and supports reasoning with some

---

[9]https://accumulo.apache.org/.
[10]http://rdf4j.org/.

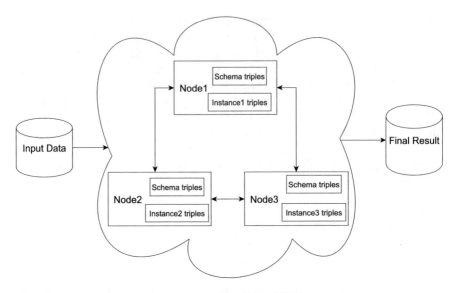

Fig. 6.2 Generic architecture for Hadoop- and Spark-based RDF reasoning systems

RDFS and OWL Horst [379] rules. WebPIE implements intra-query parallelism, that is, the evaluation of each rule is performed in parallel. The parallelism consists of partitioning the input in several chunks and processing each chunk by a different processor. The initial version of WebPIE supported only partial RDFS reasoning, but it was later extended to support the OWL Horst fragment. The research contribution consisted of showing how certain rules could be evaluated efficiently with MapReduce by exploiting certain properties of current datasets (i.e., a relatively small size of terminological knowledge compared to the assertional one). Each rule is encoded using the MapReduce primitives and executed with one or more Hadoop programs. The system reads in as its input a series of (compressed) RDF triples, performs the materialization, and returns another list of files which contains the inferred triples. Each rule is hardcoded; therefore the system cannot be easily extended to support more rules. In the largest experiments, it was able to compute the materialization of 100 billion triples. The system however suffers from two major limitations: First, it cannot be quickly extended to other rulesets since each rule is hardcoded in the program. Second, the system does not index the derivation. This means that after the computation of WebPIE has finished, the user must load its output into an RDF engine in order to query the results efficiently.

Bonatti et al. [50] leveraged annotated logic programs to incorporate provenance and trust in linked data reasoning. The authors annotate whether a piece of linked data should be trusted, ignored, or used with a numeric ranking in a reasoning procedure that employs part of the OWL 2 RL/RDF rule set. In addition to a number of desired formal properties such as monotonicity and decidability, the algorithm is designed based on a shared-nothing distributed architecture to support large-scale linked data. In this architecture, a master machine is used to partition the data and task, to request tasks executions, to pull tasks results, and to broadcast global knowledge. A number of slave machines are used to execute concrete tasks and can exchange data between each other when necessary. Each slave machine is assigned with an approximately equal number of triples/quads. Due to the design of the approach, most of the expensive tasks can be performed in an embarrassingly parallel manner, significantly reducing the data exchange between slave machines. A prototype system is implemented based on a shared-nothing distributed platform where several independent machines are involved. Although this implementation is not based on Hadoop, it is pretty close to a Hadoop system with one master distributing and coordinating the tasks among the slaves. The behavior of embarrassing parallelism has also been observed in evaluation, in which a dataset of 1.11 billion triples/quads is used. Evaluation shows that the distributed reasoning and inconsistency checking time is reduced, on average, by 40–50% when the number of slaves is doubled. The speedup for distributed ranking is less significant. The reduction of ranking time diminishes when more and more slaves are used.

QueryPIE [388, 392] is a backward chaining, top-down reasoner that supports OWL Horst and partial OWL 2 RL/RDF. The computation can be performed either on a single, multi-core machine or be distributed across several machines that communicate to each other using a message passing library. The system implements two major contributions: a permanent tabling technique (which is rebranded as hybrid reasoning [392]) and a parallel variant of the well-known QSQ-R algorithm [4]. The tabling technique consists in materializing a consistent part of the terminological knowledge and indexing it in main-memory so that it can be retrieved quickly. This prematerialization is useful to prune the search space at query time and reduces the inference process to the calculation of only assertional data. The parallel variant of QSQ is introduced to speed up the top-down evaluation of the rules. The parallelism is interquery: this means that the system evaluates several rules concurrently and synchronization is introduced only during a few stages. The algorithm presented in [388] is incomplete (interestingly, the source of incompleteness is the same as that which affected the original presentation of QSQR). The algorithm was later fixed in [392]. In a subsequent work, some of the original authors interleaved sequential execution with parallel ones. The sequential code is reserved for "hard" rules which require joins between multiple intensional predicates. Simpler rules, which only require either no join or only joins between extensional and intensional predicates, are executed in parallel. The system is implemented in Java. It relies on a distributed computing framework, called Ajira [391], to execute the computation in parallel. The paper [392] reports the execution of single-pattern queries using a LUBM dataset of ten billion triples on a single machine. Later, another evaluation was conducted on multipattern queries [386]. In terms of input size, this system scales well since it can handle KBs with billions of triples. However, its main limitation is that it stores the inferred tuples in main memory, and this precludes the execution of queries which produce a number of intermediate answers whose size exceeds the available main memory.

6.5   Spark-Based RDF Reasoning Systems

Several scalable RDF reasoning systems have been implemented on top of the
Apache Spark [429] cluster computing platform. For example, Reasoning on
SPARK (RSPARK) [217] is a system that was designed to perform forward
chaining reasoning on the Spark ecosystem. The goal and functioning of this system
are very similar to WebPIE, and the only difference is related to the infrastructure
used (Hadoop for WebPIE, and SparK for RSPARK). The system performs TBox
reasoning (i.e., executes only rules that derive new schema), and then performs
ABox reasoning (i.e., executes all other rules). RSPARK executes the rules one
at a time. Before doing so, it reorders the execution order of the rules to reduce
the possibility that inference derived at a later stage can serve as input of rules
already executed. The rules that perform TBox reasoning are executed only once.
This means that the reasoner can potentially be incomplete because it will be unable
to produce TBox inference which required some ABox inference first. In order
to execute the rules, the system represents the triples into $< key, value >$ pairs
which are then stored in Resilient Distributed Datasets (RDDs). RDDs are the data
structures which are manipulated by the Spark's operators. Overall, the functioning
is similar than the one proposed in WebPIE, with the only difference being that
Spark is a more efficient framework. Interestingly, it appears that this system does
not perform dictionary encoding and works directly on raw strings. The system was
evaluated using a knowledge base of about 860 million triples, and its performance
on this input was compared with WebPIE. The results show that the system is about
three times faster. Unfortunately, the evaluation in [217] was conducted with only
five machines. It is not clear how the system would scale either with a larger cluster
or with larger datasets.

Cichlid [155] implements RDFS and OWL Horst rulesets on top of Spark.
Reasoning over these rulesets is an iterative process where the rulesets are applied
repeatedly until no new triples are produced. Triples are represented in the form
of RDDs, and the implementation of the rules involves Spark operations such as
filter, map, join, union, and distinct. Schema triples are broadcast to all the nodes
so that shuffling data across the nodes can be avoided and a local join can be
performed. Apart from optimizing expensive join operations, another issue that
needs to be handled is the elimination of duplicate triples that get generated due to
the repeated application of rules. In Cichlid, a partial duplicate elimination strategy
is followed to reduce the shuffling of data across the nodes. In the case of OWL
Horst rule implementation, data is preshuffled to optimize joins. In this step, RDDs
are partitioned and cached in memory before the join operation is invoked. This
helps in reducing the data sent over the network during the join operation. Another
optimization from Cichlid is to implement a smart transitive closure [239] for
transitive rule reasoning. Rules involving *owl:sameAs* are optimized by maintaining
a sameAs table that contains concepts related by the *owl:sameAs* property. The last
optimization is the usage of Tachyon, an in-memory file system for storing heap
objects such as RDDs. A 17-node cluster with each node having two Xeon quad

2.4 GHz processors and 24 GB RAM is used for the experiments. LUBM, WordNet, and DBpedia datasets are used with triples ranging from 1.9 million to 200 million. Performance results are compared with WebPIE. It turns out that for RDFS ruleset, Cichlid is ten times faster than WebPIE, and whereas for OWL Horst ruleset, Cichlid is six times faster than WebPIE. As the number of nodes in the cluster increases from 1 to 16, Cichlid's runtime decreases by 8 times as compared to the 2.3 times decrease in WebPIE.

RORS [246] is a distributed Spark-based RDFS and OWL Horst reasoner that implements a locally optimal execution strategy. All the 27 rules that RORS implements are divided into four categories: SPO rules, type rules, sameAs rules, and schema rules. There are interdependencies among the rules. If the input to rule R_i is dependent on the output from rule R_j, then we can say that R_i depends on R_j. A rule dependency graph for each of the four rule categories is constructed based on these dependencies. A depth-first search on the rule dependency graph gives several rule execution orders. Among them, the longest order that involves as many rules as possible is picked as the optimal execution order. In order to optimize the join operations in Spark, the schema rules, which are less in number, are copied to all the nodes in the cluster using the *broadcast* feature of Spark. RORS used the LUBM dataset to run experiments on a five-node cluster with one master and four slave nodes. Five datasets are generated from LUBM with triples varying from 1.4 to 27.6 million. The performance of RORS has been compared with RSPARK [217] and Cichlid [155]. RORS is 30% faster when compared to RSPARK and infers triples 26% faster when compared to Cichlid. On the downside, some of the rule optimization strategies are specific to the LUBM dataset. In a follow-up work of Liu et al. [247], they extended their experiments to the DBpedia dataset and showed that the performance improvements over RSPARK remain the same.

SPOWL [245] is another Spark-based OWL 2 RL/RDFS reasoner. The assumption in this work is that ontologies have small TBox and large ABox axioms. The first step is to use a tableaux reasoner such as Pellet[11] or HermiT[12] to classify the TBox axioms, that is, to compute the complete subsumption hierarchy of all the concepts in the ontology. This allows SPOWL to support axioms that are beyond OWL 2 RL/RDFS. The next step is to load all the ABox data to a distributed file system such as HDFS. The final step is to transform the classified TBox axioms into Spark programs and run them iteratively on the loaded ABox facts until no new facts can be generated. Axioms in the ontology are represented as Spark RDDs. Individuals of a class C are stored in an unary RDD C_{rdd}, and individuals connected by a property P are stored in a binary RDD P_{rdd}. Partitioning the data in this manner offers the advantage of accessing only the relevant pieces while implementing the reasoning. With these RDDs in place, implementing a subsumption relation such as $C \sqsubseteq D$ in Spark is as easy as using the Spark's RDD union feature to merge C_{rdd} and D_{rdd} into D_{rdd}. Apart from this, SPOWL makes use of Spark's built-in optimizations

---

[11]https://github.com/stardog-union/pellet.

[12]http://www.hermit-reasoner.com/.

such as caching the data, partitioning the data before a join, and the DAG for parallelizing the reasoning. SPOWL used a nine-node cluster for its experiments. Each node has a quad core 2.5 GHz processor with 16 GB of RAM. LUBM is used as the dataset for the experiments. The dataset size varies from LUBM-400 (data from 400 universities) to LUBM-2000 (data from 2000 universities). The TBox of LUBM contains 43 classes, 32 properties, and around 200 axioms. The loading and reasoning time in SPOWL for LUBM-400 to LUBM-2000 grows linearly and is faster than WebPIE.

6.6   Shared Memory RDF Reasoning Systems

A generic architecture for shared-memory-based RDF reasoning systems is presented in Fig. 6.3. In this architecture, resources such as memory and computing time are shared between the threads in the system. So, generally, lock-based techniques are used by the threads to achieve mutually exclusive access to the resources. However, some other approaches make use of lock-free data structures and these approaches are naturally faster than the lock-based approaches. Goodman et al. [143] studied RDFS reasoning over a shared memory machine with multi-threaded processors. All processes are performed completely in memory by utilizing the global shared memory, on the Cray XMT supercomputer. In particular, the authors present an algorithm for encoding RDFS triples, represented in N-Triples or N-Quads format, into a set of 64-bit integers, thus mapping strings into integers. Dictionary encoding is highly optimized for parallel processing, while the final representation consists of triples encoded as integer values, and the mappings from each unique string to its corresponding integer value and vice versa. This in-memory representation is used for RDFS closure computation. RDFS closure is based on a previously presented algorithm, although the approach is altered in order to reduce memory usage. Specifically, triples are stored in a global hash table, with the new approach optimizing the use of hash key values in order to include information about the availability of each slot. In addition, RDFS reasoning is based on processing the entire dataset instead of using queues that contain matching triples for each rule. Subsequently, RDFS closure is transformed into a graph representation to facilitate SPARQL query answering. An algorithm called *Sprinkle SPARQL* is used in order to identify matching triples and calculate final results by combining all

Fig. 6.3 Generic architecture for shared memory RDF reasoning systems

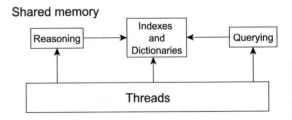

intermediate results. Experimental results showed that the system is able to scale up to 512 processors while handling 20 billion triples completely in memory using the Cray XMT supercomputer. In particular, dictionary encoding handled up to 16.5 billion triples, with compression ratios ranging from 3.2 to 4.4, speedups ranging from 2.4 to 3.3, and a maximum throughput of up to 561 MB/s. RDFS closure generated 20.1 billion unique triples, requiring 40% less memory at the cost of a 11–33% increase in computation time, with speedups ranging from 6 to 9 and throughput of 13.7 (resp. 21.7) million inferences/second including (resp. ignoring) I/O. SPARQL queries showed speedups ranging from 4.3 to 28 for complicated queries, while authors point out that *Sprinkle SPARQL* did not outperform all evaluated alternatives, for simple queries, as it comes with a significant overhead.

Heino and Pan [181] reported their work on RDFS reasoning on massively parallel hardware. They use forward chaining based on the six RDFS entailment rules. Their evaluation uses two real-world datasets, DBPedia and YAGO2 Core. To improve efficiency and scalability, a few optimizations have been employed, such as encoding the strings in RDFS documents into 64-bit integers. The approach has been implemented in both multicore CPU and multicore GPU with shared main memory. The CPU implementation uses four 8-core CPUs and the GPU implementation uses a 20-core GPU. Evaluation shows that when the number of the CPU cores used is doubled, the CPU kernel time is reduced by half, with up to 16 cores. It also shows an interesting comparison between the CPU implementation and the GPU implementation, in which the latter has a shorter kernel time but not longer overall time. The authors explained that this is because GPU has more cores, but the data needs to be copied back and forth between the main memory and GPU's global memory.

DynamiTE [390] is a parallel engine that performs materialization of inference considering the minimal RDF fragment [276]. The system first performs a full materialization (when the data is initially loaded into the system) and then incrementally updates the materialization after new data is added or removed. The full materialization is executed using standard Datalog semi-naive evaluation. The incremental updates can be executed either using D-Red [159] or with a bookkeeping algorithm that stores counters next to each derivations. The system is implemented in Java and exploits multicore parallelism. The knowledge base is indexed on various permutations of the triples and stored on disk using multiple B-Tree data structures. The system was evaluated using LUBM benchmark datasets [157] with up to one billion triples. The performance was compared against WebPIE, and the results indicated that DymamiTE was able to produce higher throughputs due to less overhead. The best performance was obtained with the counting algorithm. Unfortunately, this algorithm does not work properly with recursive rules [274].

Motik et al. [272] proposed an approach for parallelizing materialization of datalog programs. It covers general datalog programs and is further adapted to languages such as RDFS and OWL 2 RL. The authors extend the classical datalog materialization algorithm, that is, the *semi-naive* algorithm [4], to a parallel variant. They provided a strategy of indexing RDF triples in memory. This indexing strategy results in an effective join operation. The following process briefly describes the algorithm: (a) Initially, a global iterator is provided, in which all facts (including the new added ones) are ordered according to a strict total order. (b) Any free thread captures a fact F from the global iterator and attempts to match it to the body atoms in all rules. For example, when a thread is applying the rule (1), it attempts to match F to each $B_i (1 \leq i \leq n)$, and all B_j where $j < i$ (resp. $j \geq i$) can only be matched to the facts having a lower (resp. Higher or equal) order than B_i. (c) Step 2 is repeated until all threads generate no more facts. The global order helps to avoid generating redundant facts. The other critical issue for this method is how to implement the operations of accessing facts through the global iterator, inserting new facts, and checking if a new fact is already existing. In this work, the authors propose a new indexing strategy for RDF triples, which results in high efficient joining operations. In the core of the materialization algorithm, any free thread obtains the next fact from the global iterator and applies rules on a special fact set.

The RDFox system [273] has been developed for testing concurrency overhead and scalability by comparing with current state of the art systems. It is essentially an OWL 2 RL management system on datalog programs. It is also an in-memory reasoner. Since RDFox is a datalog reasoner, the evaluated ontologies should first be translated into datalog programs. The experimental results show the following: First, RDFox performs better than other serial systems both on materialization and data importing on most datasets. Second, the fraction of the work performed in parallel ranges from 88 to 98% when 32 threads are available (according to Amdahl's law). This means, in most cases, parallelizing reasoning pays off. Third, in practice, the memory-based approach is sufficient for real datasets like DBpedia. However, from the proposed results, there are still cases that result in memory exhaustion. The main reason behind this is that the algorithm leads to the memory usage that increases with the number of threads.

6.7 Influence on Other Semantic Web Languages

The success of scalable RDFS reasoning approaches in terms of openly available systems that have been evaluated on massive datasets and peer-reviewed at well-known conferences has encouraged the use of similar approaches to other Semantic Web languages such as OWL Horst, OWL 2 EL, OWL 2 RL, and also non-monotonic reasoning. Among these, we have already discussed in this chapter the systems and approaches that implement the rulesets of OWL Horst and OWL 2 RL along with RDFS. We will briefly look at primarily Hadoop- and Spark-based approaches to implement the rules in OWL 2 EL and non-monotonic reasoning. We will also highlight the difficulty in implementing the rulesets when moving from a lower expressive language such as RDFS to a higher expressive language such as OWL 2 EL.

MapReduce algorithms were proposed for description logics $\mathcal{EL}^+$, $\mathcal{EL}^{++}$ (formal logic underpinning for OWL 2 EL), and fuzzy-$\mathcal{EL}^+$ in [255, 278, 342], and [440], respectively. But the proposed algorithms were not evaluated and implementations are often not provided. Although an implementation and evaluation was discussed in [441], it was not promising. It turns out that using MapReduce and the Hadoop framework for implementing OWL 2 EL rules is inefficient and does not scale well to large ontologies. This is due to the following reasons:

- There are a lot more interdependencies among the OWL 2 EL rules when compared to RDFS rules which result in increased communication overhead among the nodes in the cluster.
- In RDFS reasoning, there are limited schema triples and several instance triples. This means that it is possible to replicate schema triples across all the nodes in the cluster.

In practice, large $\mathcal{EL}^+$ bio-medical ontologies such as SNOMED CT[13] contain several millions of schema data (also referred to as TBox axioms). So replicating the schema data in such ontologies is as good as having duplicates of the entire ontology on all the nodes in the cluster. However, other approaches to distributed reasoning in $\mathcal{EL}^+$ such as Peer-to-Peer approach [280] and a Spark implementation [277] have yielded better results. The architecture of the Peer-to-Peer approach is shown in Fig. 6.4. Each rule type is assigned to a particular group of nodes called subclusters. These subclusters only communicate with specific subclusters that are working on dependent rules. Rules are applied iteratively until no new inferences are produced. U[X], R[r], and Q[r] are the result set, role (property) set, and intermediate role set, respectively. In general, the use of the Hadoop framework for non-monotonic reasoning has given better results. Tachmzidis et al. [375] presented the first step towards scalable non-monotonic reasoning, focusing on defeasible reasoning. The main idea lies on the fact that there is only one variable in the body of the rule. Thus, all predicates of the body have a common argument on which they can be joined in order to decide on the applicability of the rule. Tachmazidis et al. [374] further extended the work to allow for more than one variable in the rules.

---

[13]http://www.snomed.org/snomed-ct.

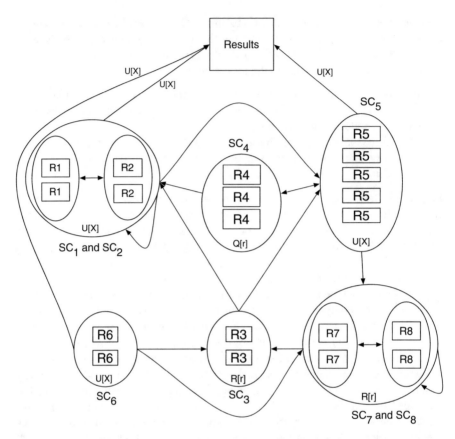

Fig. 6.4 Node assignment to rules and dependency among the completion rules. A rectangle represents a node in the cluster and inner ovals represent subclusters. Outer ovals enclosing SC_1/SC_2, and SC_7/SC_8 show their tighter input–output relationships. The set (U[X], R[r], or Q[r]) affected by the rule is shown within the enclosing oval. For simplicity, only one node is shown to hold results. ©Springer International Publishing Switzerland 2015. Reprinted with permission

Chapter 7
Benchmarking RDF Query Engines and Instance Matching Systems

Standards and benchmarking have traditionally been used as the main tools to formally define and provably illustrate the level of the adequacy of systems to address the new challenges. In this chapter, we discuss benchmarks for RDF query engines and instance matching systems. In practice, benchmarks are used to inform users of the strengths and weaknesses of competing tools and approaches, but more importantly, they encourage the advancement of technology by providing both academia and industry with clear targets for performance and functionality.

This chapter starts by presenting the *principles* described in the literature for benchmark development and the *dimensions* of an RDF benchmark, namely, *query workloads*, *performance metrics*, and employed *datasets* or *data generators* (in the case of synthetic benchmarks). We then provide a comprehensive overview of the existing RDF benchmarks (*real*, *synthetic*, and *benchmark generators*) with an analysis using the aforementioned dimensions. We will also discuss the advantages and disadvantages of the existing frameworks.

7.1 Benchmark Definition and Principles

7.1.1 Overview

Benchmarks are used to evaluate the performance of systems. Unfortunately, and despite the long tradition of systems and benchmarks, according to [256], there are still some key issues such as:

- There is *no single recipe on how to do performance evaluation right*.
- There are *many ways to do it wrong*.
- There are a *number of best practices* but *no broadly accepted standard* on how to design a benchmark.

© Springer International Publishing AG 2018
S. Sakr et al., *Linked Data*, https://doi.org/10.1007/978-3-319-73515-3_7

The above are especially true for RDF *query engines* since work in this domain has only started no more than 10 years ago. The questions one could (and should) ask when starting a performance evaluation are [256]:

- The *datasets* to use
- The *workload/queries* to consider
- The *key performance indicators* to measure and *how* those should be measured

In the literature, there are three different categories of benchmarks: (a) *microbenchmarks*, (b) *standard benchmarks*, and (c) *real-life applications*.

Microbenchmarks are *specialized, stand-alone pieces of software* that can be used to test a *particular* functionality of a large system. For instance, in databases a microbenchmark can test a *single* query operator such as *selection, join*, and *union*, among others. The advantages of microbenchmarks are that they (a) are *very focused* since they test a specific operator of the system and (b) they come with a *controllable data* and *workload* (i.e., set of queries). The datasets can be *synthetic* and/or *real* that should have different *value ranges* and *value distributions/correlations*. Furthermore, datasets come in *different sizes* in order to challenge systems regarding *scalability*. Queries can be of different *size* and *complexity*. Size refers to the *number of query operators* involved in the query, whereas *complexity* refers to the *types of query operators* involved in the query. Queries should allow a *broad range* of *parameters* in order to challenge the systems under test. The disadvantages of this category of benchmarks is that they neglect the larger picture since they do not test the whole system, and hence the results of experiments might not be correct. Furthermore, they do not consider the flow of costs of specific operations to the cost of the system, and the results of such benchmarks cannot be applied in a straightforward manner and are also difficult to generalize. Last but not least, microbenchmarks do not use standardized metrics. To conclude, microbenchmarks are useful for detailed, in-depth analysis, have a very low setup threshold, and are very easy to run. Nevertheless they cannot be very useful for optimizations in large-scale systems since they do not consider the complete workflow.

The second category of benchmarks, *standard benchmarks* have been used to test the performance of relational, object-oriented, and object-relational database systems. The family of TPC benchmarks [382] can be considered as a very good example of this kind of benchmarks. A number of such benchmarks have been considered to test XML query engines [54] such as **XBench** [427], **XMach-1** [48], and **XMark** [344]. Another family of standard benchmarks are the SPEC benchmarks [102] with the key aim of comparing systems' performance across many different technologies, architectures, implementations, memory systems, I/O subsystems, operating systems, clock rates, bus protocols, compilers, libraries, and application software.

The advantages of standard benchmarks are that they mimic real-life scenarios that respond to real needs. For instance, TPC is a business-oriented benchmark. These benchmarks are publicly available and well defined and provide scalable datasets and workloads with very well-defined metrics. On the other hand, they are outdated since standardization is a very lengthy process, for instance, it took 7 years for XQuery to become a standard, and benchmarks for TPC are continuously evolving. In general, standard benchmarks are very large and complicated to run. They consider a limited dataset variation since they target a very specific type of data, a limited workload since they are focusing on the application used to develop the benchmark, and finally, the systems are often optimized for the benchmarks and not necessarily for other use cases.

7.1.2 Benchmark Development Methodology

Standard benchmarks such as TPC[1] follow a *development methodology* that focuses on primarily two main categories: *management* and *methodological* activities. Management activities focus on *organizational protocols* that are needed to control the process of development of the benchmark. Methodological activities focus on the *principles*, *methods*, and *steps* for benchmark creation.

In the Benchmark Development phase, one could identify (a) the *roles* and *bodies* involved in the development of the benchmark; (b) the *design principles*, that is, the fundamental rules that direct the development of a benchmark; and finally, (c) the *development process* meaning the series of steps that are followed to develop a benchmark. The majority of benchmarks have not been developed with a clear methodology in mind: the purpose was to check the query evaluation performance of systems for different but not always representative workloads.

In this section, we are going to discuss briefly the set of Transaction Processing Performance Council (TPC) state-of-the-art benchmarks for relational database management systems. TPC is a nonprofit corporation focused on developing *data-centric benchmark standards* and disseminating objective, verifiable performance data to the industry. The goal of TPC is to "create, manage and maintain a set of fair and comprehensive benchmarks that enable end-users and vendors to objectively evaluate system performance under well defined consistent and comparable workloads" [302]. The design principles of TPC-C, the mostly used benchmark of the family of TPC benchmarks that focuses on transactions are shown in Table 7.1 [240]. A benchmark is also accompanied by *metrics* that are essential for assessing the overall performance of the system. Such metrics are related to (a) *system performance*, (b) *price/performance*, and (c) *energy/performance*, a metric to measure the energy consumption of system components. TPC provides consistent methodologies for computing the price of the benchmarked system, licensing of software, maintenance, etc. Table 7.2 presents the TPC metrics per benchmark.

A set of desirable attributes for a benchmark have been proposed in the literature. More specifically, Weicker [407] stated that "A good benchmark is written in a high-level language, making it portable across different machines; is representative of some programming style or application; can be measured easily; has wide

---

[1]http://www.tpc.org/.

Table 7.1 TPC-C design principles

Principle	Comment
Relevant	The benchmark is meaningful for the target domain
Understandable	The benchmark is easy to understand and use
Good metrics	The metrics defined by the benchmark are linear, orthogonal, and monotonic
Scalable	The benchmark is applicable to a broad spectrum of hardware and software configurations
Coverage	The benchmark workload does not oversimplify the typical environment
Acceptance	The benchmark is recognized as relevant by the majority of vendors and users

Table 7.2 TPC metrics

Benchmark	Metrics
TPC-D	Transaction rate (tpmC), price per transaction ($/tmpC)
TPC-E	Transactions per second (tpS)
TPC-H	Composite query per hour performance metric (QpH@Size), price per composite query per hour performance metric ($/ QpH@Size)

distribution". Gray [148] stated that a domain-specific benchmark should meet four important criteria: *relevance*, *portability*, *simplicity*, and *scalability*. Levine [240] adds *understandability*, *good metrics*, and *coverage* to the relevance and scalability attributes to define the desirable set of attributes. Huppler [192] proposed a different set of attributes where he suggests that *relevance*, *repeatability*, *fairness*, *verifiability*, and *economy* are properties that a good benchmark should have. Gathering all this information, one could summarize that according to literature, the desirable attributes a benchmark should have are:

- **Relevant/Representative**. The benchmark should be based on realistic use case scenarios and must reflect the needs of the use case.
- **Understandable/Simple**. The results and workload are easily understandable by users.
- **Portable/Fair/Repeatable**. No system should benefit from the benchmark, and it must be deterministic and provide a "gold standard" since systems must be able to check the correctness of the results.
- **Metrics**. Metrics should be well defined in order for developers and system users to be able to assess and compare the systems under test.
- **Scalable**. The datasets considered by the benchmark should be in the order of billions of objects in order to address extremely large datasets.
- **Verifiable**. The benchmark must allow verifiable results in each execution.

7.1.3   Choke Points

A benchmark exposes a system to a workload and should identify the technical difficulties of the system under test. Boncz et al. [51] coined the term *choke*

Table 7.3 TPC-H choke points [51]

CP1	Aggregation Performance	Ordered aggregation, small group-by keys, interesting orders, dependent group-by keys
CP2	Join Performance	Large joins, sparse foreign keys, rich join order optimization, late projection
CP3	Data Access Locality (materialized views)	Columnar locality, physical locality by key, detecting correlation
CP4	Expression Calculation	Raw Expression Arithmetic, Complex Boolean Expressions in Joins and Selections, String Matching Performance
CP5	Correlated Sub-queries	Flattening sub-queries, moving predicates to a sub-query, overlap between outer query and sub-query
CP6	Parallelism and Concurrency	Query plan parallelization, workload management, result reuse

points that denote the set of *technical difficulties* whose resolution will significantly improve the performance of a product. The authors analyzed the TPC-H workload, a 20-year-old benchmark (superseded by TPC-DS) that is still influential, using business-oriented queries and concurrent modifications. The workload consists of 22 queries that capture (most of) the aspects of *relational query processing*. The result of the analysis of Boncz, Neumann, and Erling was the definition of *28 choke points* that were grouped into *six categories*. Table 7.3 presents those categories.

The work of Kotsev et al. [224] has been based on the choke points shown in Table 7.3 and proposed a set of choke points for RDF benchmarks shown below:

- CP_1 **Join Ordering** This choke point tests (a) if the engine can evaluate the trade-offs between the time spent to find the best execution plan and the quality of the output plan and (b) the ability of the engine to consider cardinality constraints expressed by the different kinds of schema constraints (e.g., functional and inverse functional properties)
- CP_2 **Aggregation** Aggregations are implemented with the use of subselects in the SPARQL query; the optimizer should recognize the operations included in the subselects and evaluate them first.
- CP_3 **Optional and Nested Optional Clauses** This choke point tests the ability of the optimizer to produce a plan where the execution of the optional triple patterns is the last to be performed since optional clauses do not reduce the size of intermediate results.
- CP_4 **Reasoning** This choke point tests the ability of the engine to handle efficiently RDFS and OWL constructs expressed in the schema.

Table 7.4 Query characteristics

Simple filters	Unbound predicates	LIMIT	REGEX	CONSTRUCT
Complex filters	Negation	ORDER BY	UNION	ASK
≥ 9 TPs	OPTIONAL	DISTINCT	DESCRIBE	

- CP_5 **Parallel Execution of Unions** This choke point tests the ability of the optimizer to produce plans where unions are executed in parallel.
- CP_6 **Filters** This choke point tests the ability of the engines to execute as early as possible those filter expressions to eliminate a possibly large number of intermediate results.
- CP_7 **Ordering** This choke point tests the ability of the engine to choose query plan(s) that facilitate the ordering of results.
- CP_8 **Geospatial Predicates** This choke point tests the ability of the system to handle queries for geospatial data.
- CP_9 **Full Text** This choke point tests the ability of the systems to handle queries that involve the evaluation of regular expressions on data value properties of resources.
- CP_{10} **Duplicate Elimination** This choke point tests the ability of the system to identify duplicate entries and eliminate them during the creation of intermediate results.
- CP_{11} **Complex Filter Conditions** This choke point tests the ability of the engine to deal with negation, conjunction, and disjunction efficiently (i.e., breaking the filters into conjunction of filters and execute them in parallel).

The authors also proposed a set of *characteristics* that can be used to describe the workload of the various benchmarks. Table 7.4 presents those features that will be used for describing the benchmarks in this chapter. Each of these characteristics is essential for the aforementioned choke points.

7.2　Benchmarks for RDF Query Engines

In this section, we discuss the state-of-the-art benchmarks that have been developed for RDF query engines. We distinguish between *real benchmarks* (Sect. 7.2.1), *synthetic benchmarks* (Sect. 7.2.2), and *benchmark generators* (Sect. 7.2.3).

Table 7.5 UniProtKB queries [285]

Characteristic	Queries							
	Q_1	Q_2	Q_3	Q_4	Q_5	Q_6	Q_7	Q_8
Simple filters								
Complex filters								
>9 TPs		✓	✓	✓		✓	✓	✓
Unbound predicates								
Negation								
OPTIONAL								
LIMIT								
ORDER BY								
DISTINCT								
REGEX								
UNION								
DESCRIBE								
CONSTRUCT								
ASK								

7.2.1   Real Benchmarks

7.2.1.1   UniProt

UniProt[2] is a *comprehensive, high-quality*, and freely accessible resource of protein sequence and functional information [322]. The UniProt Schema is comprised of several ontologies and more specifically of the UniProt Core Vocabulary, BIBO (journals), ECO (evidence codes), and Dublin Core (metadata). The UniProt Core Vocabulary contains 124 classes and 113 Properties. The UniProt dataset is a very large dataset containing approximately 13 billion triples with 2.5 billion distinct subjects and 2 billion distinct objects. The dataset is not accompanied by a set of queries. Nevertheless, Neumann and Weikum defined a set of eight queries to test the RDF-3X engine [285]. The queries were very simple as they were focused mostly on testing the ability of systems to find the optimal *join ordering* since the system aims at optimizing join processing for RDF data (Table 7.5). The queries also addressed only the Choke Point **CP1** (*Join Ordering*) since the majority of queries were simple and focused solely on identifying the optimal join order in the query plan. The most complex query, Q_8, contains 12 joins and 7 queries contain more than 7 joins. Table 7.6 shows an overview of the choke points addressed by UniProt queries.

---

[2]http://www.uniprot.org/help/query-fields.

Table 7.6 UniProtKB queries choke points

Query	CP_1	CP_2	CP_3	CP_4	CP_5	CP_6	CP_7	CP_8	CP_9	CP_{10}	CP_{11}
Q_1	✓										
Q_2	✓										
Q_3	✓										
Q_4	✓										
Q_5	✓										
Q_6	✓										
Q_7	✓										
Q_8	✓										

7.2.1.2 YAGO (Yet Another Great Ontology)

YAGO[3] is a *high-quality multilingual knowledge base* [371] derived from Wikipedia,[4] WordNet,[5] and GeoNames.[6] The schema of YAGO contains ten million entities from the aforementioned ontologies, and it associates the WordNet taxonomy with the Wikipedia Category System. YAGO contains approximately 120 million triples about schema entities with 2.625 million links to DBpedia through Wikipedia entities. Similar to UniProt, YAGO is not accompanied with a representative set of queries. Nevertheless, Neumann and Weikum [285] proposed a set of representative queries to evaluate the RDF-3X query engine [285]. These queries are more complex than the ones proposed for YAGO, but they are still simple SELECT queries that focus on *join ordering, negation,* and *duplicate elimination.* The characteristics of the queries are shown in Table 7.7, and the choke points they address can be found in Table 7.8. One can see that the YAGO queries address all the choke points related to *join ordering* (CP_1) but also to *parallel execution of unions* (CP_5), the *efficient execution of filters* (CP_6), *duplicate elimination* (CP_{10}), and *complex filter conditions* (CP_{11}). Regarding join ordering that is tackled by all the proposed queries, all queries contain more than five joins whereas the most complex one contains eight joins.

7.2.1.3 Barton Library

Barton Library[7] is a dataset from the MIT Simile Project that develops tools for library data management.[8] It contains records that compose an RDF-formatted

---

[3] https://old.datahub.io/dataset/yago.

[4] https://en.wikipedia.org.

[5] https://wordnet.princeton.edu/.

[6] http://www.geonames.org/.

[7] http://simile.mit.edu/rdf-test-data/.

[8] http://web.mit.edu/dspace-dev/www/simile/.

Table 7.7 YAGO queries characteristics

Characteristic	Queries							
	A_1	A_2	A_3	A_1	A_2	A_3	C_1	C_2
Simple filters			✓					
Complex filters								
>9 TPs		✓						
Unbound predicates								
Negation				✓		✓	✓	
OPTIONAL								
LIMIT								
ORDER BY								
DISTINCT			✓	✓		✓	✓	✓
REGEX								
UNION			✓					
DESCRIBE								
CONSTRUCT								
ASK								

Table 7.8 YAGO queries choke points

Query	CP_1	CP_2	CP_3	CP_4	CP_5	CP_6	CP_7	CP_8	CP_9	CP_{10}	CP_{11}
A_1	✓										
A_2	✓										
A_3	✓				✓	✓				✓	
B_1	✓									✓	✓
B_2	✓				✓						
B_3	✓									✓	✓
C_1	✓				✓					✓	✓
C_2	✓									✓	

dump of the MIT Libraries Barton catalog and was converted from raw data stored in an old library format standard called MARC (Machine Readable Catalog). The Barton Library dataset schema contains *common types* as well as *primitive types*, and it contains approximately 45 million RDF triples. Similar to YAGO and UniProt, the Barton Library Dataset does not come with a representative set of queries. Abadi et al. [2] provided a workload of seven queries (in SQL) that were used to assess the proposed approach of the authors regarding the use of systems that employ the *vertical partitioning* approach. Neumann and Weikum provided the SPARQL version of those queries in their work in [285]. The queries employ *simple filters* and test the performance of the query engine in the case of *duplicate elimination*. Table 7.9 presents the characteristics of the Barton Queries, and the choke points these address are shown in Table 7.10. The queries are as difficult as the ones proposed in YAGO and UniProt, but the queries still do not address the more

Table 7.9 Barton queries [2]

	Queries						
------------------	Q_1	Q_2	Q_3	Q_4	Q_5	Q_6	Q_7
Characteristic							
Simple filters		✓	✓	✓		✓	
Complex filters							
>9 TPs							
Unbound predicates							
Negation					✓		
OPTIONAL							
LIMIT							
ORDER BY							
DISTINCT	✓	✓				✓	
REGEX							
UNION						✓	
DESCRIBE							
CONSTRUCT							
ASK							

Table 7.10 Barton queries choke points

Query	CP_1	CP_2	CP_3	CP_4	CP_5	CP_6	CP_7	CP_8	CP_9	CP_{10}	CP_{11}
A_1										✓	
Q_2					✓					✓	
Q_3					✓						
Q_4					✓						
Q_5	✓				✓						
Q_6	✓			✓	✓				✓		
Q_7	✓										

challenging choke points such as complex filters, negation, and parallel execution of joins, among others.

In addition to the aforementioned real benchmarks, other benchmarks include the Linked Sensor Data [307] and WordNet. The Linked Sensor Data contains expressive descriptions of approximately 20,000 weather stations in the United States, divided up into multiple subsets, that reflect weather data for specific hurricanes or blizzards from the past. The schema of the dataset contains information about temperature, precipitation, pressure, wind, speed, humidity, links to GeoNames, and links to observations provided by MesoWest (meteorological service in the United States). The dataset is very large as it contains more than one billion triples. WordNet is a large lexical database of English, developed under the direction of George A. Miller (Emeritus), widely used in a variety of applications. The schema contains nouns, verbs, adjectives, and adverbs which are grouped into sets of cognitive synonyms (synsets), each expressing a distinct concept. The synsets are interlinked by means of conceptual-semantic and lexical relations. The resulting network of meaningfully related words and concepts can be navigated with the browser. The dataset contains approximately 1.9 million triples. Neither the Linked Sensor Data nor WordNet contains representative query workloads. Nevertheless they have been used by a set of systems for performance benchmarking.

7.2.2 Synthetic RDF Benchmarks

7.2.2.1 Lehigh University Benchmark (LUBM)

LUBM [157] is the first benchmark for RDF engines that was intended to facilitate the evaluation of Semantic Web repositories and is widely adopted by the data engineering and Semantic Web communities. It focuses on evaluating the performance of query optimizers and *not ontology reasoning* as in Description Logic systems. LUBM's ontology Univ-Bench is of *moderate size* and *complexity*, and describes universities and departments and related activities. The benchmark offers a *scalable synthetic data generator* and supports *extensional queries*, queries that request only *instance* and not schema information. It also proposes a set of *performance metrics* so that systems can assess their performance.

The LUBM schema consists of 43 classes, 32 object properties, and 7 datatype properties and uses only the `owl:inverseOf`, `owl:transitiveProperty`, `owl:someValuesFrom`, and `owl:intersectionOf` OWL Lite constructs. It is expressed in OWL Lite, since the authors wanted to develop a benchmark to address the ability of systems to perform simple reasoning. Figure 7.1 shows the LUBM ontology schema. LUBM's data generator produces synthetic extensional data that conform to the LUBM ontology that are generated using the **UBA** (**Univ-Bench** Artificial Data Generator) that supports *random* and *repeatable* data generation during which *instance* of *classes* and *properties* are randomly produced. In the data generation, the *minimum unit* of data generation are *universities* that have *departments*, *employees*, and *courses*. In order to make data more realistic, a number of restrictions were applied during data generation (i.e., minimum 15 and maximum 25 departments per university, the undergraduate student/faculty ratio is between 8 and 14). Data generated by the tool are repeatable for the universities: a user specifies a seed for the random number generator employed in the data-generation process who can also configure the serialization and representation model.

The LUBM benchmark proposes *14 realistic queries* that are written in SPARQL 1.1. Two design criteria were followed for the specification of the LUBM queries. First, the *input size* was taken under consideration, that is, the *proportion* of the *class instances involved* and *entailed in the query* to the *total dataset instances*. The second was the *selectivity* that is highly dependent on the *input dataset size*, which is defined as the *estimated proportion* of the class instances that *satisfy the query criteria*. The *query complexity* is measured on the basis of the number of classes and properties involved in the query, and hence the same query under different implementations, that is, RDF and relational, might have different complexities. LUBM queries also consider *class* and *property hierarchies* in order to compute the

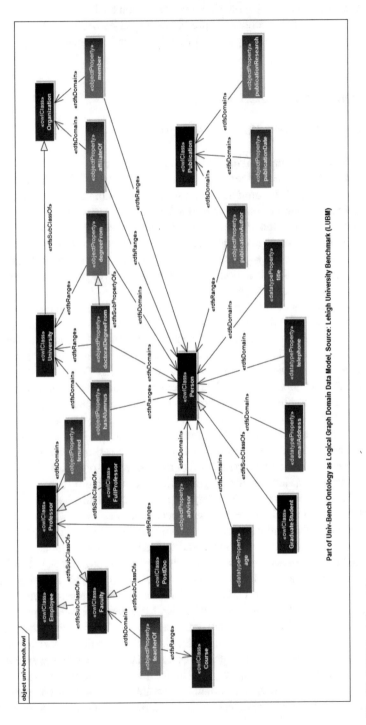

Fig. 7.1 LUBM ontology schema

correct and complete query results, and hence *logical inference* is required to obtain all query answers. LUBM queries are very simple SPARQL queries that mainly address *join ordering* (choke point CP_1) and *reasoning* (choke point CP_4)—see Table 7.11. The performance metrics proposed by LUBM are:

- *Load time* is the time needed to parse, load, and reason for a dataset.
- *Repository size* is the size of all files that constitute the repository.
- *Average time* is the time needed for executing a query ten times (warm run).
- *Query completeness and soundness* measures the degree of completeness of a query answer as the percentage of entailed unique answers.
- *Combined metric* combines query response time with answer completeness and answer soundness to essentially measure the trade-off between query response time and completeness of results in order to show how reasoning affects query performance.

7.2.2.2 SP₂Bench

SP₂Bench [345] benchmark proposed a language-specific benchmark to test the most common SPARQL constructs, operator constellations, and RDF access patterns. SP₂Bench provides a *scalable synthetic data generator* that produces DBLP documents in RDF, mimicking key characteristics of the original DBLP dataset that also contain blank nodes and RDF containers. Similar to LUBM, it supports extensional queries (i.e., queries that request instances and not schema information) and proposes performance metrics. The schema considered in SP₂Bench is an extract of the DBLP 2008 schema shown in Listing 7.1. The authors studied DBLP data in order to determine the probability distribution for selected attributes per

Table 7.11 LUBM queries choke points

Query	CP_1	CP_2	CP_3	CP_4	CP_5	CP_6	CP_7	CP_8	CP_9	CP_{10}	CP_{11}
Q_1											
Q_2	✓										
Q_3				✓							
Q_4	✓			✓							
Q_5				✓							
Q_6				✓							
Q_7	✓										
Q_8	✓										
Q_9	✓										
Q_{10}				✓							
Q_{11}				✓							
Q_{12}	✓			✓							
Q_{13}				✓							
Q_{14}											

Listing 7.1 SP$_2$Bench schema

```
<!ELEMENT dblp (article | inproceedings | proceedings | book |
                incollection |phdthesis | masterthesis | www)* >
<!ENTITY %field author | editor | title | booktitle | pages
                | year | address | journal |volume | number |
                month | url | ee | cdrom | cite | publisher |
                note | crossref | isbn | series | school |
                chapter >
<!ELEMENT article (%field)*>
<!ELEMENT inproceedings (%field)* >
```

Table 7.12 Probability distributions for DBLP schema classes and properties

	Article	Inproc.	Proc.	Book	WWW
author	0.9895	0.9970	0.0001	0.8937	0.9973
cite	0.0048	0.0104	0.0001	0.0079	0.0000
editor	0.0000	0.0000	0.7992	0.1040	0.0004
isbn	0.0000	0.0000	0.8592	0.9294	0.0000

document classes that forms the basis for generating class instances. This study revealed that only a *few of the attributes* are repeated for the same class resulting in datasets that are very well structured. Table 7.12 shows probability distributions for the classes and properties followed by the SP$_2$Bench data generator. The authors applied *bell-shaped Gaussian* curves to approximate input data usually used to model *normal distributions*, and *power law distribution* to model the *number of class instances over time*.

The SP$_2$Bench data generator produces *synthetic extensional data* that conforms to the DBLP schema and takes into account data approximation as reflected in the Gaussian curves. It also uses *random functions* that are based on a fixed seed making data generation *deterministic*. The generator also employed existing external vocabularies to describe resources in a uniform way such as FOAF, Semantic Web for Research Communities (scientific publications) [373], and Dublin Core [107] and produces *blank nodes* and RDF containers to capture all aspects of the RDF data model. The data generator also accepts as input either the triple count or year up to which the data is generated and always ending up in a consistent state.

SP$_2$Bench proposes 17 queries, where 5 queries are essentially modifications of the basic 12 ones. All queries are provided in natural language, with available SPARQL 1.0 and SQL translations. The authors aimed to cover the majority of SPARQL constructs including DISTINCT, ORDER By, LIMIT, and OFFSET and focused mostly on SELECT and ASK SPARQL forms. SP$_2$Bench queries are more complex than the LUBM ones, especially as it has a very broad range of features and covers the majority of the choke points discussed earlier. Table 7.13 presents the benchmark's queries characteristics and the choke points that those queries address.

One can observe that most of the queries address the *join ordering* choke point (CP$_1$) with the most complex query having eight joins. The majority of

Table 7.13 SP$_2$Bench queries characteristics

Characteristic	Queries											
	Q_1	Q_2	Q_{3abc}	Q_4	Q_{5ab}	Q_6	Q_7	Q_8	Q_9	Q_{10}	Q_{11}	Q_{12abc}
Simple filters			✓	✓	✓							✓
Complex filters						✓		✓				✓
>9 TPs		✓				✓	✓	✓				✓
Unbound predicates						✓	✓					
Negation								✓				
OPTIONAL		✓				✓	✓					
LIMIT											✓	
ORDER BY		✓									✓	
DISTINCT				✓	✓	✓	✓	✓			✓	
REGEX												
UNION								✓	✓			✓
DESCRIBE												
CONSTRUCT												
ASK												✓

queries also contain *complex filters* (choke point CP$_6$) with the most complex query containing two filters. Finally, *duplicate elimination* is addressed by 6 out of the 14 queries. Examining the characteristics of the SP$_2$Bench queries, one can see that the queries consider a number of features, more than the ones considered by LUBM. Furthermore, SP$_2$Bench considers different performance metrics than those of LUBM (Table 7.14).

- *Loading time*, the time needed to parse, load, and reason using the tested system for a dataset.
- *Per-query performance*, the performance of each query.
- *Global performance* lists the arithmetic and geometric mean of queries. It is computed by multiplying the execution time of all 17 queries, penalize queries that fail with 3600s penalty, and compute the 17th root of the result.
- *Memory consumption* reports the high watermark of main memory consumption and reports the average memory consumption of all queries.

7.2.2.3 Berlin SPARQL Benchmark (BSBM)

BSBM[9] is built around an e-commerce use case, with a query mix that emulates the search and navigation patterns of a user looking for a product of interest focusing on an enterprise setting where multiple clients concurrently execute workloads [44]. The benchmark aims at allowing the comparison of SPARQL engines across

---

[9]http://wifo5-03.informatik.unimannheim.de/bizer/berlinsparqlbenchmark/spec/index.html.

Table 7.14 SP$_2$Bench queries choke points

Query	CP$_1$	CP$_2$	CP$_3$	CP$_4$	CP$_5$	CP$_6$	CP$_7$	CP$_8$	CP$_9$	CP$_{10}$	CP$_{11}$
Q$_1$	✓										
Q$_2$	✓						✓				
Q$_{3abc}$						✓					
Q$_4$	✓					✓				✓	
Q$_{5ab}$	✓					✓				✓	
Q$_6$	✓		✓			✓					✓
Q$_7$	✓		✓			✓				✓	
Q$_8$	✓				✓	✓				✓	✓
Q$_9$					✓					✓	
Q$_{10}$											
Q$_{11}$							✓				
Q$_{12abc}$	✓									✓	

different architectures (relational and/or RDF), challenging forward and backward chain reasoning engines, measuring SPARQL query performance, and not (so much) reasoning. BSBM offers a *data generator* that supports the creation of arbitrarily large datasets and a *test driver* that executes sequences of SPARQL queries.

The BSBM schema is a *relational* schema that simulates an e-commerce use case where products are offered by several vendors and consumers post reviews for those products (Fig. 7.2). The main relations are *Product*, *Offer*, and *Review*, each relation carrying a number of attributes; relations are connected through relationships that carry different cardinality constraints. Every product has a type from a product hierarchy that is not fixed (depends on the dataset size). Its depth and width depend on the chosen scale factor *n*:

$$d = 1 + \frac{round(\log(n))}{2}$$

The hierarchy's branching factor is computed as follows:

$$bf_r = \begin{cases} 1 + round(\log(n)) * \text{ for the root} \\ 8 \qquad\qquad\qquad\qquad\qquad \text{otherwise} \end{cases}$$

Instances of the different product types are assigned a variable number of product features, computed as *lowerBound* and *upperBound* with

$$lowerBound = \frac{35 \times i}{\left(d \times \frac{(d+1)}{2} - 1\right)}$$

$$upperBound = \frac{75 \times i}{\left(d \times \frac{(d+1)}{2} - 1\right)}$$

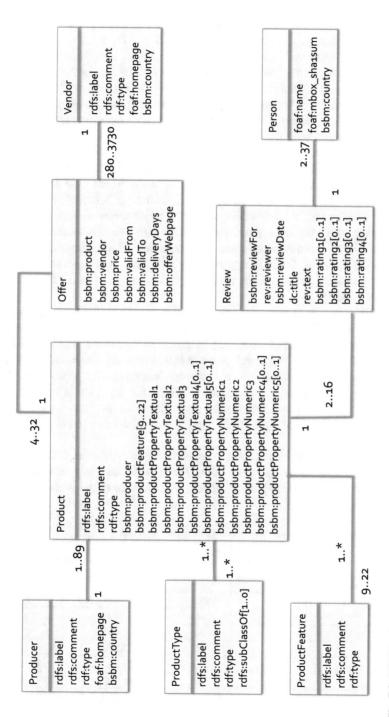

Fig. 7.2 BSBM schema

The set of possible features for a given product type are the union of the type and all its supertypes. For the generation of BSBM datasets, a set of assumptions was considered: First of all, for all products that are of the same type, they also have same set of features. For a given product, its features are chosen from the set of possible features with a hard-coded probability of 25%. A normal distribution with a mean of $\mu = 50$ and standard deviation $\sigma = 16.6$ is employed to associate products with producers. Vendors are associated to countries following hard-coded distributions and the size of offers is $n \times 20$ distributed over products following a normal distribution with fixed parameters: $\mu = \frac{n}{2}$ and $\sigma = \frac{n}{4}$. Finally, offers are distributed over vendors following a normal distribution with fixed parameters $\mu = 2000$ and $\sigma = 667$. The size of reviews per product is ten times the scale factor n, datatype property values (*title* and *text*) are between 50 and 300 words. Each review has up to four ratings, each rating is a random integer between 1 and 10, and a rating is missing with a hard-coded probability of 10%. Reviews are distributed over products with a normal distribution depending on dataset size and following $\mu = \frac{n}{2}$ and $\sigma = \frac{n}{4}$. The number of reviews per reviewer follows normal distribution with $\mu = 20$ and $\sigma = 6.6$. Reviews are generated until all reviews are assigned a reviewer and the countries of the reviewers follow the same distribution as the countries of vendors.

The BSBM data generator produces synthetic instances of class Product that conform to the BSBM Schema. Table 7.15 provides an indicative number of instances for different dataset sizes. BSBM proposes 12 queries, given in natural language, SPARQL and SQL, and *query mixes* where each mix emulates the search and navigation patterns of a customer looking for a product. BSBM queries are more complex than the ones of SP$_2$Bench and exhibit a variety of characteristics and address more choke points than the previous benchmarks. Tables 7.16 and 7.17 present the BSBM queries characteristics and choke points, respectively.

As one can observe, the most complex query is Q_2 with *11 joins, 3 OPTIONAL* clauses, *3 filters*, and *1 unbound variable*. Query Q_8 is the query with the most *OPTIONAL* clauses. Regarding *choke points*, *join ordering* (CP$_1$) is addressed by

Table 7.15 Indicative number of instances for different dataset sizes

Total #triples	250K	1M	2M	100M
#products	666	2785	70,812	284,826
#product features	2860	4745	23,833	47,884
#product types	55	151	731	2011
#producers	14	60	1422	5618
#vendors	8	34	722	2854
#offers	13,320	55,700	1,416,240	5,696,520
#reviewers	339	1432	36,249	146,054
#reviews	6660	27,850	708,120	2,848,260
Total #instances	23,922	92,757	2,258,129	9,034,027

Table 7.16 BSBM queries characteristics

Characteristic	Queries											
	Q_1	Q_2	Q_3	Q_4	Q_5	Q_6	Q_7	Q_8	Q_9	Q_{10}	Q_{11}	Q_{12}
Simple filters	✓		✓	✓			✓	✓	✓	✓		
Complex filters					✓	✓						
>9 TPs		✓		✓			✓	✓		✓		
Unbound predicates		✓								✓		
Negation		✓										
OPTIONAL		✓	✓				✓	✓				
LIMIT	✓		✓	✓	✓					✓		
ORDER BY	✓		✓	✓	✓			✓		✓		
DISTINCT	✓				✓					✓		
REGEX						✓						
UNION				✓						✓		
DESCRIBE												
CONSTRUCT											✓	
ASK												

Table 7.17 BSBM queries choke points

Query	CP_1	CP_2	CP_3	CP_4	CP_5	CP_6	CP_7	CP_8	CP_9	CP_{10}	CP_{11}
Q_1	✓				✓	✓			✓		
Q_2	✓										
Q_3	✓					✓	✓				
Q_4	✓				✓	✓	✓				
Q_5	✓				✓	✓			✓		
Q_6						✓			✓		
Q_7	✓		✓			✓					
Q_8	✓					✓	✓				
Q_9						✓					
Q_{10}	✓				✓	✓			✓		
Q_{11}					✓						
Q_{12}	✓										

the majority of the queries with the most complex query containing 11 joins. Furthermore, the queries include *filters* (CP_6) in order to test the ability of the engines to execute as early as possible to eliminate a possibly large number of intermediate results. The most complex query contains three filters, and the most complex filter contains arithmetic expressions. Finally *duplicate elimination* (CP_7) is also addressed by the BSBM queries.

BSBM also proposes more complex *performance metrics* than the ones proposed by LUBM and SP$_2$Bench benchmarks. More specifically, the performance metrics proposed are:

- *Query Mixes per Hour (QMpH)*: Measures the number of complete BSBM query mixes answered by a system under test and for a specific number of clients running concurrently against the system under test
- *Queries per Second (QpS)*: Measures the number of queries of a specific type handled by the system under test in a second. The value is calculated by dividing the number of queries of a specific type within a benchmark run by the total execution time of those queries.
- *Load Time:* Time to load the dataset in the RDF or relational repositories. This time includes the time to create the appropriate data structures and indices.

7.2.2.4 Semantic Publishing Benchmark (SPB)

SPB is an industry-motivated benchmark built on a scenario that involves a media/publisher organization that maintains semantic metadata about its journalistic assets. It is designed to reflect a scenario where a large number of aggregation agents provide the heavy query workload, while at the same time a steady stream of editorial agents implement update operations that insert and delete creative works. Journalists use the aggregation agents to query existing creative works and use the retrieved data in order to create new ones using the editorial agents. The Semantic Publishing Benchmark includes:

- A *scalable synthetic data generator* that uses ontologies and reference datasets provided by BBC, to produce sets of instances of BBC ontologies that mimic characteristics of the original real input datasets. The data generator supports the creation of arbitrarily large RDF datasets in the order of billions of triples that mimic the characteristics of the reference BBC datasets.
- The workload in SPB is defined by the simultaneous execution of editorial and aggregation agents, simulating a constant load generated by end-users, journalists, editors, or automated engines. The workload is designed to reflect a scenario where a large number of aggregation agents provide the heavy query workload, while at the same time a steady stream of editorial agents implement update operations that insert and delete creative works. The SPB queries are defined in a way that tackle the choke points presented earlier that each RDF store needs to address in order to satisfy the requirements raised from real-world use cases. SPB queries are extensional queries (i.e., queries that request instances and not schema information).
- Similar to the previous benchmarks, it proposes performance metrics that describe how fast an RDF database can execute queries by simultaneously running aggregation and editorial agents.

SPB was built to satisfy a set of requirements set by the use case in question. More specifically, the requirements were (i) testing storage and processing of RDF data, (ii) support for schema languages, and (iii) loading data expressed in different RDF formats. In (i) the idea is to test the ability of engines to store data in different RDF graphs support SPARQL 1.1 standard query language for querying and updating RDF data. In (ii) the objective is to check whether the RDF engine provides support for RDFS to obtain the correct and complete set of answers as well as optional support for the RL profile of Web Ontology Language (OWL2 RL). Finally for (iii) the idea is to examine whether the RDF engine provides support for the various RDF serialization formats (n-quads, ntriples, RDF/XML, etc.).

SPB uses seven core and three domain RDF ontologies provided by BBC. The former define the main entities and their properties required to describe essential concepts of the benchmark, namely, creative works, persons, documents, BBC products (news, music, sport, education, blogs), annotations (tags), provenance of resources, and content management system information. The latter are used to express concepts from a domain of interest such as football, politics, and entertainment, among others. The ontologies are relatively simple: they contain a few classes (74), 29 and 88 datatype and object properties, respectively, and shallow class and property hierarchies. More specifically, the class hierarchy has a maximum depth of 3 whereas the property hierarchy has a depth of 1. Figure 7.3 shows an excerpt of the ontology employed by SPB. SPB also uses reference datasets that are employed by the data generator to produce the data of interest. These datasets are snapshots of the real datasets provided by BBC. The reference datasets are collections of entities describing various domains and are snapshots of the real datasets of BBC considering sport events (football competitions and teams, formula one competitions and teams), politicians (UK Parliament Members), place names from the GeoNames ontology, and person data from DBpedia. The GeoNames and DBPedia reference datasets have been included for further enriching the annotations with geolocations to enable the formulation of geospatial queries, and person data.

The SPB data generator produces RDF descriptions of creative works that are valid instances of the BBC ontologies presented previously. A creative work is described by a number of data value and object value properties; a creative work also has properties that link it to resources defined in reference datasets: those are the about and mentions properties, and their values can be any resource. One of the purposes of the data generator is to produce synthetic large (in the order of billions of triples) datasets in order to check the ability of the engines to scale. The generator models three types of relations in the data:

- *Clustering of data.* The clustering effect is produced by generating creative works about a single entity from reference datasets and for a fixed period of time. The number of creative works starts with a high peak at the beginning of the clustering period and follows a smooth decay toward its end. The data generator produces major and minor clusterings with sizes (i.e., number of creative works) of different magnitude. An example of clusterings of data could be news items that are about events starting with a high number of journalistic assets related

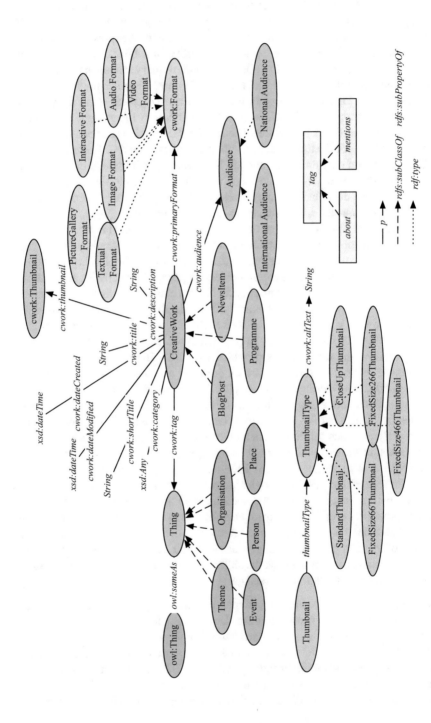

Fig. 7.3 Core BBC ontology

to them and following a decay in time as they reach the end of time period, a tendency that mirrors a real-world scenario in which a "fresh" event is popular and its popularity decreases as time goes by.

- *Correlations of entities.* This correlation effect is produced by generating creative works about two or three entities from reference data in a fixed period of time. Each of the entities is tagged by creative works solely at the beginning and end of the correlation period, and in the middle of it, both are used as tags for the same creative work. By default fifty correlations between entities are modeled for 1 year period.
- *Random tagging of entities.* Random data distributions are defined with a bias toward popular entities created when the tagging is performed, that is, when values are assigned to about and mentions creative work properties. This is achieved by randomly selecting a 5% of all the resources from reference data and mark them as popular when the remaining ones are marked as regular. When creating creative works, 30% of them are tagged with randomly selected popular resources, and the remaining 70% are linked to the regular ones. This random generation of data concerns only one-third of all generated data; the remaining data is generated with correlations and clustering effects modeled as previously described.

The SPB data generator operates in a sequence of phases (see Fig. 7.4 that presents data generation flow in SPB):

1. Ontologies and reference datasets are loaded in an RDF repository.

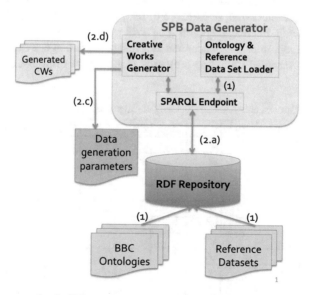

Fig. 7.4   Data generation in SPB

2. All instances of the domain ontologies that exist in the reference datasets are retrieved by means of predefined SPARQL queries that will be used as values for the about and mentions properties of creative works.
3. From the previous set of instances, the popular and regular entities are selected.
4. The generator produces the creative works according to the three properties discussed previously.

As mentioned previously, the SPB query workload is designed to reflect a scenario where a large number of aggregation agents provide the heavy query workload requesting creative works, while at the same time a steady stream of editorial agents implement update operations that insert and delete creative works. SPB *aggregation queries* are defined in a way that tackle the choke points discussed earlier that each RDF store needs to address in order to satisfy the requirements raised from real-world use cases. *Editorial* queries are simple update queries that consider only *insert* and *delete* operations (Table 7.18).

Most of the choke points are addressed by SPB queries that focus mostly on *join ordering*, *reasoning* for *class*, and *property hierarchies* as well as *ordering* and *duplicate elimination*.

Table 7.19 shows the SPARQL features that each of the queries in the SPB query mix implement. Query Q1 is a very complex query that contains 11 optionals with 4 of them having nested optional clauses. Query Q3 contains the majority of the SPARQL features (except aggregates, group by, and regular expressions in filters).

Aggregation agents simulate the retrieval operations performed by journalists, end-users, or automated search engines by executing a mix of aggregation queries of type: aggregation, search, statistical, full-text, geo-spatial, analytical, drill-down, and faceted search. Each aggregation agent will execute a mix of those query types in a constant loop, until the benchmark run finishes. Each agent executes a query and waits for a response (or a time-out); after receiving the response, the next query

Table 7.18 SPB queries and their corresponding choke points

Query	CP_1	CP_2	CP_3	CP_4	CP_5	CP_6	CP_7	CP_8	CP_9	CP_{10}	CP_{11}
Q_1	✓		✓	✓			✓			✓	
Q_2			✓	✓		✓					
Q_3			✓	✓	✓	✓				✓	
Q_4	✓			✓		✓	✓			✓	
Q_5	✓			✓		✓	✓			✓	
Q_6	✓			✓				✓		✓	
Q_7	✓			✓							
Q_8	✓		✓	✓							
Q_9		✓		✓			✓				
Q_{10}	✓			✓	✓					✓	
Q_{11}	✓			✓	✓		✓			✓	
Q_{12}				✓			✓				

Table 7.19 SPB queries characteristics

Characteristic	Queries											
	Q_1	Q_2	Q_3	Q_4	Q_5	Q_6	Q_7	Q_8	Q_9	Q_{10}	Q_{11}	Q_{12}
Simple filters		✓										
Complex filters			✓	✓	✓							
>9 TPs	✓	✓	✓					✓				
Unbound predicates			✓									
Negation												
OPTIONAL	✓	✓	✓					✓				
LIMIT	✓		✓	✓				✓			✓	✓
ORDER BY	✓		✓	✓	✓				✓		✓	✓
DISTINCT	✓		✓	✓	✓				✓	✓	✓	
REGEX												
UNION		✓								✓	✓	
DESCRIBE												
CONSTRUCT	✓	✓	✓	✓				✓				
ASK												

is executed (queries executed by agents are not of the same type). Query order of execution is pseudorandomly chosen following an even distribution for each query defined in the benchmark's configuration.

Editorial agents simulate the editorial work performed by journalists, editors, or automated text annotation engines by executing SPARQL insert, update, and delete operations. Insert operations generate new creative work descriptions (content metadata) following the models discussed earlier. Update operations update an existing creative work. Update operation consists of two actions, executed in one transaction, following the BBC's use case for update of a creative work. First action is to delete the context where a creative work description resides along with all its content. Second is to insert the same creative work (using its current ID) with all its properties—current and updated ones. Delete operations delete an existing creative work. Delete operation will erase the context where a creative work resides along with all of its content. Similar to aggregation queries, each editorial agent will execute a mix of editorial operations in a constant loop, until the benchmark run has finished. Editorial operations executed by an agent are chosen pseudorandomly following the distribution: 80% INSERT operations, 10% UPDATE operations, 10% DELETE operations. Such distribution follows a similar to live datasets pattern where a massive amount of new data is added to the database (inserts and updates) and a minor amount of data deleted from it.

The performance metrics proposed by SPB describe how fast an RDF database can execute queries (by simultaneously running aggregation agents) while at the same time executing editorial operations (by simultaneously running editorial agents) and operating over an amount of generated data in the RDF database. SPB outputs two types of performance metrics:

1. *Minimum, Maximum,* and *Average execution times* for each individual query and editorial operation during the whole benchmark run
2. *Average execution rate per second*for all queries and editorial operations

The benchmark produces two query execution reports. The first reports (a) the *duration of bulk load*, the *Duration of Measurement Window*, the *number of Complete Analytical mixes*, the *number of Complete Interactive mixes*, and finally the *number of Complete Update Operations.* The second report provides information for each query the *Arithmetic Mean Execution Time, Minimum Execution Time, 90th% Average Execution Time*, and the *number of executions.*

7.2.3 Benchmark Generators

7.2.3.1 DBPedia SPARQL Benchmark (DBSB)

DBSB [269] provides a *generic methodology* for SPARQL Benchmark Creation. It is based on (a) *flexible data generation* that mimics an input data source, (b) *query-log mining*, (c) clustering of queries, and (d) SPARQL queries *feature analysis*. DBSB follows a *schema agnostic* methodology, but the authors demonstrate their approach using the DBpedia Knowledge Base. The proposed approach was applied on various sizes of the DBPedia Knowledge Base and proposes a query workload based on real queries expressed against DBPedia. The working assumptions of DBSB data generation are:

- The output datasets should have similar characteristics as the input dataset, that is, the output dataset should respect the number classes, properties, value distributions, and taxonomic structures (schema hierarchies).
- It should support varying output dataset sizes.
- Characteristics such as indegree and outdegree of nodes in datasets of varying sizes should be similar.
- The data-generation process should be easily repeatable in order for systems to be able to test their performance.

The design of DBSB was motivated by the following ideas: first of all, *large datasets* are produced by duplicating all triples and changing their namespace. *Small datasets* are produced by:

1. Removing triples in a way that would preserve the properties of the original graph.
2. Using a seed-based method based on the assumption that a representative set of resources is obtained by sampling across classes. More specifically, for each selected element in the dataset, its concise bound description (CBD) is retrieved

and added in the queue. This process is repeated until the number of triples is reached.

The goal of DBSB query analysis is to detect prototypical queries that were sent to a DBPedia SPARQL endpoint using similarity measures and, more specifically, *string similarity* and *graph similarity*. The approach is based on a four-step query analysis and clustering approach:

1. Select queries executed frequently on the input data.
2. Strip common syntactic constructs (namespace, prefixes).
3. Compute query similarity using string matching.
4. Compute query clusters using a soft graph clustering algorithm where clusters are used to devise the benchmark query generation patterns.

Determining the query selection from the DBpedia query logs to be considered in DBSB was a difficult process. The authors used the DBpedia SPARQL query logs that comprised of 31.5 million queries, all requested in a 3 month period. The initial set of queries was reduced by considering *query variations* and *query frequency*. In the former case, the authors used a standard way to name variables to reduce differences among queries (promoting query constructs such as DISTINCT and REGEX). In the latter case, queries with low frequency were discarded since they do not contribute to the overall query performance. The result of this reduction were 35,965 queries out of the initial set of 31.5 million queries. After the reduction of queries from the initial set, authors proceeded with *string stripping* when all SPARQL keywords and common prefixes were removed from the queries. The authors then computed the similarity of the stripped queries using the Levenshtein string similarity measure, with a 0.9 threshold. In order to compute the similarity of the queries, authors used the LIMES framework [288]. The use of LIMES reduced by 16.6% the time needed for the computation of the query similarity that would normally require the computation of the Cartesian product of queries. Once the query similarity is computed, the authors applied graph clustering with the goal of identifying similar groups of queries out of which prototypical queries will be generated. The BorderFlow algorithm was used [289] to compute the clusters that follows a seed-based approach. The result was 12,272 query clusters where 24% of the clusters contained a single query; the authors ended up selecting all the clusters that contained more than 5 queries, considering them as the most representative ones.

Out of the selected clusters, the most interesting SPARQL queries were picked based on (a) the ones that are the most frequently asked and (b) those that cover the most SPARQL *features*. The features that the authors consider are shown in Table 7.20. In the table, for each feature we also provide the choke point that it implements. Using these features, 25 representative queries are selected, where for each of the features, the part of the query to be varied (IRI or filter condition) was manually selected to produce a set of *query templates*. For each of these query templates, 1000 values were chosen to substitute the parameters in the template.

Table 7.20 DBSB SPARQL features

F_1	Overall number of triple patterns	Test the efficiency of join operations	CP_1
F_2	SPARQL pattern constructors (UNION and OPTIONAL)	Handle parallel execution of Unions	CP_5
		Perform OPTIONALs as late as possible in the query plan	CP_3
F_3	Solution sequences and modifiers (DISTINCT)	Efficiency of duplication elimination	CP_{10}
F_4	Filter conditions and operators (FILTER, LANG, REGEX, STR)	Efficiency of engines to execute filters as early as possible	CP_6, CP_9

Table 7.21 Structural features in WatDiv

F_1	Triple pattern count	Number of triple patterns in SPARQL Graph Patterns
F_2	Join vertex count	Number of RDF terms (IRIs, literals, blank nodes) and variables that are subjects or objects of multiple triple patterns
F_3	The degree of a join vertex v is the number of triple patterns whose subject or object is v	

This method ensures that the executed queries during the benchmark differ and the queries always return non-empty results.

7.2.3.2 Waterloo SPARQL Diversity Test Suite

This work [14] stress tested existing RDF engines to reveal a wider range of query requirements as established by web applications. The contribution of this work is threefold. First of all, the authors define two classes of query features used to evaluate the variability of workloads and datasets: *structural* and *data-driven*. Structural refers to, for instance, the number of triple patterns considered in the query, whereas data-driven refers to the query selectivity and result cardinality. A second contribution is the in-depth analysis of existing SPARQL benchmarks using the structural and data-driven features. Finally, the implementation of the WatDiv TestSuite can be used to stress existing RDF engines in order to reveal a wider range of query requirements. Table 7.21 shows the different structural features considered in WatDiv.

The *join vertex degree* and *join vertex count* provide a good characterization of the structural complexity of a query that is not provided by the number of triple patterns: for instance, two queries with the same set of triple patterns can have different structures as can be shown in Fig. 7.5. The join vertex type plays an important role in the behavior of RDF engines to determine efficient query plans. For instance, star queries promote efficient merge joins and allow the construction

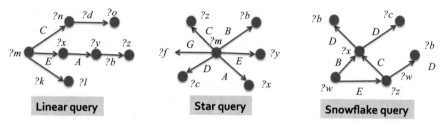

Fig. 7.5 Examples of different queries for the same triple patterns

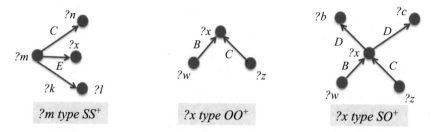

Fig. 7.6 WatDiv join vertex types

of bushy plans. Aluc et al. [14] identified three (mutually nonexclusive) types of join vertices shown below where triple pattern (s, p, o) is incident on x.

Vertex x of type SS^+ if for all triple patterns $(s, p, o)^*$, x is the subject
Vertex x of type OO^+ if for all triple patterns $(s, p, o)^*$, x is the object
Vertex x of type SO^+ if for all triple patterns $(s, p, o)^*$, $(s', p', o')^*$, $x = s \wedge x = o'$

Figure 7.6 provides a graphical representation of the join vertex types considered in WatDiv. It is well known from query optimization that a system's choice on the most efficient query plan depends on (a) characteristics of the dataset and (b) the query structure. If the system relies on selectivity estimations and result cardinality, the same query will have a different query plan for dataset(s) of different sizes.

Regarding the data-driven features, the authors have identified the following:

- *Result Cardinality* $CARD(\bar{A}, G)$ is defined as the number of solutions in the result of the evaluation of a graph pattern $\bar{A} = <A, F>$ over graph G.
- Filter Triple Pattern Selectivity (f-TP Selectivity) $SEL_G^F(tp)$ is defined as the ratio of distinct solution mappings of a triple pattern tp to the set of triples in graph G. The mean and standard deviation of f-TP selectivities of triple patterns is important for distinguishing queries whose triple patterns are almost equally selective from queries with varying f-TP selectivities.

The Result Cardinality and f-TP selectivity are not sufficient data-driven features. For instance, the authors observed that it might be the case that intermediate solution mappings will not make it to the final result (e.g., due to filters or more restrictive joins), and the overall selectivity of a graph pattern can be determined by a single very selective triple pattern. To address these shortcomings of the aforementioned data-driven features, the authors introduced two new ones: the *BGP-Restricted f-TP selectivity* and the *Join-Restricted f-TP selectivity*:

- *BGP-Restricted f-TP selectivity* $SEL_G^F(tp \mid \bar{A})$ assesses how much a triple pattern contributes to the overall selectiveness of the query and is a fraction of distinct solution mappings for a triple pattern that are compatible with some solution mapping in the query result.
- *Join-Restricted f-TP selectivity* $SEL^F(tp \mid x)$ assesses how much a filtered triple pattern contributes to the overall selectiveness of the joins that it participates in. More specifically, for a join vertex X and a triple pattern tp incident on x, the x-restricted f-TP of tp over graph G is the fraction of distinct solution mappings compatible with a solution mapping in the query result of the sub-query that contains all triple patterns incident to x.

WatDiv also proposed a Test Suite that comprises of a *data generator* and a *query generator*. The data generator allows users to define their own dataset controlling (a) the *entities* to include, (b) the topology of the graphs allowing one to mimic the real types of data distributions in the web, (c) the *well-structuredness*[106] of entities, (d) the probability of entity associations, and finally (e) the cardinality of property associations. The data generated by the WatDiv generation process are not relational as is the case with the previous RDF benchmarks, since the entities *do not have* the same set of attributes.

In addition to the WatDiv data generator, WatDiv offers a *Query Template Generator* that is highly parameterized since the user can specify the number of templates to use for the generation of queries, the characteristics of the query templates such as the number of triple patterns, in addition to the types of joins and filters in the triple patterns. The template generator traverses the WatDiv schema using a random walk and generates a set of query templates. It is then, the responsibility of the *query generator* to produce the actual queries by instantiating the query templates with terms (IRIs, literals, etc.) from the RDF dataset to produce the number of queries as specified by the user.

7.2.3.3   FEASIBLE

FEASIBLE [332] proposed a feature-based benchmark generation approach from real queries using *structure-* and *data-driven*-based features that are similar to WatDiv Test Suite. The authors followed a novel sampling approach for queries based on *exemplars* and *medoids* in order to produce a workload that consists of SELECT, ASK, CONSTRUCT, and DESCRIBE SPARQL queries. The query features considered by FEASIBLE are *number of triples* and *number of join vertices*, where the authors distinguished between *star*, *path*, *hybrid*, and *sink* vertices (see Fig. 7.7) where the Join Vertex Degree is the sum of incoming and outgoing edges

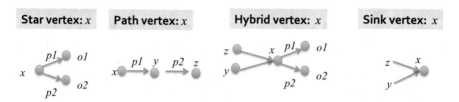

Fig. 7.7 Types of join vertices

of the vertex. The authors also considered the *triple pattern selectivity*, that is, the ratio of triples that match the triple pattern over all triples in the dataset.

FEASIBLE follows a three-step benchmark generation process. First, the dataset is cleaned in order to obtain a reliable benchmark. Second, the feature vectors are normalized, meaning that the query representations are normalized so that all queries are in a unit hypercube. Third, queries are selected following the idea of exemplars [288]. Dataset cleaning is focused on the removal of erroneous and zero-result queries from the set of real queries used to generate the benchmark and excludes all syntactically incorrect queries. During this phase, nine SPARQL operators such as UNION, DISTINCT, OPTIONAL, etc. are attached to the queries along with seven query features (join vertices, join vertex count, etc.). The queries are mapped to a vector of length 16 which stores the query features during the normalization phase. For example, for binary SPARQL clauses (e.g., UNION is either used or not used), stored value is 1, otherwise the value 0 is stored. All nonbinary feature vectors are normalized by dividing their value with the overall maximum value in the dataset, and query representations are associated with values between 1 and 0.

At the last phase, query selection is implemented by selecting exemplars (points that represent a portion of the space) that are as far as possible from each other. In order to do this, the authors computed an *l*-size partition of a set of cleaned and normalized queries L such that (a) the average distance between two points in two different elements in the partition is high, (b) the average number of points within a partition is small, and (c) the point that is close to the average of each partition and includes it in the benchmark is selected. Given the partitions, exemplars are selected that are as far as possible from each other. The initial set of queries L is partitioned by mapping every point of L to one of these exemplars to compute a partition of the space. Then, the medoid of each of the space partitions is used as a query in the benchmark.

7.2.4 Dataset Structuredness

The real and synthetic benchmarks discussed in the previous sections have been used extensively in the last years for testing the performance of the majority of RDF query engines. Duan et al. [106] studied thoroughly the different benchmarks and presented interesting results of their study. More specifically, they found that real benchmarks have little in common with real RDF datasets, and therefore evaluation results of the different engines might not reflect how well (or bad) systems do regarding RDF query processing. Authors proposed a set of metrics and used those to report on the different RDF benchmarks. These metrics are:

- *Average* and *distribution* of the RDF graph's *indegree* and *outdegree* that describe the graph structure
- *Number* of *dataset subjects, objects,* and *properties*
- *Number* of *types, average type properties,* and *type properties distribution* that characterize the schema
- *Average number of instances per type* and *instance distribution*
- *Number of triples*

In terms of the indegree and outdegree, the authors note that some of the datasets have a power law-like distribution of indegree/outdegree (BSBM, DBPedia, and Barton datasets). The authors also noted that the average number of properties of a subject or an object is between 1 and 10, while a small number of entities have very large numbers of indegree and outdegree. Regarding standard deviation of the average outdegree for most datasets, it is for almost all datasets relatively large (in the order of many hundreds). The average outdegrees of LUBM and SP2Bench are not a function of dataset sizes, since the average outdegree remains almost constant across datasets whose sizes span across four orders of magnitude. This fact is the same for the indegrees of datasets.

Regarding the number of objects and subjects, BSBM, SP2Bench,WordNet, Barton, YAGO, and DBpedia datasets have more objects than subjects; this is not the case for LUBM and UniProt, where the opposite holds. In terms of properties, most datasets have around 100 distinct properties, with the exception of DBpedia which has almost 3 orders of magnitude more properties. Most datasets have only a few types (less than 100), with the exception of DBpedia and the YAGO datasets. Most datasets have less than 20 properties per type (on average) with the exception of DBpedia that has more than 40 properties per type.

The authors conclude their discussion by pointing out that they could not provide any useful insights regarding their findings about those primitive metrics: UniProt is the dataset with the most triples, LUBM the dataset with the largest average indegree, DBpedia has the most properties, and YAGO has the most types. The primitive metrics that the authors used to characterize the existing benchmarks could not really describe the structure of the datasets, and therefore they proposed one complex metric for characterizing the dataset structure: *structuredness*. The level of structuredness of a dataset D, with respect to a *type T*, is determined by *how well the instances* of T conform to type T. If each instance of T has the properties defined in T, then the dataset has *high structuredness* with *respect to T*. As a metric, structuredness permeates every aspect of data management, since it can be used while deciding (a) appropriate data representation format (e.g., relational for structured and XML for semi-structured data), (b) organization of data (e.g.,

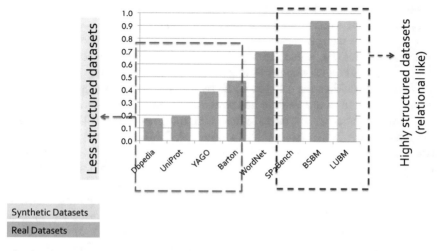

Fig. 7.8 Structuredness of benchmark datasets

dependency theory and normal forms for the relational model, and XML), and (c) data indexes (e.g., B+-tree indexes for relational and numbering scheme-based indexes for XML) and the language to query the underlying datasets (e.g., using SQL for the relational and XPath/XQuery for XML). The authors showed that the datasets produced by synthetic benchmarks such as BSBM, LUBM, and SP2Bench are highly structured with a structuredness that is close to 1, and hence the datasets are close to relational data (see Fig. 7.8). Real datasets cover the whole spectrum of structuredness. The authors proposed an approach for producing datasets that cover the whole range of structuredness in order to produce data that can be used for testing RDF query engines. The idea was to turn every dataset into a benchmark. The benefit here is that there is no need to synthetically generate values since the actual data values in the dataset can be used. Furthermore, there is no need to synthetically generate queries since those that run on the original dataset can also be used in the produced dataset. The authors were able to produce data that is closer to real-world data with their approach that can be used to test the performance of a large number of engines.

Benchmark generators such as the Waterloo and Feasible took into consideration the results of the authors when designing and developing their dataset generators in order to produce data that resemble more real RDF datasets.

7.3   Benchmarks for Instance Matching Systems

The instance matching problem has been considered for more than half a decade in Computer Science [111] and has been mostly considered for relational data. There has been significant work on instance matching techniques for relational data [194, 242, 358]. In this context the problem is well defined: the data is well structured and the focus of the approaches was on discovering differences between values of relation attributes (i.e., value variations). Consequently, the proposed solutions did not have to focus on variations in structure or semantics but simply focus on value variations. In addition, the data processed by the proposed algorithms is dense and usually originated from a very limited number of, well curated, sources.

The first approaches, for instance, matching for general Web of Data, addressed the problem for XML data [231]. In principal, XML data may exhibit strong structural variations (as no schema is necessarily imposed); however, solutions proposed for XML have typically assumed that the data conform to the same schema (i.e., data from different schemas need to be mapped to a common schema before performing instance matching) [231]. Thus, the structural variations between instances are limited to the instance level (e.g., number of occurrences, optional elements, etc.) and not at the schema level. Finally, the proposed methods focus on data that are typically dense. For Linked Data, the picture is different since they are described by expressive schemas that carry rich semantics expressed in terms of the RDF Schema Language (RDFS) and the OWL Web Ontology Language. RDFS and OWL vocabularies are used by nearly all data sources in the LOD cloud. According to a recent study[10] 36.49% of LOD use various fragments of OWL, so it is imperative that we consider the constraints expressed in such schemas when developing instance matching tools and benchmarks.

Consequently, the variations in the huge number of data sources are value, structural, as well as logical [180]. As far as semantics are concerned, when paired with a suitable reasoning engine, Linked Data allows implicit relationships to be inferred from the data [180], which was not possible with relational data and XML data. Due to these reasons, instance matching systems that have been designed for relational or XML data cannot fully exploit the aforementioned heterogeneities and thus failed to deliver good matching results.

Furthermore, according to [180], there exist specific requirements that distinguish the Linked Data from other instance matching workloads, which arise from the autonomy of data sources and the uncertainty of quality-related meta-information. Thus, it is required to assess data quality in order to resolve inconsistencies. The large variety of instance matching techniques requires their comparative evaluation to determine which one is best suited for a given context. Performing such an assessment generally requires well-defined and widely accepted benchmarks to determine the weak and strong points of the proposed techniques and/or tools. An instance matching benchmark consists of different *test cases*, where each test case addresses a different kind of requirement. A test case comprises of the *source* and *target datasets*, the *reference alignment (or gold standard or ground truth)* which contains the correct alignments between the source and the target dataset, and the *evaluation metrics* or *key performance indicators (KPIs)*.

---

[10]http://linkeddatacatalog.dws.informatik.uni-mannheim.de/state/.

7.3.1 Datasets

Datasets are the raw material of a benchmark. In the case of instance matching benchmarks, each test case contains a source dataset and a target dataset, which are compared to identify "matched" instances. Datasets are characterized by (a) *their nature (real or synthetic)* and the (b) *variations appearing in the dataset.*

Real datasets are those that contain real data and can be used either as a whole (i.e., the entire ontology with its instances) or partly (i.e., only a part of the ontology and the corresponding data instances, without any modifications). Real datasets are widely used in benchmarks since (a) they offer realistic conditions for addressing heterogeneity issues and (b) they have distributions that reflect real-world situations. The disadvantage of using real datasets in benchmarks is that they often do not come with adequate reference alignments, so a manual or semiautomatic process of reference alignment creation must be undertaken, which often leads to incomplete or incorrect reference alignments.

Synthetic datasets are generated using automated data generators. Such generators may be used to create a dataset from scratch, or to create a dataset based on existing datasets. Those generators try to overcome the problem of unrealistic data distributions during synthetic data generation by starting from a real dataset (which is either preselected) and creating a synthetic dataset by applying "transformations" over the source (real) dataset. This way, the generated (synthetic) dataset is closely based on the actual data, and thus can be claimed to enjoy realistic distributions. Synthetic datasets are useful because (a) they offer fully controlled test conditions; (b) they have accurate reference alignments (as they are synthetically generated); and (c) they allow setting the focus on specific types of heterogeneity problems in a systematic manner. These characteristics play a crucial role when the scope of the benchmark is to test specific features of the systems. The disadvantage of synthetic datasets is that if the generation is not done by considering characteristics of real data, then the datasets produced usually come with unrealistic distributions.

7.3.2 Variations

Variations correspond to the differences that exist (or are applied, in the case of synthetic datasets) between the matched instances of the source and target datasets. Datasets (and benchmarks) may contain different kinds of variations. Variations are classified as *value*, *structural*, and *logical variations* [118, 119].

Value variations address differences in the data level, which can occur due to typographical errors, differences in the format (e.g., different date and number formats), name style abbreviations, etc. Multilingualism is also considered a type of value variation. This is a useful feature, as the Linked Data cloud is multilingual by nature.

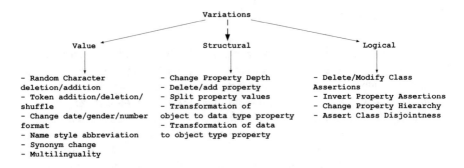

Fig. 7.9 Data variations [118, 119]

Structural variations refer to differences in the structure of the Linked Data schemas. These variations can occur, for example, because of the deletion of properties, or by splitting two properties, or by the transformations of datatype properties to object properties, etc.

Finally, *logical variations* come from the semantically rich constructs of the RDF/OWL languages [55, 260]. Such variations can be quite complex and are mostly related to the interplay between the schema and instance level, where the instance matching systems can get hints for or against the match of two web resources by applying reasoners and by using schema information. An example of such a variation appears when an instance is modified in a way that is classified under disjoint classes in the source and target schema(s).

Figure 7.9 shows the types of variations that occur in real and implemented in synthetic datasets. The common case in real benchmarks is that the datasets to be matched contain different types and combinations of variations. On the other hand, synthetic datasets may be purposefully designed to contain specific types of variations in an effort to illustrate all the common cases of discrepancies that appear in reality between individual descriptions.

7.3.3 Reference Alignment

A reference alignment (known also as ground truth or gold standard) is considered as the "correct answer sheet" of the benchmark and is used to judge the completeness and soundness of the matched instances produced by the benchmarked matching algorithms. Benchmarks that use synthetic datasets can produce automatically reference alignments during the (systematic) generation of the target dataset. In the case of real datasets, the reference alignment can be either manually curated or (semi-)automatically generated. In the first case, domain experts manually find the matches between the datasets, whereas in the second, supervised systems and crowdsourcing techniques can be used in finding the matches. This process is often time consuming and error prone since experts might miss matching entities and probably results in incomplete gold standards.

7.3.4 Key Performance Indicators

The evaluation metrics or key performance indicators for systems under test are used to determine and assess the systems behavior and performance. Various metrics have been proposed for different benchmarks. The most widely known benchmarks are those proposed by the Transaction Processing Performance Council (TPC) [382]. The metrics that TPC benchmarks employ are related to performance and efficiency (e.g., throughput source rows processed per second, transaction rate, transactions per second, Query-per-Hour Performance, etc.) [284]. Instance matching is usually an offline process, and hence although performance is important, it is crucial for instance matching systems to return good quality results. Therefore, evaluation metrics focus mostly on *Precision, Recall*, and *F-measure* [145]. Precision is the fraction between the correct answers of the tested system and the total number of answers in its result set. Recall is the fraction between the correct answers of the tested system and the total number of correct answers reported in the reference alignment. Thus, precision is more about how many errors are contained in the dataset (false-positive answers), while recall counts how many correct answers are missing (false-negative answers). F-measure is the harmonic mean of recall and precision.

7.3.5 Real Benchmarks

In this section we describe the benchmarks that employ real datasets (or parts of real datasets) without introducing synthetically produced variations. An overall evaluation of those benchmarks is shown in Table 7.23.

7.3.5.1 A-R-S 2009

This work [113] proposed by OAEI in 2009 consists of three different datasets: the AKT-Eprints archive that contains information about papers produced within the AKT project[11]; the Rexa dataset[12] that includes computer science research literature, people, organizations, venues, and data about research communities; and

---

[11]http://www.aktors.org/.

[12]www.rexa.info.

Dataset	foaf:Person	sweto:Publication
AKT-Eprints	564	283
Rexa	11,050	3721
SWETO-DBLP	307,774	983,337

Table 7.22 Characteristics of A-R-S benchmark datasets

the SWETO-DBLP dataset,[13] a publicly available dataset listing publications from the computer science domain. All three datasets were structured using the SWETO-DBLP ontology.[14]

The benchmark implements the following three test cases: matching instances of (a) AKT-Eprints to instances in Rexa dataset (**TC1**), (b) AKT-Eprints instances to DBLP (**TC2**), and (c) Rexa to DBLP instances (**TC3**). The benchmark focuses on matching instances of two classes foaf:Person and sweto:Publication for fairly *small datasets*. Table 7.22 shows the number of instances of the benchmark datasets.

The benchmark addresses the following two challenges: (a) *ambiguous labels* since person names and paper titles coincide and (b) *noisy data*. The *gold standard* is manually created through a time-consuming and error-prone process that contained 777 mappings for **TC1**, 544 for **TC2**, and 1540 for **TC3**. The A-R-S was used by five systems, namely, DDim [283], RiMOM [433] FBEM [367], HMatch [182], and ASMOV [198]. Not all systems were able to publish results for all the test cases, for instance, DSSim did not publish any results for **TC2** and **TC3**. This implies that DSSim was not able to process the largest dataset, that is, DBLP. Similarly, the ASMOV system reported only results for **TC1** that considered the smaller datasets. Regarding the quality of the results, the systems report worse results when called to match instances of foaf:Person than when called to match foaf:Publication instances. The reason is that the former contain *structural variations* that stress the systems under test that reported low F-measure. To conclude, there are systems that exhibit good results, such as RiMOM, and others that do not have very good results like FBEM and DSSim; this makes this benchmark one of the most balanced ones.

From the overall evaluation of the ARS benchmark (see Table 7.23), we observed that it is a benchmark which tests the ability of the systems to scale, but at the same time contains a possibly erroneous reference alignment. Another characteristic of ARS is that it does not contain any logical variations, which means that systems did not have to consider schema information to match the instances.

---

[13] http://lsdis.cs.uga.edu/projects/semdis/swetodblp/.

[14] https://datahub.io/dataset/sweto-dblp.

Table 7.23 Overall evaluation of real instance matching benchmarks

	A-R-S	DI 2010	DI 2011
Scalability	1M	6K	NA
Reference alignment	✓	✓	✓✓
Value variations	✓	✓	✓
Structural variations	✓	✓	✓
Logical variations	✗	✗	✗
Multilinguality	✗	✗	✗

Table 7.24 Characteristics of DI 2010 datasets

Ontology	Characteristics
DailyMed	Marketed drug labels for 4308 drugs
Diseasome	Information about 4212 disorders and genes
DrugBank	Information about more than 5900 drugs
SIDER	Marketed 996 drugs, recorded adverse drug reaction

7.3.5.2 Data Interlinking (DI) 2010

DI 2010 [114] is one of the benchmarks proposed by OAEI in 2010. DI 2010 is a benchmark that focuses on instance matching techniques and tools for the health-care domain, and its datasets contain information about drugs. Table 7.24 presents the domain ontologies and their characteristics.

The task posed by the DI 2010 benchmark is to *interlink* the input datasets, that is, to create `owl:same-as` links between the matching instances. The DI benchmark was the first real benchmark where the reference alignment was created in a *semiautomatic way*. In order to produce the alignment, Silk [400] and LinQuer [177] interlinking systems were used; the format employed was the one used by IIMB 2009.

RiMOM [403] and ObjectCoRef [190] reported results for the benchmark and for OAEI 2010. ActiveGenLink [196] and GenLink [195] reported in 2013 and 2012 additional results for the benchmark. From the reported results, one can observe that RiMOM returns better results for recall and worse results for precision, whereas it is the opposite for ObjectCoRef. In other words, RiMOM did report most of the correct results, but it also had a large number of false positives. On the other hand, ObjectCoRef did not contain many of the correct results in its result set, but also did not report any false positives. Both ActiveGenLink and its ancestor GenLink report very good results [195, 196]. The difference in the performance of the systems lies in how systems were benchmarked: RiMOM and ObjectCoRef conducted *blind evaluations* so they had *no a priori knowledge* of the complete reference alignment (*unsupervised systems*). On the other hand, ActiveGenLink and GenLink used the existing reference alignments in order to learn the linkage rules (*supervised learning systems*).

The DI 2010 benchmark uses small datasets (in the order of thousands of instances, smaller than the ARS benchmark), and it also *does not consider any logical variations*, so systems did not need to conduct any reasoning in order to compute the links between instances. A comparative evaluation of DI 2010 with ARS is shown in Table 7.23.

7.3.5.3   Data Interlinking (DI) 2011

DI 2011 [115] is the second benchmark in the series of Data Interlinking benchmarks from OAEI. This benchmark focuses on retrieving New York Times subject headings links[15] with DBpedia [96] locations, organizations, and people, Freebase [125] locations, organizations, and people, and GeoNames [133] locations. The *reference alignment* is based on existing links in the New York Times dataset. Hence, the provided mappings *are accurate* but *may not be complete*. The existing links were removed from the dataset, and the goal of the benchmark was the discovery of the missing links.

AgreementMaker [89], Zhishi.links [293], and SERIMI [23] systems were benchmarked with DI 2011. ActiveGenLink [196] and GenLink [195] reported in 2013 and 2012 additional results for the benchmark. All systems reported good results for DI 2011. The most prominent reason is that the datasets employed by the benchmark are well known and of good quality. Furthermore, the benchmark considered only *value* and *structural* variations and no *logical* ones that add a significant complexity to the systems. Unfortunately, the datasets of the benchmark were not available; hence it was impossible to assess the size of the datasets.

7.3.5.4   Overall Evaluation of Real Benchmarks

Table 7.23 presents a summary of the overall evaluation of the real benchmarks we discussed in the previous section. We can see that there is one benchmark that tests the ability of the systems to scale, namely, the ARS benchmark, but still tested over a very small number of instances (1M instances). Furthermore, none of the real benchmarks consider logical, that is, schema variations but mostly consider value and structural ones. Last but not least, the first two benchmarks included reference alignments that contained errors, while the last one (DI 2011 [115]), contained an error-free reference alignment, due to the fact that the links between the datasets were already included in the New York Times dataset. Regarding the last point, it is still an open issue for the research community to provide a reliable (semi-)automated mechanism to create good quality reference alignments for real datasets.

---

[15]https://researchbuzz.me/tag/new-york-times/.

7.3.6   Synthetic Benchmarks for Instance Matching Systems

In this section we will discuss all *synthetic benchmarks* that have been proposed for testing Instance Matching Systems for Linked Data.

7.3.6.1   IIMB 2009

This work [113] is the first synthetic instance matching benchmark proposed for Linked Data and introduced by OAEI. The benchmark was created using the ontology developed in the context of the OKKAM project [299] that contains actors, sports persons, and business firms. The ontology is *small* (6 classes and 47 datatype properties, 200 instances). The benchmark is divided into *37 test cases*, each one implementing a set of the variations presented in Fig. 7.9. More specifically, the test cases implement *value* variations such as typographical errors, use of different formats, etc., *structural* variations, for example, property deletion and change of property types, among others, and finally *logical* variations like subsumption assertions and modified class assertions. Out of the 37 test cases, only 7 contain a combination of the aforementioned variations. Listings 7.2 and 7.3 depict examples of value and structural variations in IIMB 2009, respectively. The former shows an example of value variations where typographical errors have been used to obtain the transformed instance of the target dataset and the latter depicts an example of structural variations, where datatype properties from the source instance have been transformed into object properties of the target instance. Examples of logical variations are shown in Listing 7.4. The type of the source instance has been altered in the target dataset; if the tested instance matching systems can infer from the ontology schema that class "sportsperson" is a subclass of class "Thing" and the two instances share the other properties, one can conclude that the two instances refer to the same person.

Listing 7.2   IIMB 2009: Example of value variations

```
Original Instance

<#i1> a :Actor .
<#i1> :wikipedia-name ''James Anthony Church'';
        :cogito-name ''Tony Church'';
        :cogito-description ''James Anthony Church (Tony Church) (
            May
        11, 1930 - March 25, 2008) was a British Shakespearean
            actor,
        who has appeared on stage and screen'' .

Transformed Instance

<#i1> a :Actor .
<#i1> :wikipedia-name ''qJaes Anthonodziurcdh'';
```

```
: cogito−name  ''Toty  fCurch'';
: cogito−description  ''Jpes  Athwobyi  tuscr( n Tons Courh)
       pMay
yls/1,9  3i−mcr  25, 200hoa s Bahirtishwaksepearnactdor, woh
hmwseappezrem  yo  nytmlaenn  dscerepnq'' .
```

Listing 7.3 IIMB 2009: Example of structural variations

```
Original Instance

<#i1> a : Actor ;
        : cogito−name  ''Wheeler Dryden'';
        : cogito−first_sentence  ''George Wheeler Dryden (August
           31, 1892 in

                                London − September 30, 1957 in
                                   Los Angeles)
                                was an English actor and film
                                   director,
                                the son of Hannah Chaplin and
                                   ...)'' ;
        : cogito−tag  ''Actor'' .

Transformed Instance
<#i2> a : Actor ;
        : cogito−name  ''Wheeler Dryden'';
        : cogito−first_sentence  <#i3> ;
        : cogito−tag  <#i4> .

<#i3> : hasDataValue  ''George Wheeler Dryden (August 31, 1892
        in London − September 30, 1957 in Los Angeles) was an
           English
        actor and film director, the son of Hannah Chaplin and
           ...)'' .

<#i4> : hasDataValue  ''Actor'' .
```

Listing 7.4 IIMB 2009: Example of logical variations

```
Original Instance

<#i1> a : Sportsperson ;
        : wikipedia−name  ''Sammy Lee'' ;
        : cogito−first−sentence  ''Dr. Sammy Lee (born August 1,
           1920)
        is the first Asian American to win an Olympic gold'';
        : cogito−tag  ''Sportperson'' ;
        : cogito−domain  ''Sport'' .

Transformed Instance

<#i1> a : owl:Thing ;
        : wikipedia−name  ''Sammy Lee'' ;
```

```
:  cogito−first −sentence   ''Dr. Sammy Lee (born August 1,
      1920)
is  the  first  Asian  American  to  win  an  Olympic  gold'';
:  cogito−tag  ''Sportperson''  ;
:  cogito−domain  ''Sport''  .
```

The reference alignment for each test case is automatically created and thus
is accurate without any errors or missing answers. The reference alignment is
represented in an RDF/XML file (see Listing 7.5) and follows the API/EDOL
format [95] that contains the match in the form of a cell, where each cell includes
the *matched instances*, the *measure element* (in that case a float value always equal
to 1.0), and a *relation element* (which is the equal sign "="). The same format is also
used in all the benchmarks of OAEI that will be discussed in the following.

Listing 7.5   IIMB 2009: Example of logical variations

```
<Cell>
  <entity1  rdf : resource = '' http ://www. okkam . org / ens / id1 / ''>
  <entity2  rdf : resource = '' http :// islab . dico . unimi . it / iimb / abox .
      orl#ID3 ''/>
  <measure  rdf : datatype = '' http ://www.w3. org /2001/XMLSchema# float '
      ' >1.0</ measure >
  <relation >=</ relation >
</Cell>
```

The systems that participated in the IIMB benchmark 2009 campaign are the
Aflood [349], ASMOV [198], DSSim [283], HMatch [68], FBEM [367], and
RiMOM [433]. In 2012, authors of the Oto System reported results for the IIMB
2009 Benchmark [94]. The overall reported results [94, 113] provided interesting
conclusions. Systems are able to address test cases that consider *value* variations
relatively easily (except DSSim), whereas they do not return good results for those
that consider combinations of variations. We can conclude that for the majority of
the systems the benchmark was easy since they were all shown to have good results.
A comparison of the benchmark with the other synthetic ones is shown in Table 7.25
of which the benchmark is balanced with two main disadvantages. The first disadvantage is that the datasets are very small (only up to 200 instances), so it cannot
be used to test the scalability aspect of the instance matching systems. The second
is that the logical variations employed to obtain the test cases are only for testing
the ability of the systems to understand subsumption relationships and anonymous
classes. The benchmark does not address any complex schema constructs.

7.3.6.2   IIMB 2010

This work [114] proposed by OAEI is a benchmark employing synthetic datasets,
and the second synthetic benchmark of the IIMB benchmark. It was based on the
Freebase Ontology [125] of which the benchmark included a small version (363
instances) and a larger one (1416 instances). The small version of the Freebase

Table 7.25 Overall evaluation of synthetic benchmarks

	IIMB 2009	IIMB 2010	PR 2010	IIMB 2011	Sandbox 2012	IIMB 2012	RDFT 2013	ID-REC 2014	SPIMBENCH 2015	AUTHOR 2015	ONTOBI	LANCE
Scalability	200	1400	860	4000	375	1500	430	2650	1,000,000	8500	13,700	>>1,000,000
Reference alignment	✓	✓	✓	✓	✓	✓	✓	✓	✓	✓	✓	✓
Value variations	✓	✓	✓	✓	✓	✓	✓	✓	✓	✓	✓	✓
Structural variations	✓	✓	✓	✓	✗	✓	✓	✓	✓	✓	✓	✓
Logical variations	✓	✓	✗	✓	✗	✓	✗	✗	✓	✗	✓	✓
Multilinguality	✗	✗	✗	✗	✗	✗	✓	✓	✗	✓	✗	✓

Ontology consists of 29 classes, 32 objects, and 13 datatype properties, while the large version considers 81 classes. IIMB 2010 contains a larger volume of instances, compared to IIMB 2009, but still remains a small-scale instance matching benchmark. The benchmark is divided into 80 test cases (all of them addressing the variations presented in Fig. 7.9, except multilinguality).

Listing 7.6 shows an instance in the source ontology and its transformed instance in the target ontology obtained from the former by applying a set of variations discussed previously. For this particular example, the tested systems had to consider *schema level information* and more precisely the `rdfs:subClassOf` hierarchy shown also in Listing 7.6. In particular, the combination of the facts that (a) class "Character" is a subclass of class "Creature", (b) property "created_by" is the inverse property of "creates", (c) property "acted_by" is a sub-property of "featuring", and (d) class "Creature" is a subclass of class "Thing", one can conclude that the two instances possibly refer to the same real matching process. The reference alignment was automatically created using the same format as IIMB 2009 (see Listing 7.5). Moreover, the benchmark was created using the SWING Tool [119], a benchmark generator.

Listing 7.6 IIMB 2009: Example of logical variations

```
Schema Hierarchy

Original Instance

Character a rdfs:Class ;
          rdfs:subClassOf Creature .
Creature a rdfs:Class ;
          rdfs:subClassOf Thing .

created_by a rdf:Property ;
          owl:inverseOf creates .

acted_by a rdf:Property ;
          rdf:subPropertyOf featuring .

<#i1> a Character ;
      created_by <#i2> ;
      acted_by <#i3> ;
      name ''Luke Skywalker'' ;
      name ''Mark Hamill'' ;
      name ''George Lucas'' .

<#i2> a Creature .
<#i3> a Creature .

Transformed Instance

<#i4> a Creature ;
      featuring <#i6>
      name ''Luke Skywalker'' ;
```

```
       name  ''Mark  Hamill '' ;
       name  ''George  Lucas ''  .

<#i5> a  Creature  ;
       creates  <#i4>  .

<#i6> a  Thing  .
```

The systems that participated in OAEI IIMB 2010 were ASMOV [199], RiMOM [403], and CODI [296]. All systems reported excellent results for the test cases that considered value and logical variations. The systems did not report good results for test cases that considered *structural transformations* and even worse in cases considering *combinations of transformations*. In addition to those systems, LINDA [47] reported results for the smaller ontology considered in the benchmark. LINDA reports very good results in precision, but not so good when it comes to recall: it includes almost all the correct results in the result set, but it also includes many false results (false negatives) in it.

The results illustrate that the systems were not ready to deal with the scenario that include combinations of transformations, which is actually the most realistic one. An overall evaluation of IIMB 2010 is shown in Table 7.25. The main points here are that if compared to IIMB 2009, it is more voluminous but still a small scale benchmark and that both benchmarks consider the same type of variations (value, structural and logical). IIMB 2010 is the benchmark that considers all the different types of *logical variations* as presented in Fig. 7.9.

7.3.6.3 Person-Restaurants (PR) 2010

(PR) 2010 [114] was also proposed in 2010 as the second synthetic benchmark of OAEI. This benchmark was created by using datasets from the Febrl project [116] and the Fodor and Zagat's Restaurant Guide [123]. The benchmark was built around two test cases: the first concerns matching persons in the dataset from Febrl project, and the second aims at matching restaurants in the Fodor and Zagat dataset. The target datasets in both test cases are constructed using *value* and *structural* but *not logical variations*, this is mostly due to the fact that the datasets were relational and transformed to RDF. Another difference with the IIMB 2009 benchmark is that IIMB 2010 considers *clustering mappings*, that is, $1 - n$ mappings in the reference alignment. This means that one instance from the source could be a match with more than one instances from the target dataset. This fact adds an additional difficulty to the systems under test since, in order to provide good performance results, they must discover all possible matchings for a source instance. The datasets considered in the benchmark are small, since they contain only a limited number of instances (not up to 600). The benchmark, as in the case of IIMB 2009 and 2010 does not consider a data generator so as to produce larger target datasets from the source one. Similar to those benchmarks, the reference alignment follows the same format as IIMB 2009 (see Listing 7.5).

The systems that used PR 2010 were ASMOV and ASMOV-D [199], CODI [296], LN2R [328], ObjectCoRef [190], and RiMOM [403], in addition to LINDA [47]. More than half of the systems, in addition to LINDA system, exhibit bad performance especially in the test case concerning the Febrl project dataset. This is because some systems could not handle the fact that they had to match one source dataset instance to multiple target dataset instances.

The interested reader can refer to Table 7.25 for an overall evaluation of the benchmark. PR 2010 considers *value* and *structural* but not complex variations such as logical ones or multilinguality. It is a challenging benchmark though, since it was the first benchmark to consider $1 - n$ mappings in the reference alignment.

7.3.6.4 IIMB 2011

IIMB 2011 [115] is the third IIMB benchmark proposed by OAEI in 2011. The Freebase Ontology was again used as the schema of the datasets (as was the case also in IIMB 2010). Another common feature shared between IIMB 2011 and IIMB 2010 is that they were both created using the SWING tool [119].

The test cases implemented by IIMB 2011 use the same *value, structural*, and *logical* variations as well as combinations of the above as in IIMB 2010. The reference alignments were created automatically, without any errors or missing results and use the same format as IIMB 2009. The maximum number of instances for the test cases was approximately 4K, unlike previous benchmarks that contained up to 1400 instances. No systems that participated in the OAEI Challenge 2010 reported any results except CODI [296] which is able to handle large datasets that depict complex transformations. The benchmark as shown in Table 7.25 implements all kinds of data transformations, but it also is the "most voluminous" one when compared to others.

7.3.6.5 Sandbox 2012

The Sandbox 2012 benchmark was proposed by OAEI in 2012 [7] and was again created using the Freebase Ontology. The benchmark contains a very small number of instances (approximately 400), and all the test cases it implements consider *only value variations*. Reference alignments were automatically created, using the same format as all the previous OAEI benchmarks. Sandbox 2012 was admittedly a fairly benchmark to work with. It was created with a simple dataset that has been specifically conceived to provide examples of some specific matching problems (like name spelling and other controlled value variations). It was intended as a test for tools that are in the initial phases of their development process and/or for tools that are facing focused tasks. The results for Sandbox and for systems LogMap and LogMap Lite [202], in addition to SBUEI [376], are presented in [7]. The systems reported very good performance results since the benchmark is not a challenging one and does not present significant technical difficulties to the systems.

7.3.6.6   IIMB 2012

IIMB 2012 [7] proposed by OAEI was considered as the *enhanced Sandbox Benchmark*. It was based on the Freebase Ontology and contained various kinds of test cases including value, structural, and logical variations. The SWING benchmark generator was used in the creation of the benchmark, just as it was used in IIMB 2010 and IIMB 2011. All variation types described in Fig. 7.9 have been used in the generation of the target dataset.

The systems that participated in the IIMB 2012 benchmark were LogMap and LogMap Lite [202], SBUEI [376], and Semsim [7]. The results for this benchmark for different systems are reported by Aguirre et al. [7]. In general the systems reported very good results but failed to address test cases that consider the combination of structural and logical variations. Table 7.25 presents an overall evaluation of IIMB 2012. As one can notice, IIMB 2010, IIMB 2011, and IIMB 2012 are very similar. They all contain the same types of variations (since all of them have been created with SWING), and furthermore they use the Freebase Ontology, with IIMB 2011 being the most voluminous of all.

7.3.6.7   RDFT 2013

RDFT 2013 [146] was created by extracting data from DBpedia. It is divided into five test cases, where the first considers only value variations for the target dataset, the second structural variations, the third on language variations (English to French), and the last two contain combinations of the above. RDFT is the first synthetic benchmark for IM proposed by OAEI that contained multilingual datasets. It is also the first synthetic benchmark that conducted the so-called blind evaluations, that is, evaluations of participating systems were not aware of the reference alignment when running the test. This means that the systems could not optimize their results (e.g., by running learning algorithms), since they were not aware of the correct matches. They were only given training data in order to "train" their systems with the particular needs of each test case. Last but not least, one of the proposed test cases contained clusters of mappings, that is, $1 - n$ mappings, which was also the case in the PR 2010 benchmark.

The systems that reported results for the RDFT benchmark are LilyIOM [146] LogMap [203], RiMOM [439], and SLINT+ [290]. All systems exhibited good performance when dealing with test cases that did not consider combinations of variations. Performance drops when different kinds of transformations are combined together except for RiMOM, whose precision and recall was close to 1.0. This suggests that a key challenge for instance matching tools is to work in the direction of improving the combination and balancing of different matching techniques in one dataset. Furthermore, systems seem to handle multilinguality well when the English and French languages are considered. To conclude, this benchmark also does not address the ability of the systems to handle large datasets since the size of the considered data instances (the maximum number being around 430) is very limited.

7.3.6.8   ID-REC 2014

This work was proposed in OAEI 2014 with two tasks, namely, the identity recognition task ("id-rec" task) and the similarity recognition task ("sim-rec" task). Here, we will analyze the first benchmark task only. The "id-rec" benchmark contains one test case where the participants are asked to match books from the source dataset to the target dataset. Constraints are expressed in terms of OWL constructs. The source dataset contains 1330 instances described using 4 classes, 5 datatype properties, and 1 annotation property. The target dataset contains 2649 instances described using 4 classes, 4 datatype properties, 1 object property, and 1 annotation property. Primarily, the main kind of transformation that was performed into the source data was to transform the structured information into an unstructured version of the same information. Specifically, labels are substituted with a set of keywords taken from the instance description. Furthermore, data was translated from Italian to English and vice versa.

The problem of matching structured data with a semistructured or unstructured version of such data is still an open issue for the research community, and that was the reason why the quality of the reported alignments were in general not very high. The systems that have reported results for this benchmark were InsMT and InsMTL [214] and LogMap and LogMap-C [204] in addition to RiMOM-IM [351]. The majority of the systems (i.e., all except RiMOM) either reported fairly good results for precision and bad results for recall or vice versa. This means that the systems either returned very few results that were correct, but at the same time missed a lot of correct results (high precision—low recall), or returned many results, the majority of which were wrong (high recall—low precision). Other characteristics of the benchmark include blind evaluations and the fact that the reference alignment contained $1 - n$ mappings, something that proved to create difficulties for systems.

In conclusion, the instance matching (see Table 7.25) benchmark did not contain logical variations. This means that the semantics expressed at the schema level were not considered when the matching process was performed. The benchmark did not address the ability of systems to handle large datasets since it contains a small number of instances.

7.3.6.9   SPIMBench 2015

SPIMBench 2015 was OAEI 2015 SPIMBENCH track [75] that included 3 test cases, namely, *value-semantics ("val-sem")*, *value-structure ("val-struct")*, and *value-structure-semantics ("val-struct-sem")*, all created using the benchmark generator SPIMBENCH [338]. The source and target datasets have been produced by altering a set of source data with the aim to generate descriptions of the same entity where *value-based*, *structure-based*, and *semantics-aware* transformations are employed in order to create the target data. The target dataset is produced in a way such that an instance in the source dataset can have none or one matching counterpart in the target dataset. The ontology contains 22 classes, 31 datatype properties, and 85 object properties. From those properties, one is an inverse functional property and two are functional properties. The test cases are available in two different scales, namely, the "sandbox" scale that contains 10,000 instances and the "mainbox" scale that contains 100,000 instances. The participants of these tasks were LogMap [205] and STRIM [215]. For evaluation, a reference alignment was available which contains a set of expected matches.

Both systems have presented good results [75] with consistent behavior for the "sandbox" and the "mainbox" tasks, a fact that shows that both systems can handle different sizes of data without reducing their performance. LogMap's performance showed a bigger drop for tasks that consider structure-based transformations (val-struct and val-struct-sem). Also, it produces links that are quite often correct (resulting in a good precision) but fails in capturing a large number of the expected links (resulting in a lower recall). STRIM's performance drops for tasks that consider semantics-aware transformations (val-sem and val-struct-sem) as expected. The probability of capturing a correct link is high, but the probability of a retrieved link to be correct is lower, resulting in a high recall but not equally high precision.

7.3.6.10   ONTOlogy Matching Benchmark with Many Instances (ONTOBI)

ONTOBI is a synthetic benchmark [431] that uses the schema and datasets from DBpedia, and it is not introduced by OAEI. It is divided into 16 test cases, which contain *value*, *structural*, and *logical* variations, as well as *combinations* thereof. Logical variations are only limited to "expanded structure" and "flatten structure", without exploiting any other construct of the RDF or OWL languages. Another issue of the ONTOBI benchmark is that the only system that has reported results for the benchmark is the MICU system [430], which was created by the authors of ONTOBI. Thus, we consider ONTOBI as an isolated benchmark, and we will not be commenting further on the results of their system.

Table 7.25 shows the overall evaluation of the ONTOBI benchmark. It is worth noting that ONTOBI only includes a few logical variations, which are the most expensive type (in terms of computational resources). As far as equity is concerned, we cannot possibly know since no other system has reported results for this benchmark, other than MICU system.

7.3.7 Overall Evaluation of Synthetic Benchmarks

Table 7.25 shows a summary of the evaluation of the synthetic instance matching benchmarks that have been presented so far. It is obvious that each benchmark has been created for a specific reason. For example, the IIMB series and SPIMBENCH 2015 ("sandbox" version) of OAEI benchmarks have all been created to test the ability of the systems to cope with different kinds of variations, that is, data, structural, and logical, but they are all limited in volume (up to 10K instances). PR, RDFT, and ID-REC benchmarks test the ability of the systems to cope with $1 - n$ mappings. Furthermore, SPIMBENCH, RDFT, ID-REC, and Author benchmarks of OAEI evaluations also include multilingual tests. Sandbox is considered to be a trivial benchmark, with no special challenges, with the aim of attracting new systems to the instance matching track of OAEI. ONTOBI seems not to consider many logical variations and does not test the ability of the systems to use the semantic information of the accompanied schemas when those are used to perform the matching task.

The question that remains to be answered by looking at the overall picture of synthetic benchmarks is related to the size of the considered datasets: even though the number of instances that are uploaded in the Linked Data cloud is in the order of billions of triples, all the proposed synthetic benchmarks consider small datasets (at the range of thousands of instances). Before addressing that question, it is interesting to have a look at the real benchmarks that have been published so far.

7.4 Instance Matching Benchmark Generators for Linked Data

In this section, we will present the existing benchmark generators that have been used for the creation of various instantiations of instance matching benchmarks. They are *deterministic frameworks* that take some input parameters and return *synthetically created benchmarks*, that is, *source, target datasets*, and *reference alignments*. The benchmark generators that we will present in this section are SWING [119], SPIMBENCH [338], and LANCE [337].

7.4.1 SWING

SWING [119] is the first *general domain agnostic*, framework for creating benchmarks for instance matching algorithms and tools. It takes as input a source dataset expressed in RDF/OWL format and returns various transformed ontologies (schema and instances), accompanied with a reference alignment for every test case created. It has been implemented as a Java application, and it is available at http://code.

google.com/p/swing. A benchmark is created by SWING in three phases: First, in the *data acquisition* phase the appropriate datasets/ontologies are selected from the Linked Data cloud and enriched with appropriate schemas. The ontology enrichment phase is necessary because Linked Data ontologies are usually poor in semantic information, so they are enriched by adding more OWL constructs. In the *data transformation phase*, the schemas and the instances are transformed by employing *value, structural*, and *logical variations* to the source ontologies. The last phase is the *data evaluation* phase, where reference alignments are created for each test case, and the instance matching tools are tested with the created benchmarks. SWING [119] implements all variations presented in Fig. 7.9.

7.4.2 SPIMBENCH

SPIMBENCH [338] is a *domain-specific* benchmark generator that implements *value*, *structural*, and *logical variations* that can be also combined into *simple* and *complex* transformations. A simple transformation involves a combination of variations from the same category, whereas combining variations from different categories results in a complex transformation.

SPIMBENCH uses extensively the SWING [119] library of variations to implement the set of *value*, *structural* variations that it supports. SPIMBENCH takes as input an *ontology* (schema and instances), a *set of parameters* that describe the characteristics of the *source* and *target* datasets of the produced benchmark, more specifically:

- The *size* of the source and target datasets
- The *percentage* of the source instances to be transformed in order to produce the *target* instances
- The *type of value/structural/logical* variation as well as its *difficulty*

SPIMBENCH puts great emphasis on the logical variations and is the *first benchmark framework* to support *complex logical variations* that go *beyond the standard RDFS constructs*. These are primarily used to examine if the matching systems take into consideration *OWL axioms* to discover matches between instances that can be found only when considering schema information. These constructs are, namely:

- Instance (in)equality
  - `owl:sameAs`
  - `owl:differentFrom`
- Class and property equivalence
  - `owl:equivalentClass`, `owl:equivalentProperty`

- Class and property disjointness
  - `owl:disjointWith`
  - `owl:AllDisjointClasses`
  - `owl:propertyDisjointWith`
  - `owl:AllDisjointProperties`
- Class and property hierarchies
  - `rdfs:subClassOf`
  - `rdfs:subPropertyOf`
- Property constraints
  - `owl:FunctionalProperty`
  - `owl:InverseFunctionalProperty`)

SPIMBENCH extends the data generator of the Semantic Publishing Benchmark (SPB) [224] and produces RDF descriptions of metadata about journalistic assets called *creative works* that are valid instances of classes of the real-world BBC ontologies that are considered by SPB. SPIMBENCH is an open source framework and is available at http://www.ics.forth.gr/isl/spimbench/.

7.4.3 LANCE

LANCE [337] is a *domain and schema agnostic* framework for assessing instance matching techniques for RDF data that are published with an associated schema. LANCE supports a set of test cases based on transformations that distinguish different types of matching entities. LANCE is a *descendant* of SPIMBENCH and supports the *value-based* (typos, date/number formats, etc.), *structure-based* (deletion of classes/properties, aggregations, splits, etc.), and *semantics-aware* test cases. Semantics-aware test cases allow testing the ability of instance matching systems to be tested by using the semantics of RDFS/OWL axioms to identify matches and include tests involving instance (in)equality, class and property equivalence and disjointness, property constraints, and complex class definitions. The novelty of LANCE lies in the fact that it produces a *weighted gold standard* that is based on *tensor factorization*, and it also supports *varying degrees of difficulty* for the proposed transformations as well as *fine-grained evaluation metrics*.

The main difference between SPIMBENCH and LANCE, among others, is that LANCE is *domain independent* and *schema agnostic*: it can accept any linked dataset and its accompanying schema as input to produce a target dataset implementing test cases of varying levels of difficulty. LANCE supports *simple combination* test cases implemented using the aforementioned variations applied on *different triples referring to the same instance*, as well as *complex combination* test cases implemented by *combinations of individual transformations for the same triple*. LANCE is open source and is available at http://www.ics.forth.gr/isl/lance/.

Chapter 8
Provenance Management for Linked Data

The term *Provenance* refers to the origin of information and is used to describe *where* and *how* the data was obtained. Provenance is versatile and could include various types of information, such as the source of the data, information on the processes that led to a certain result, date of creation or last modification, and authorship. Recording and managing the provenance of data is of paramount importance, as it allows supporting *trust mechanisms*, *access control* and *privacy policies*, *digital rights management*, *quality management and assessment*, in addition to *reputability*, *reliability* and *accountability* of data sources. In this chapter, we discuss the provenance management for Linked Data and present the different provenance models developed for the different fragments of the SPARQL standard language for querying RDF datasets. In addition, we discuss the different models for relational provenance that set the basis for RDF provenance models and proceed with a thorough presentation of the various provenance models for the different fragments of the SPARQL query language.

8.1 An Overview of Provenance Models

In the context of scientific communities, provenance information is used in the proof of the correctness of results and in general determines the quality of scientific work. In this respect, provenance is not an end in itself, but a means towards answering a number of questions concerning data as well as processes that manage this data. The absence, or non-consideration, of provenance can cause several problems; interesting examples of such *provenance failures* can be found in [80]. One such case was the publication, in 2008, of a document regarding the near bankruptcy of a well-known airline company; even though the document was 6 years old, and thus irrelevant at the time, the absence of a date in the document caused panic, and the company's share price fell by 75%.

© Springer International Publishing AG 2018
S. Sakr et al., *Linked Data*, https://doi.org/10.1007/978-3-319-73515-3_8

Understanding where and how a piece of data is produced (its provenance) has long been recognized as an important factor in determining the quality of a data item particularly in data integration systems [402]. Thus, it is no surprise that provenance has been of concern within the Linked Data community where a major use case is the integration of datasets published by multiple different actors [45]. The W3C Linking Open Data initiative (LOD)[1] has boosted the publication and interlinkage of massive amounts of datasets on the Semantic Web as RDF data, queried with the SPARQL query language [314]. Together with Web 2.0 technologies (e.g., mashups), they have essentially transformed the web from a publishing-only environment into a vibrant place for information dissemination where data is exchanged, integrated, and materialized in distributed repositories behind SPARQL endpoints. The unconstrained publication, use, and interlinking of datasets that is encouraged by the Linked Open Data initiative is both a blessing and a curse. On the one hand, it increases the added-value of interlinked datasets by allowing the re-use of concepts and properties, but on the other hand, the unmoderated data publication raises various additional challenges including making the need for clear and efficient recording of provenance even more imperative for resolving problems related to data quality, data trustworthiness, privacy, digital rights, etc. [122, 173].

Provenance becomes even more important in the context of LOD, which promotes the free publication and interlinking of large datasets in the Semantic Web [20, 40]. The LOD cloud is experiencing rapid growth since its conception in 2007; hundreds of interlinked datasets compose a knowledge base which currently consists of more than 31 billion RDF triples. Such datasets include ontologies created from DBpedia[2] or other sources,[3] data from e-Science, most notably in the area of life sciences,[4] Web 2.0 information mashups [234], and others.

The work on provenance and Linked Data builds upon prior work in the database, e-Science and distributed systems communities. Moreau provides an extensive review of the literature by contextualizing it with respect to the web [266]. Regarding *provenance models*, there exist two main models for provenance: *workflow provenance* and *data provenance*. In this chapter we are focusing on *data provenance* models in the style as described by Cheny et al. [81], that is, *provenance of data in the result of declarative queries*. This is different from workflow provenance [126] (e.g., OPM4), which typically describes procedural data processing, and where operations are usually treated as black boxes [362] due to their complexity. As a result, workflow provenance is in general less fine-grained than data provenance.

Data provenance has been widely studied in several different contexts such as databases, workflows, distributed systems, Semantic Web, etc. Moreau [266] explored the different aspects of provenance in the aforementioned communities.

---

[1]linkeddata.org.

[2]http://www.dbpedia.org.

[3]http://www.informatik.uni-trier.de/~ley/db.

[4]http://www.geneontology.org/.

Likewise, Cheney et al. [81] provide an extended survey that considers the provenance of query results in relational databases regarding the most popular provenance models (why, where, and how). In the same context, Tan [377, 378] considered the problem of supporting data provenance in scientific applications by providing some background on previous research and some discussions on potential future directions.

Research on data provenance can be categorized depending on whether it deals with *updates* [27, 62, 121, 129, 164, 397] or *queries* [62, 81, 92, 132, 150, 209, 275, 397]. Compared to querying, the problem of provenance management for updates has not been studied thoroughly. Another important classification is based on the underlying data model, relational [60, 62, 129, 150, 275, 397] or RDF [27, 92, 132, 164, 173, 209, 424], which determines whether the model deals with the SQL or SPARQL operators, respectively. Despite its importance, only a few works deal with the problem of update provenance, and even fewer consider the problem in the context of SPARQL updates [27, 164]. A third categorization stems from the expressive power of the employed provenance model, for example, *how*, *where*, and *why*, among others. The last dimension deals with the fragment of the SPARQL query language studied, and more specifically whether it includes *negation* or not. Hence, we distinguish between provenance for *positive* SPARQL, SPARQL with *negation*, and SPARQL *including updates*.

8.2 Provenance Representations

Because data processing takes place across systems, there is a need to be able to interchange information about how data was combined, recombined, and processed. This has led to the development of a number of ontologies for the representation of that information including Dublin Core,[5] the Proof Markup Language (PML) [91], Provenir [327], Provenance Authoring and Versioning [84], Provenance Vocabulary [170], and OPMV [435]. These ontologies shared many common capabilities to describe various types of information about how data was combined and processed including:

- How software was executed to consume and produce data
- That data were derived from other data
- That data were composed of other data
- Who was involved in the manipulation or construction of data

These common characteristics were also evident to the broader provenance community through the development of the Open Provenance Model [268]. Given this, the World Wide Web Consortium formed a working group that developed a recommendation for the interchange of provenance on the web called PROV [153].

---

[5]http://dublincore.org/documents/dcmi-.terms/.

PROV incorporates the concepts from above and establishes a baseline for the interchange of provenance. We recommend the PROV Primer [135] as a good introduction to the concepts of PROV. A book length introduction is given by Moreau and Groth [267]. In practice, many of the ontologies described above that were precursors to PROV have now been revised to extend PROV including PML[6] and PAV [85]. Furthermore, there is a mapping between PROV and Dublin Core. The key realization here is that these ontologies provide the vocabulary to represent provenance information at differing levels of detail to enable interchange between systems. Thus, when developing a Linked Data management system, it is important to be aware that there is a difference between external, interchangeable representations and those used internally to manage data. These representations all use the common Linked Data formats, and more importantly, they rely on the URL as identifiers to point to pieces of data and describe the provenance. At the dataset level, provenance is often attached to a dataset descriptor [149] often embedded in a Vocabulary of Interlinked Datasets (VoID) file [11]. VoID is an important part of Linked Data provenance as it allows one to define what constitutes a dataset and its associated metadata. The Dataset Descriptions: HCLS Community Profile[7] provides excellent guidance on what metadata (inclusive of provenance) should be provided by linked datasets.

Within Linked Data, provenance is attached using either reification [179] or named graphs [66]. Widely used datasets such as YAGO [186] reify their entire structures to facilitate provenance annotations. Indeed, provenance is one reason for the inclusion of named graphs in the current version of RDF 1.1 [436]. Other approaches, such as nanopublications [154], extensively use named graphs to enable subsets of Linked Data to be referred to and for their provenance to be described [154].

8.3 Provenance Models

8.3.1 Relational Provenance

The inspiration to address provenance for Linked Data comes from the relational setting, where the problem has been considered for SQL queries in various works. In that setting, the various operators of relational algebra ($\sigma, \pi, \bowtie$, etc.) have been reused to denote provenance and annotate the corresponding data in a way that shows which operators were used (and how) to produce it [81, 150]. As an example, when a tuple is the result of a join between two other tuples, then its provenance annotation should be $a_1 \bowtie a_2$, where a_1, a_2 are the provenance annotations of the input tuples and $\bowtie$ is the abstract operator that corresponds to the

---

[6]http://inference-web.org/wiki/PML_3.0.

[7]http://www.w3.org/TR/hcls-dataset/.

relational join. Under this general idea, different models for the relational algebra, with different expressiveness, have been developed. An important consideration in this respect is the granularity of provenance. Some works apply provenance at the attribute level [60, 62, 131, 397], others consider provenance at the level of tuples [38, 60, 90, 136, 137, 150, 397], whereas some others study provenance at the relation level [60, 62]. Another consideration is the fragment of the relational algebra considered. The so-called *positive fragment* is simpler; this fragment allows only *filter-project-join-union* queries, that is, the monotonic part of SQL. Most works deal with this fragment (e.g., [62, 81, 150, 209]).

The seminal work in this respect is [150], where a provenance model with two abstract operators was defined. The two operators accepted by the model, + and ·, correspond to the union and natural join operators of relational algebra and have been proven to be sufficient to express the full positive fragment of SQL. In addition to the operators, two distinguished elements 0 and 1, indicating that a certain tuple is "out of" or "in" the relation (respectively) were defined. Then, the authors argued that any reasonable concretization of the above model should satisfy a number of properties, which essentially stem from the properties of relational algebra; these properties allowed proving that the structure $(K, +, \cdot, 0, 1)$, for any given set K such that $0, 1 \in K$, is a commutative semiring.

When *non-monotonic* operators, that is, (left-)outer join or relational difference, enter the picture, the problem becomes more difficult. The extra challenge in the more general case is that the existence of a tuple in the query result is sometimes due to the *absence* of a tuple. This is harder to record in the annotation of the result and is certainly not expressible in the semiring framework of [150]. Works addressing this problem (such as [16, 17, 130, 136]) proposed extensions of the semiring model with additional operators that would capture the semantics of non-monotonic operators.

Of particular interest in this respect is the work of Geerts et al. [130], whose extension included a *monus* operator that captures the semantics of relational difference. This approach thus uses three operators, namely, $\oplus$ (corresponding to + of [150]), $\otimes$ (corresponding to · of [150]), and the new $\ominus$ (the monus operator, which is used to capture relational difference). This led to a structure called *monus-semiring* (or *m-semiring* for short) which allowed the annotation of query results for the full SQL.

8.3.2 RDF Provenance

Challenges related to the representation of provenance information appear also in the context of SPARQL queries and SPARQL updates. In that case, the provenance of the constructed or inserted triples (or tuples, in general) is the combination of the provenance of the triples that were used to obtain the result. This is a complicated case, because construction in SPARQL queries and updates uses (via the graph patterns) various different operators (union, join, projection, selection). The problem with dynamic information appears when the result of a SPARQL query is pre-computed, for example, in the context of materialized SPARQL views. In such a scenario, the provenance of triples in the result of the SPARQL query needs to be revisited (and recomputed) when changes in the underlying dataset happen. Note that this is part of the more general and well-known problem of managing materialized views when the underlying data changes [158]. More importantly, the problem with the unexpected uses of provenance information is emphasized in the SPARQL case. In many cases, users may not be interested only in the result of the query but also in the provenance of the information found in the result. This provenance information can be used in various different and unexpected ways by the users, so it should not be artificially aggregated by the system under any reasonable semantics, but instead presented in the form of an abstract expression, which, in essence, "justifies" (or "explains") the presence of each triple in the result. Same arguments apply for the case where triples are inserted as part of SPARQL Update operations.

For the case of querying, examples of such works are [38, 41, 130, 131, 136, 150, 397], which are mostly focusing on queries in the relational setting (i.e., when the underlying dataset is a relational database, and the queries are expressed using SQL). Attempts for adapting this line of work for the RDF/SPARQL case have identified several problems, mainly related to the non-monotonic fragment of SPARQL [92, 380]. An indirect way of overcoming the problem appears in [442], where an extension of SPARQL is proposed, in which the user can express queries that explicitly manipulate both data and annotations (provenance). The obvious solution for solving the problem of annotating the results of queries for the RDF/SPARQL case would be to adapt the corresponding relational/SQL solutions. SPARQL, like SQL, allows monotonic operators (AND, UNION, etc.) as well as non-monotonic ones (OPTIONAL, DIFFERENCE, MINUS). Extending the relational/SQL solutions to apply in the RDF/SPARQL case was proven easy for the positive fragment [101, 380]; in particular, the classical approach of provenance semirings [150] was shown to be adequate to express provenance for the monotonic SPARQL fragment [380?]. However, as with the relational case, the approach of [150] is not adequate for the non-monotonic case. Moreover, for the RDF/SPARQL case, an additional difficulty was caused by the fact that the semantics of the DIFFERENCE and OPTIONAL operators of SPARQL [311] is slightly different than the corresponding SQL operators. In particular, when taking the SPARQL DIFFERENCE (say $P_1 \setminus P_2$), SPARQL uses bag semantics for P_1, but set semantics for P_2 (i.e., the multiplicities in P_2 are ignored). As a result, extensions to the semiring framework that capture the non-monotonic fragment of SQL, such as [130], could not be applied directly for the SPARQL case [132, 209, 380].

The first proposed approach towards solving the problem of SPARQL provenance management [92] in the presence of non-monotonic operators employs the formalism of m-semirings [130] where it uses a translation technique (from SPARQL to SQL) to overcome the discrepancy between the semantics of SPARQL and SQL. More precisely, (m, δ)-semirings are employed, which are m-semirings extended with δ, a generalization of the duplicate elimination operator that represents constant annotations [130]; this is necessary to capture the hybrid semantics of SPARQL DIFFERENCE. The approach is based on a translation of SPARQL queries into equivalent relational ones along the lines of [110]. More precisely, each triple pattern as well as each graph pattern that can appear in a SPARQL query is translated into an appropriate SQL expression; SPARQL DIFFERENCE in particular is encoded through a complex relational expression involving joins, relational set difference, and duplicate elimination. Based on this translation, any SPARQL query can be translated into a (possibly complex) SQL query. Using this translation, the result of a SPARQL query can be obtained via the result of an SQL query. Given that the provenance of the results of an SQL query (for both the monotonic and the non-monotonic fragment) can be obtained using the approach of m-semirings [136], this approach solves the problem of representing the provenance of the result of SPARQL queries.

In summary, to capture the provenance of the result of a SPARQL query, one must first translate the query into the corresponding SQL query, and take the result. The provenance of the SQL result is represented using the model of m-semirings that is described in [136]: the abstract operators of $\oplus$, $\otimes$, and $\ominus$ are used to describe the provenance and are concretized according to the application at hand (trustworthiness evaluation, data quality management, etc.). Note that the concretization should satisfy the properties of $\oplus$, $\otimes$, $and \ominus$ that are defined in [136]. The only problem with this approach is that the final abstract expression that models the provenance of the query result may be overly complicated, due to the complex translation that is necessary to obtain it. Moreover, the structure of the original SPARQL query is not always preserved during the translation, which could lead sometimes to unintuitive provenance annotations for the resulting triples.

Another effort of solving the problem of SPARQL provenance management for both the monotonic and the non-monotonic operators of SPARQL uses an algebraic structure called *spm-semirings* [132] ("spm" stands for SPARQL minus). The proposed solution is also inspired by the idea of m-semirings [136]: like m-semirings, the approach extends the original semirings framework with a new operator, $\ominus$, whose semantics are adequate for capturing SPARQL non-monotonic operators [132]. In more detail, spm-semirings accept three operators, $\oplus$, $\otimes$, $\ominus$, where the latter is used to capture SPARQL DIFFERENCE (and thus the operator OPTIONAL as well). The semantics of SPARQL DIFFERENCE are slightly different than the semantics of the corresponding SQL operator, in the sense that SPARQL DIFFERENCE employs both set and bag semantics in a hybrid manner.

The idea is to start by identifying the equivalences that should hold for SPARQL operatorsand were shown to hold for any SPARQL expressions P_1, P_2, P_3 [132, 346]. Then, spm-semirings are defined to be structures of the form $(K, \oplus, \otimes, \ominus, 0, 1)$ that satisfy the identities in Table 8.1. It can be easily seen that a structure of the form $(K, \oplus, \otimes, \ominus, 0, 1)$ is an spm-semiring if and only if the corresponding SPARQL K-annotated algebra satisfies the SPARQL equivalences.

The above formal approach shows that the semantics of $\ominus$ (as expressed in Table 8.1) cannot be captured using $\oplus$, $\otimes$ alone. This means that the inclusion of the new operator ($\ominus$) in the spm-semiring structure is unavoidable. Further, it was shown that the identities $x \otimes 0 = 0$ and $x \oplus 0 = x$ (from Table 8.1) are not

Table 8.1 Identities for spm-semirings

$x \otimes 1 = x$	$x \otimes 0 = 0$
$x \oplus 0 = x$	$x \oplus y = y \oplus x$
$x \otimes y = y \otimes x$	$(x \oplus y) \oplus z = x \oplus (y \oplus z)$
$(x \otimes y) \otimes z = x \otimes (y \otimes z)$	$x \otimes (y \oplus z) = (x \otimes y) \oplus (x \otimes z)$
$x \ominus x = 0$	$x \ominus (y \oplus z) = (x \ominus y) \ominus z$
$x \otimes (y \ominus z) = (x \otimes y) \ominus z$	$(x \ominus (x \ominus y)) \oplus (x \ominus y) = x$

necessary, in the sense that a structure $(K, \oplus, \otimes, \ominus, 0, 1)$ is an spm-semiring if and only if it satisfies all the remaining identities from Table 8.1. Finally, SPARQL query equivalences, as implied by the SPARQL semantics [311], are respected in the spm-semiring structure (and the corresponding annotations). This means that equivalent queries would lead to equivalent annotations for the (same) output triples.

The above results show that spm-semirings are adequate for developing a provenance model to capture the non-monotonic operators, but do not give any hints as to how to construct an spm-semiring, that is, the methodology that should be followed in order to define operators that satisfy the identities of Table 8.1. Towards this aim, a structure called *seba-structure* (from semiring boolean algebra) was defined, which is a hybrid structure consisting of a commutative semiring and a boolean algebra, as well as mappings between them. Seba-structures solve the above problem because they provide an easy constructive way to generate an spm-semiring; in particular, the operators $\oplus, \otimes$ stem directly from the corresponding operations of the commutative semiring in the seba-structure, whereas the $\ominus$ operator is defined constructively using the $\otimes$ operator of the semiring, the complement operator of the boolean algebra and the mappings between the semiring and the boolean algebra of the seba-structure. Further, seba-structures can be used to construct the "universal spm-semiring," that is, the most general spm-semiring. This universal structure provides a concise representation of the provenance of RDF data and SPARQL queries involved.

8.3.3 Update Provenance

Most works related to the update problem try to adapt the solutions proposed for the case of (SQL or SPARQL) querying [61, 62, 397]. This is reasonable, because the underlying problem is that of identifying the annotation of a newly constructed triple, regardless of whether this is constructed in order to be returned as the result of a query or if it is constructed in order to be added in a dataset/database. Having said that, it is also true that there are several differences that require a different approach to address this problem.

In the context of SPARQL, update provenance only considers abstract provenance models. More specifically, Avgoustaki et al. [28] proposed a new provenance model that uses algebraic expressions to represent the attribute and triple level provenance of quadruples constructed via SPARQL insert updates. Instead, other works use RDF named graphs to represent both past versions and changes to a graph [164]. This is achieved by modeling the provenance of an RDF graph as a set of history records, including a special provenance graph and additional auxiliary named graphs that store the different versions of a dataset. Compared to querying, the problem of provenance management during updates is less well-understood with all the related work dealing with the relational setting. Moreover, most existing works deal with provenance at the tuple level (the approach of [62] is an exception in this respect, as it deals with all three levels of provenance granularity, namely, at the attribute, tuple, and relation levels).

In most approaches, the creation (and insertion) of a new tuple that is "constructed" from constant values or from values taken from different tuples is assumed to take a "default" provenance (often called "empty" or "blank" provenance), indicated by a special symbol ($\perp$) [61, 397]. This loss of information on how the triple was created is an inherent problem of dealing with provenance at the tuple level; discriminating between the (different) provenance of each attribute can only be done in models that work at the attribute level. In addition, the provenance model considered is why and where provenance, rather than how provenance; as a result, these works do not consider how the tuple was created (i.e., the transformations that the source data underwent), only the origin of the source data. Given these shortcomings, the only case that these works essentially address is when a tuple is copied from one table (or database) to another; in this case, the provenance records the origin of the original tuple [61, 397]. Another related approach is [151], where schema mappings are used to express the provenance of a tuple; this tuple can be inserted from the user of the database or it can be copied from another database. It is worth mentioning that this model is more expressive than why provenance or lineage, since it relies on the properties of semirings (see [150]). The problem of identifying the provenance tag of an inserted triple is quite similar to the problem of computing the provenance of the result of a SPARQL query, but raises some additional complications.

One important complication arises because of the fact that inserted triples are actually placed in some user-defined named graph. This is in contrast to the case of triples produced via inference (which are placed in custom, system-defined graphs, such as named graphs representing graphsets [308]) and is also different from triples constructed via SPARQL queries (which are not placed in any named graph whatsoever). This fact raises some complications as related to the representation of provenance: named graphs are no longer adequate for this purpose. To be more specific, it has been argued that named graphs (or their extension via graphsets [121]) can be used to store the provenance of a triple [66, 67]. Despite the inherent difficulties of modeling a complex provenance label (such as those occurring during complex inference paths) via a named graph, it is, in principle, possible to associate each such label with a distinct URI, which plays the role of the corresponding named graph (and represents the triple's provenance); thus, the above argument is valid for the case of inference and simple SPARQL queries. However, this is no longer the case when it comes to modeling the provenance of newly inserted triples. In fact, SPARQL Update statements explicitly specify the named graph where the newly inserted triple should be placed. As a result, two triples with a totally irrelevant provenance label may be forced to coexist in the same named graph.

8.4 Provenance in Data Management Systems

Provenance within Linked Data management systems builds heavily on the work of the database systems community [81]. Miles defined the concept of *provenance query* [263] in order to only select a relevant subset of all possible results when looking up the provenance of an entity. A good example of a classic database system that handles provenance is Perm [137], which can compute, store, and query in a relational manner. Provenance was computed by using standard relational query rewriting techniques. Perm supports the calculation of provenance both when queried for (the lazy approach) or when a new relation is created or data is inserted (the eager approach) depending on settings. Recently, Glavic showed that the provenance captured within such a standard relational system can be represented and interchanged using PROV [295].

An important point is that these traditional database approaches [43, 208] assume a strict relational schema, whereas RDF data is by definition schema-free. To address these issues, a number of authors have adopted the notion of annotated RDF [121, 385]. This approach assigns annotations to each of the triples within a dataset and then tracks these annotations as they propagate through either the reasoning or query processing pipelines. Formally, these annotated relations can be represented by the algebraic structure of communicative semirings, which can take the form of polynomials with integer coefficients [150]. Zimmermann et al. [442] propose to annotate a triple with temporal data and a provenance value. Such provenance value refers to the source of a triple. The authors use a standard triple-oriented data model and include temporal and provenance annotation. A triple takes the form of (Subject, Predicate, Object, Annotation), that is, N-Quad (Chap. 2). Such statements can be stored in any triple store supporting N-Quads. Zimmermann et al. also proposed a model to describe provenance of inferred triples with the logical operators $\vee$ and $\wedge$. Consider the following data:

```
(chadHurley; worksFor; youtube) : chad
(chadHurley; type; Person) : chad
(youtube; type; Company) : chad
(Person; sc; Agent) : foaf
(worksFor; dom; Person) : wrokkend
(worksFor; range; Company) : workont
```

It is possible to infer the following triple:

(chadHurley; type; Agent) : (chad ∧ foaf ∧ workont)
∨ (chad ∧ foaf)

which logically is equivalent to:

(chadHurley; type; Agent) : chad ∧ foaf

The proposed method to describe provenance of inferred triples could be possibly leveraged to trace provenance in query execution; however this avenue was not explored by the authors. Zimmermann et al. also proposed a query language that allows provenance information to be incorporated in the query execution. The basic idea to query over provenance values is similar to named graphs in SPARQL. The query incorporates information on the annotation, which is then taken into account during the execution.

A similar approach is described by Udrean et al. [385]. The authors extend the RDF schema for temporal, uncertainty, and provenance annotations. The main focus of this work is to develop a theoretical model to manage such metadata information. The authors also proposed a query language that allows querying over such metadata. Contrary to the previous solution, here the authors annotate predicates with provenance information. In a similar way Nguyen et al. [291] proposed to use a singleton property instead of RDF reification or named graphs to describe provenance. A triple would then take the form (Subject, Predicate : Annotation, Object). Such annotation added to a predicate could be later tracked to deliver a trace of the query execution; however it is not included in the work. Udrean et al. [385] also proposed a query language to include provenance information in the query execution process. A query then takes a form similar to their annotated triple, that is, (Subject, Predicate : Annotation, Object). Query schema proposed in this work is not fully compatible with SPARQL. Queries can by expressed in SPARQL but the annotations are not taken into account in such a case.

Ding et al. considered tracking provenance from the database perspective at a molecule level [100]. They defined RDF molecule as the finest and lossless sub-graph resulting from the graph decomposition, which boils down to triples if there are no blank nodes involved. In the case the dataset contains blank nodes, triples sharing the same blank node are placed in the same molecule. They consider provenance at the document level which means that molecules are annotated with the source URI. Their implementation is similar to previous approaches as they store data in the form of quads in a statement table. Likewise, the final output of their system consists of query results and a list of documents (URIs) which provided the triples used in the query execution.

The RDFProv [76] system allows to manage and query provenance that results from scientific workflows. RDFProv proposes a solution to manage scientific workflow provenance by representing it as triples. Chebotko et al. [76] proposed two algorithms to map a provenance ontology into a relational database system. The first algorithm uses database views, while the second one instead of using views uses tables, and thus it replicates all data and results in more complex update operations since all independent relations have to be modified separately. To map an ontology, first of all, they store all data in a statement table; additionally for each *type* (class of resources) they create three auxiliary views/relations co-locating triples to address different kinds of workloads. The three views are as follows:

- A view for all instances of the *type*
- Subject(i,p,o) for triples whose subjects belong to the *type*
- Object(s,p,i) for triples whose objects belong to the *type*

To optimize the execution they create B+-tree indexes on columns (s, p, o), (s, o), and (p) of the statement table. Similar indexes are created on the auxiliary relations in case tables are employed.

As Damásio et al. have noted [92], many of the annotated RDF approaches do not expose the how provenance (i.e., how a query result was constructed). The most comprehensive implementations of these approaches are [385, 442]. However, they have only been applied to small datasets (around ten million triples) and are not aimed at reporting provenance polynomials [150] (i.e., algebraic structures representing, using relational algebra operators, how data is combined) for SPARQL query results, focusing instead on inferred triples. Annotated approaches have also been used for propagating trust values [171]. Other recent work, for example, [92, 132], has looked at expanding the theoretical aspects of applying such a semiring-based approach to capturing SPARQL.

Contrary to the previous approaches, TripleProv [424] extends a native triple store [423] to allow storing, tracing, and querying provenance information in processing RDF queries. TripleProv returns a description of the way the results of an RDF query were derived; specifically it gives an explanation of which pieces of data and how they were combined to produce the answer of a query. The system also allows the query execution to be tailored with provenance information [426]. The user can input a provenance specification of the data that he wants to use to derive the answer. For example, if he is interested with articles about "Obama," but he wants the answer to come only from sources attributed to "US News."

As an input to the system, the user provides a query he wants to execute (workload query) and an RDF query describing provenance of the data he wants to be used in query processing (provenance query)—see Fig. 8.1. The query execution

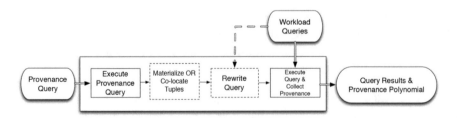

Fig. 8.1 TripleProv: Executing provenance-enabled queries; both a workload and a provenance query are given as input to a triple store, which produces results for both queries and then combine them to obtain the final results and the provenance polynomial [425]. ©2015 VLDB Endowment. Reprinted with permission

process can vary depending on the strategy. Typically the system starts with executing the provenance query, then it optionally pre-materializes or co-locates data. Afterwards, TripleProv executes the workload queries; at the same time, it collects information of entities used during the query execution and the way they are combined. The system returns:

- Results of the workload queries, restricted to those which are following the provenance specification
- The provenance polynomial describing the way the results were derived

TripleProv [426] provides detailed information on each piece of data used to produce the answer and the exact way it contributed to the results. To express this information, the system uses the notion of a provenance polynomial, which is an algebraic structure describing how the data was combined. A provenance polynomial provided by TripleProv allows the system to pinpoint and trace back the exact pieces of data used to produce the answer and the exact way of how those pieces of data were combined. In order to express the way the pieces of data were combined, TripleProv uses two basic algebraic operators: the first one ($\oplus$) to represent a union, and the second ($\otimes$) to represent a join.

Figure 8.2 shows a simple star query (Basic Graph Pattern) and a provenance polynomial pinpointing how each part of the query is tackled. In this example the first triple pattern is satisfied with lineage l1, l2, or l3, while the second has been satisfied with l4 or l5; the third was processed with elements having a lineage of l6 or l7, and the last one was processed with elements from l8 or l9. The triples were joined on variable ?a, which is expressed by the join operation ($\otimes$) in the polynomial.

TripleProv allows RDF queries to be tailored with provenance information [426]. The user can provide to the system a description of the data which will be used in the query processing. Such description (provenance query) is expressed in the same way as the workload query. The query workload together with the provenance query is used to give a provenance-enabled query. Such provenance-enabled query returns results of the workload query, limited to those derived from the data described by the provenance query.

Considering the query from Fig. 8.2, which is a workload query, we would like to retrieve results of this query, but using only data attributed to government and

Fig. 8.2 TripleProv: Provenance polynomial represents how the data is combined to derive the query answer using different relational algebra operators (e.g., UNION, JOINS) [425]

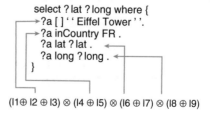

```
select ? lat ? long where {
   →?a [ ] '' Eiffel Tower ''.
   →?a inCountry FR .
     ?a lat ? lat .   ←
     ?a long ? long . ←
}
```

$(l1 \oplus l2 \oplus l3) \otimes (l4 \oplus l5) \otimes (l6 \oplus l7) \otimes (l8 \oplus l9)$

verified by the Paris Tourist Office. The following provenance query can express such description of data:

```
SELECT ? ctx WHERE {
         ? ctx prov:wasAttributedTo <government> .
         ? ctx prov:wasVeryfiedBy <PartisTouristOffice> .
       }
```

Sending those two queries to TripleProv will give to the user information about the geolocation of the Eiffel Tower in France; the information will be obtained from the data following the provenance description. Additionally, TripleProv will provide a trace of how particular pieces of data were combined to deliver the results.

VOLT [323] is a transparent SPARQL proxy system which is capable of computing the provenance of query results. VOLT acts as a SPARQL endpoint; a query is issued to the proxy which interacts with the real SPARQL endpoints, then the proxy returns the results to the client along with the provenance information. VOLT features property functions,[8] that is, properties that execute a piece of underlying code to produce results. Such code is serialized as a graph, which enables the user to trace back the way the results were produced. VOLT also records all SPARQL queries and other invoked functions. Any information used to produce the results is stored as a provenance graph and serialized in a form of RDF triples. Moreover, such provenance information is also persisted along with cached triples. This allows the system to provide it to the end user without recomputation and to invalidate stale cache.

Halpin and Cheney have shown how to use SPARQL Update to track provenance within a triple store without modifications [164]. They model provenance of an updated graph as a set of history records. Similar to the version control systems, they persist the state of provenance graph at a specific version. To track provenance of update, along with the requested data update, they list a sequence of operations. These operations create named graphs containing triples that describe provenance information. They consider cases of insert and delete operations on a single known named graph. To store provenance of graph creation, the authors proposed the following operations:

```
CREATE g;   —  the requested operation; create the graph g
CREATE g_v0;  —  and initial version v0 of the graph

             —  insert provenance information to the prov named graph
INSERT DATA { GRAPH prov {
             g version g_v0,   —  version of the graph g
             g current g_v0,   —  current version of the graph g
             u1 type create,   —  type of the operation
             u1 output g_v0,   —  link to the output graph
             —  additional metadata about the operation
             u1 meta mi,(metadata ...)
}}
```

---

[8]https://jena.apache.org/documentation/query/extension.html#property-functions.

To store provenance of deleting a graph, the authors proposed the following operations:

DROP g; — *the requested operation; drop the graph g*

— *remove link to the current version*
DELETE WHERE {GRAPH prov {g current g_vi}};

INSERT DATA { GRAPH prov {
       ui type drop, — *type of the operation*
       ui input g_vi, — *link to the removed version*
       — *additional metadata about the operation*
       ui meta mi,(metadata ...)
}}

Halpin and Cheney define similar translations for other operations. Such stored provenance information can be used by systems like TripleProv [424, 426] in tracking provenance of the query execution, as well as in restricting query execution to data that follow some provenance specification, for example, versions modified by John within a specific period of time.

Chapter 9
Conclusions and Outlook

Congratulations! We have covered the technical details of storing, querying, reasoning, and provenance management of Linked Data in the previous eight chapters that we have just walked over. This chapter will briefly summarize our journey before providing some insights and highlights on some of the open challenges and research direction for advancing the state-of-the-art of Linked Data toward achieving the ultimate vision of the Semantic Web Domain.

9.1 Conclusions

In the early days of the human history, data and information management were mainly relying on oral communication and the human brain. The invention of several mediums (e.g., paper-based, digital-based) allowed human knowledge to be recorded and passed on through generations. In the last few decades, the World Wide Web has dramatically changed the practice of data and knowledge sharing by removing the barriers for publishing and accessing documents as part of a global information space. Nowadays, intelligent information management of the huge web-scale data has become one of the biggest challenges. Data and information integration for efficient search, querying, and reasoning is the major challenge that needs to be addressed. Since 2006 the Linked Data was put forward as a main component for achieving the Semantic Web vision. In principle, Linked Data concepts and technologies have evolved to play a significant role in the Semantic Web vision for moving the document-oriented web into a web of Interlinked Data. Currently, the Linked Data term is used to refer to a set of best practices for publishing and connecting structured data on the web. As a result, recently, knowledge graphs have been gaining increasing momentum as a new concept of connecting and linking massive amounts of data from different sources. For example, big Internet giants (e.g., Google, Facebook, Microsoft) have been building their own knowledge graphs. It is expected that various applications in several

© Springer International Publishing AG 2018
S. Sakr et al., *Linked Data*, https://doi.org/10.1007/978-3-319-73515-3_9

application domain will be introduced from academic and industrial research that would further spur the development of new methods and technologies to capitalize the massively growing amounts of data and information in the World Wide Web.

In practice, with the increasing adoption rate of Linked Data for data integration across information spaces, the quest for efficiency and scalability in processing RDF data has begun since few data collections of (open) Linked Data Cloud with a dozen millions of triples published. While there have been a lot of achievements in storing, querying, and reasoning over RDF data (billions of triples in one processing box or trillions of triples are made possible so far), the hunger for larger data collections and more complicated data integration and processing pipelines has just begun. Therefore, we are witnessing new challenges for Linked Data management systems to be conquered in years to come. Before giving the outlook for such challenges, let us conclude the state of the art that we have discussed in previous chapters.

To build an RDF data management system, the simplest approach is using relational databases to store the data, for example, "statement tables" design pattern for storing RDF statements. From first few implementations, it shows that naive ways for using relational database as a blackbox have displayed several shortcomings in terms of achieving the performance and scalability of most use cases or datasets in reality. However, later generations of this approach (e.g., **Virtuoso** and **Oracle Semantic Store**) have significantly improved the performance by designing more complicated table layouts associated with tailored indexing structures or even stored functions. Along with such strategies, alternative storage structures such as index permutations, property tables, vertical partitioning, graph-based storage, and binary storage have been proposed (Chap. 3). Among them, index permutations is pretty much the same with traditional statement tables but focusing on building faster access pattern by exhaustively indexing all possible patterns. The further modifications are exploiting data distribution of RDF graphs to partition the data in favor of collocating data items that retrieved together a query. Property tables and vertical partitioning are two approaches of this kind. Moving further way from traditional relational database design, graph-based storage and binary storage provide completely different storage structures with different focuses. Graph-based systems like **gStore** or **TurboHOM++** exploit the graph structure to build data structures that favor the graph exploration queries, for example, subgraph matching. On the other hand, binary systems like **TripleBit** and **BitMat** exploit the fast bitwise and compact bit/byte representations to be able to fit as much data into the main memory to achieve better performance and scale a bit better to a certain dataset size. In the systems developed based on such approaches, the storage and query processing of RDF datasets are managed on a single node, they remain limited by the computational power and memory capacities of a single machine. Therefore scaling the systems vertically in terms of adding more processing cores and adding more memory will soon hit its upper limits.

The distributed processing infrastructure has been exploited to remedy the limitations of single node processing. In particular, with the potential of a high degree of parallelism, a distributed system can satisfy the performance demands of complex SPARQL queries on very large RDF collections. Along this line, several distributed RDF processing systems based on popular distributed processing platforms such as Hadoop and Spark have been developed. Such systems partition a large RDF data collection among several processing nodes which then query a subgroup of partitions in parallel. While such a system offers massive parallel processing capabilities with larger aggregated memory size, it might incur significant intermediate data shuffling when answering complex SPARQL queries that span multiple disjoint partitions (Chap. 4). To overcome the communication overhead in the distributed setting, several systems of this kind leverage the generic parallel processing platform such as NoSQL databases, Hadoop, and Spark which provide facilities for partitioning data and coordinating the processing among distributed nodes. However, the generic parallel processing platforms have their own shortcomings which motivated several systems such as Triad, Trinity.RDF, DiploCloud, and DREAM to build their own underlying infrastructure to serve their requirements. On top of that, federated query processing which enables answering RDF queries over multiple uncoordinated SPARQL endpoints also provides a scaling option in a loosely coupled infrastructure. However, these techniques introduce much more communication overhead in comparison to its counterparts which can coordinate in a more controlled setting.

In practice, processing stream data in RDF model requires new data and query model. In addition, the stream data poses a new challenge in extending RDF data model to capture temporal properties of the data (Chap. 5). As the data model is different, the query paradigm for continuous queries and complex event processing over stream data requires a new query language design on top of SPARQL query grammar. Moreover, the simple extension of RDF processing engine does not deliver the expected performance in terms of high update rate and low query latency. This inspired a new research trend in the Semantic Web community to combine the work on stream processing or complex even processing with RDF query engines. There is quite a good amount of work that deals with the emerging challenges of RDF stream data in the last 10 years such as C-SPARQL, CQELS, SPARQL$_{stream}$, and EP-SPARQL. Such systems show that to meet the performance and scalability demands motivated by use cases such as the Internet of Things and Smart Cities, key research and engineering efforts need to move beyond traditional RDF processing which is read-intensive and pull-based querying.

Along the line with the demand of scaling out, distributed processing paradigm sounds even more appealing for computing-intensive process like reasoning over RDF data (Chap. 6). Reasoning on shared-nothing architecture has been gathering momentum with the rise in popularity of modern big data processing systems (e.g., Hadoop, Spark) and the continuous drop in hardware prices. These approaches overcome the limitations of vertical scaling on single node, that is, querying and reasoning over large knowledge graphs can only be supported by increasing the RAM, CPU capacity, and storage. Some systems can offer some reasoning features, for example, computing materialization, on very large sets with the size of a dozen billions or even trillions of triples. Still, these achievements can only cover simple reasoning profiles such as RDFS or RDF++ which are considered not very complex to parallelize.

Along with developing RDF engines, there is a parallel line of work on proliferation of RDF systems to identify the strong and weak points of these systems.
This line of work has created several RDF benchmarks to verify the advantages,
disadvantages, and limitations of the existing systems and provide the basis for the
development of the next-generation systems of this kind. Each RDF benchmarking
system commonly provides a set of datasets and workload/queries to validate the
key performance indicators to measure how the RDF engines perform. Chapter 7
surveyed principles described in the literature for benchmark development and the
dimensions of an RDF benchmark, namely, query workloads, performance metrics,
and employed datasets or data generators (in the case of synthetic benchmarks).
Based on such principles, there are various RDF benchmarks (real, synthetic, and
benchmark generators) that have been developed to serve several needs of system
developers and users. They provide systematic validation tools for developers and
users to identify the strengths and weaknesses of competing tools and approaches.
Beyond that, the benchmarking systems have encouraged the advancement of
technology by providing both academia and industry with clear targets for performance and functionality. To help the developers and users to choose which
existing benchmarking systems to fit their needs, the chapter gives an analysis on
the advantages and disadvantages of each system to distinguish them based on the
surveyed measuring dimensions.

The workload of processing a query on RDF data is not only dictated by the size
of the RDF collections but also the nature of the query and data itself. For instance,
provenance-driven query poses more computing demand on the data processing
engine due to the complicated structure of provenance data. Therefore, the problems
of dealing with provenance within Linked Data Management Systems have attracted
a significant amount of interest and work in terms of modeling provenance, representing queries, and building efficient processing engines. Chapter 8 presented the
different provenance models developed for the different fragments of the SPARQL
standard language for querying RDF datasets. It covered the different models
for relational provenance which laid the foundation for RDF provenance models
associated with the different fragments of the SPARQL query language. The main
challenges within the area of provenance remain in efficient distributed systems
capable of handling the overhead introduced by the incorporation of provenance
information.

9.2   Outlook

In general, the openness of the web and the continuous increase in numbers of
linked datasets have provided several advantages. On the other hand, these created
several issues that need to be addressed. For example, the majority of RDF storage
and querying systems have mainly focused on efficiently executing conjunctive
SPARQL pattern matching queries. Although such querying constructs represent
the backbone of the SPARQL query language, SPARQL allows for much more

expressive queries including transitive closures, optional clauses, and aggregate queries. Efficiently executing such types of queries over massive RDF datasets is an open challenge that still needs to be addressed. In addition, with the high heterogeneity of available RDF datasets, no single set of design decisions or system architecture will ever represent a clear winner for complex SPARQL workloads [15]. Therefore, RDF management systems will increasingly have to incorporate self-tuning and dynamic data repartitioning capabilities such that they can adapt to changing data characteristics and workload. We believe that these topics will attract significant interest in the near future. Another interesting research avenue revolves around advance data processing features, like in-build data analysis and machine learning functions tailored for RDF data, hypothetical queries, etc. Additionally, the capacity to store, trace, and query provenance information should become a standard feature of any RDF data processing system. Moreover, we believe that hybrid systems that combine slow and fast changing RDF data will attract many researchers.

In general, RDF is less expressive than OWL and reasoning over RDF data using RDFS entailment rules can be an embarrassingly parallel operation. Due to these factors, several RDF reasoners were able to achieve scalable and efficient reasoning. However, there are some challenges to RDF reasoning. Although there are several RDF benchmarks and data generators (see Chap. 7), none of them focus on reasoning performance. They benchmark other operations on RDF data such as querying and instance matching. Reasoning benchmarks can be used to compare the different scalable RDF reasoning systems. The next challenge is the lack of scalable reasoning systems that can work across several different rulesets. The state of the art in this domain (see Chap. 6) focuses on specific rulesets such as RDFS, OWL 2 RL, OWL Horst, and OWL 2 EL. Users working on different Semantic Web languages have to switch between the ruleset-specific scalable reasoning systems. Instead, it would be convenient to have one scalable reasoning system that can take any ruleset as input and generate the necessary algorithms after analyzing the dependency among the rules [281]. The third challenge is the assumption made by several scalable RDF reasoning systems that schema triples are less in number when compared to the instance triples. With the ongoing research efforts in the field of automated knowledge base construction and population, it could be possible to build knowledge graphs with a large number of schema triples. So it is important to revisit this assumption and work on alternate approaches.

The research trend for RDF Stream Data processing has been established as the main track in the Semantic Web community; however, there are several challenges that have been posed by the community. The first type of challenge is dealing with the scalability which is inspired by a lot of new parallel stream processing platforms such as Apache Storm, Spark, and Kafka Streams. The next type of challenge is how to model complex event patterns in conjunction with reasoning features, and how to process them efficiently. This type of challenge is aligned with the promoted line of work in RDF Stream Data processing community, called *Stream Reasoning*, which attracted not only researchers from database and Semantic Web but also Artificial Intelligence (AI) and Knowledge Reasoning (KR). On top of that, current work on building RDF stream processing only focuses on in-memory storage model. One promising research direction in this regard is to study the possibility of designing an efficient continuous query processing engine using a disk-based storage model or a hypoid model.

In practice, despite the many models for provenance that have been developed, there are very few systems that look into the topic of provenance-aware systems. It is important that research addresses query optimization in such systems when provenance is stored along with data. Furthermore, there is no language that can be used to query provenance. This is essential in order to be able to support all the different applications that are based on provenance. In addition, it is still an open challenge to study the data structures that should be implemented to store provenance that can then be efficiently retrieved and processed.

In general, the benchmarks that have been developed over the last years addressed the needs of the research community which focused mostly on Linked Data management. Nevertheless, the last years we have experienced a growing involvement of the industry in the publication of very large and complex datasets in various domains especially in Industry 4.0. It is though essential to develop benchmarks that use real data or at least mimic the characteristics of real datasets from various domains. Second, it is essential to produce workloads that are neither too easy, so the benchmark is not really challenging, nor too difficult, so no system will use it. Third, it is essential that benchmarks are developed using some principles that have been presented in the literature. For instance, it is essential to study the choke points for the different Linked Data Management Systems so that benchmarks are developed with those choke points in mind. Last but not least, it is crucial to develop benchmarks for all the steps of the Linked Data life cycle such that all systems can be tested with state-of-the-art, well designed benchmarks.

References

1. D.J. Abadi, D. Carney, U. Çetintemel, M. Cherniack, C. Convey, S. Lee, M. Stonebraker, N. Tatbul, S. Zdonik, Aurora: a new model and architecture for data stream management. VLDB J. **12**(2), 120–139 (2003)
2. D.J. Abadi, A. Marcus, S.R. Madden, K. Hollenbach, Scalable semantic web data management using vertical partitioning, in *Proceedings of the 33rd International Conference on Very Large Data Bases*, VLDB Endowment (2007), pp. 411–422
3. A. Abele, J.P. McCrae, P. Buitelaar, A. Jentzsch, R. Cyganiak, Linking Open Data cloud diagram 2017 (2017)
4. S. Abiteboul, R. Hull, V. Vianu, *Foundations of Databases* (Addison-Wesley, Reading, 1995)
5. M. Acosta, M.-E. Vidal, T. Lampo, J. Castillo, E. Ruckhaus, ANAPSID: an adaptive query processing engine for SPARQL endpoints, in *The Semantic Web–ISWC* (2011), pp. 18–34
6. J. Agrawal, Y. Diao, D. Gyllstrom, N. Immerman, Efficient pattern matching over event streams, in *Proceedings of the 2008 ACM SIGMOD International Conference on Management of Data, SIGMOD '08* (ACM, New York, 2008), pp. 147–160
7. J.L. Aguirre, K. Eckert, J. Euzenat, A. Ferrara, W.R. van Hage, L. Hollink, C. Meilicke, A. Nikolov, D. Ritze, F. Scharffe, P. Shvaiko, O. Svab-Zamazal, C. Trojahn, E. Jimenez-Ruiz, B. Cuenca Grau, B. Zapilko, Results of the ontology alignment evaluation initiative 2012, in *OM* (2012)
8. Z. Akar, T.G. Halaç, E.E. Ekinci, O. Dikenelli, Querying the web of interlinked datasets using VOID descriptions, in *LDOW*, vol. 937 (2012)
9. T. Akidau, R. Bradshaw, C. Chambers, S. Chernyak, R.J. Fernandez-Moctezuma, R. Lax, S. McVeety, D. Mills, F. Perry, E. Schmidt, S. Whittle, The dataflow model: a practical approach to balancing correctness, latency, and cost in massive-scale, unbounded, out-of-order data processing. Proc. VLDB Endow. **8**(12), 1792–1803 (2015)
10. S. Alexaki, V. Christophides, G. Karvounarakis, D. Plexousakis, On storing voluminous RDF descriptions: the case of web portal catalogs, in *WebDB* (2001), pp. 43–48
11. K. Alexander, M. Hausenblas, Describing linked datasets—on the design and usage of void, the vocabulary of interlinked datasets, in *Linked Data on the Web Workshop (LDOW 09), in Conjunction with 18th International World Wide Web Conference (WWW 09)* (2009)
12. R. Al-Harbi, I. Abdelaziz, P. Kalnis, N. Mamoulis, Y. Ebrahim, M. Sahli, Accelerating SPARQL queries by exploiting hash-based locality and adaptive partitioning. VLDB J. **25**(3), 355–380 (2016)
13. G. Aluc, M. Tamer Özsu, K. Daudjee, O. Hartig, chameleon-db: a workload-aware robust RDF data management system. Technical Report CS-2013-10, University of Waterloo, 2013
14. G. Aluc, O. Hartig, T. Ozsu, K. Daudjee, Diversified stress testing of RDF data management systems, in *ISWC* (2014)

© Springer International Publishing AG 2018
S. Sakr et al., *Linked Data*, https://doi.org/10.1007/978-3-319-73515-3

15. G. Aluç, M. Tamer Özsu, K. Daudjee, Workload matters: why RDF databases need a new design. Proc. VLDB Endow. **7**(10), 837–840 (2014)
16. Y. Amsterdamer, D. Deutch, V. Tannen, On the limitations of provenance for queries with difference, in *TaPP* (2011)
17. Y. Amsterdamer, D. Deutch, V. Tannen, Provenance for aggregate queries, in *PODS* (2011)
18. D. Anicic, P. Fodor, S. Rudolph, R. Stühmer, N. Stojanovic, R. Studer, A rule-based language for complex event processing and reasoning, in *Proceedings of the Fourth International Conference on Web Reasoning and Rule Systems, RR'10* (Springer, Berlin, 2010), pp. 42–57
19. D. Anicic, P. Fodor, S. Rudolph, N. Stojanovic, EP-SPARQL: a unified language for event processing and stream reasoning, in *Proceedings of the 20th International Conference on World wide web, WWW '11* (ACM, New York, 2011), pp. 635–644
20. G. Antoniou, F. van Harmelen, *A Semantic Web Primer* (MIT Press, Cambridge, 2004)
21. A. Aranda-Andújar, F. Bugiotti, J. Camacho-Rodríguez, D. Colazzo, F. Goasdoué, Z. Kaoudi, I. Manolescu, AMADA: web data repositories in the Amazon cloud, in *21st ACM International Conference on Information and Knowledge Management, CIKM'12*, Maui, 29 October–02 November 2012, pp. 2749–2751
22. A. Arasu, S. Babu, J. Widom, The CQL continuous query language: semantic foundations and query execution. VLDB J. **15**(2), 121–142 (2006)
23. S. Araujo, A. de Vries, D. Schwabe, SERIMI results for OAEI 2011, in *OM* (2011)
24. M. Armbrust, R.S. Xin, C. Lian, Y. Huai, D. Liu, J.K. Bradley, X. Meng, T. Kaftan, M.J. Franklin, A. Ghodsi, M. Zaharia, Spark SQL: relational data processing in spark, in *SIGMOD* (2015)
25. M. Atre, J. Srinivasan, J.A. Hendler, Bitmat: a main-memory bit matrix of RDF triples for conjunctive triple pattern queries, in *Proceedings of the Poster and Demonstration Session at the 7th International Semantic Web Conference (ISWC2008)*, Karlsruhe, 28 October 2008
26. S. Auer, J. Demter, M. Martin, J. Lehmann, Lodstats – an extensible framework for high-performance dataset analytics, in *Knowledge Engineering and Knowledge Management* (Springer, Berlin, 2012), pp. 353–362
27. A. Avgoustaki, G. Flouris, I. Fundulaki, D. Plexousakis, Provenance management for evolving RDF datasets, in *The SemanticWeb. Latest Advances and New Domains, ESWC* (2016)
28. A. Avgoustaki, G. Flouris, I. Fundulaki, D. Plexousakis, Provenance management for evolving RDF datasets, in *International Semantic Web Conference* (Springer, Berlin, 2016), pp. 575–592
29. R. Avnur, J.M. Hellerstein, Eddies: continuously adaptive query processing. SIGMOD Rec. **29**(2), 261–272 (2000)
30. F. Baader, U. Sattler, An overview of Tableau algorithms for description logics. Stud. Logica **69**(1), 5–40 (2001)
31. F. Baader, S. Brandt, C. Lutz, Pushing the EL envelope, in *IJCAI-05, Proceedings of the Nineteenth International Joint Conference on Artificial Intelligence*, Edinburgh, 30 July–5 August 2005, ed. by L.P. Kaelbling, A. Saffiotti (AAAI, Menlo Park, 2005), pp. 364–369
32. F. Baader, I. Horrocks, U. Sattler, Description logics, in *Handbook of Knowledge Representation*, Chap. 3, ed. by F. van Harmelen, V. Lifschitz, B. Porter (Elsevier, Amsterdam, 2008), pp. 135–180
33. B. Babcock, S. Babu, M. Datar, R. Motwani, D. Thomas, Operator scheduling in data stream systems. VLDB J. **13**(4), 333–353 (2004)
34. D.F. Barbieri, D. Braga, S. Ceri, M. Grossniklaus, An execution environment for C-SPARQL queries, in *EDBT* (2010), pp. 441–452
35. D.F. Barbieri, D. Braga, S. Ceri, E. Della Valle, M. Grossniklaus, Querying RDF streams with C-SPARQL. SIGMOD Rec. **39**(1), 20–26 (2010)

36. Z. Bar-Yossef, R. Kumar, D. Sivakumar, Reductions in streaming algorithms, with an application to counting triangles in graphs, in *Proceedings of the Thirteenth Annual ACM-SIAM Symposium on Discrete Algorithms, SODA '02* (Society for Industrial and Applied Mathematics, Philadelphia, 2002), pp. 623–632

37. C. Başca, A. Bernstein, Querying a messy web of data with Avalanche. Web Semant. Sci. Serv. Agents World Wide Web **26**, 1–28 (2014)

38. O. Benjelloun, A.D. Sarma, A.Y. Halevy, J. Widom, ULDBs: databases with uncertainty and lineage, in *VLDB* (2006)

39. T. Berners-Lee, Linked data-design issues (2006). https://www.w3.org/DesignIssues/LinkedData.html

40. T. Berners-Lee, J. Hendler, O. Lassila et al., The semantic web. Sci. Am. **284**(5), 28–37 (2001)

41. D. Bhagwat, L. Chiticariu, W.-C. Tan, G. Vijayvargiya, An annotation management system for relational databases. VLDB J. **14**, 373–396 (2005)

42. A. Bifet, G. Holmes, B. Pfahringer, R. Gavaldà, Mining frequent closed graphs on evolving data streams, in *Proceedings of the 17th ACM SIGKDD International Conference on Knowledge Discovery and Data Mining, KDD '11* (ACM, New York, 2011), pp. 591–599

43. O. Biton, S. Cohen-Boulakia, S.B. Davidson, Zoom*userviews: querying relevant provenance in workflow systems, in *Proceedings of the 33rd International Conference on Very Large Data Bases, VLDB '07*, VLDB Endowment (2007), pp. 1366–1369

44. C. Bizer, A. Schultz, The Berlin SPARQL Benchmark. Int. J. Semant. Web Inf. Syst. **5**(2), 1–24 (2009)

45. C. Bizer, T. Heath, T. Berners-Lee, Linked data-the story so far (2009)

46. C. Bizer, A. Jentzsch, R. Cyganiak, State of the LOD cloud. Version 0.3 (September 2011), 1803 (2011)

47. C. Böhm, G. de Melo, F. Naumann, G. Weikum, LINDA: distributed web-of-data-scale entity matching, in *CIKM* (2012)

48. T. Bohme, E. Rahm, XMach-1: a benchmark for XML data management, in *BTW* (2001)

49. A. Bolles, M. Grawunder, J. Jacobi, Streaming SPARQL – extending SPARQL to process data streams, in *ESWC'08* (2008), pp. 448–462

50. P.A. Bonatti, A. Hogan, A. Polleres, L. Sauro, Robust and scalable linked data reasoning incorporating provenance and trust annotations. J. Web Semant. **9**(2), 165–201 (2011)

51. P. Boncz, T. Neumann, O. Erling, TPC-H analyzed: hidden messages and lessons learned from an influential benchmark, in *TPCTC* (2013). Revised Selected Papers

52. P. Bonnet, J. Gehrke, P. Seshadri, Towards sensor database systems, in *Proceedings of the Second International Conference on Mobile Data Management, MDM '01* (Springer, London, 2001), pp. 3–14

53. M.A. Bornea, J. Dolby, A. Kementsietsidis, K. Srinivas, P. Dantressangle, O. Udrea, B. Bhattacharjee, Building an efficient RDF store over a relational database, in *Proceedings of the 2013 International Conference on Management of Data* (ACM, New York, 2013), pp. 121–132

54. S. Bressan, M.L. Lee, Y.G. Li, Z. Lacroix, U. Nambiar, XML management system benchmarks, in *XML Data Management: Native XML and XML-Enabled Database Systems* (Addison Wesley, Boston, 2003)

55. D. Brickley, R.V. Guha, RDF Schema 1.1. https://www.w3.org/TR/rdf-schema/, February 2014. W3C Recommendation

56. M. Bröcheler, A. Pugliese, V.S. Subrahmanian, DOGMA: a disk-oriented graph matching algorithm for RDF databases, in *The Semantic Web-ISWC 2009* (Springer, Heidelberg, 2009), pp. 97–113

57. A.Z. Broder, M. Charikar, A.M. Frieze, M. Mitzenmacher, Min-wise independent permutations, in *Proceedings of the Thirtieth Annual ACM Symposium on Theory of Computing* (ACM, New York, 1998), pp. 327–336

58. J. Broekstra, A. Kampman, F. van Harmelen, Sesame: a generic architecture for storing and querying RDF and RDF schema, in *The Semantic Web - ISWC 2002, First International*

Semantic Web Conference, Proceedings, Sardinia, 9–12 June 2002 (Springer, Berlin, 2002), pp. 54–68

59. F. Bry, M. Eckert, Rules for making sense of events: design issues for high-level event query and reasoning languages, in *AI Meets Business Rules and Process Management, Proceedings of AAAI 2008 Spring Symposium*, Stanford University/Palo Alto, 26 March 2008 (AAAI, Menlo Park, 2008)

60. P. Buneman, S. Khanna, W.C. Tan, Why and where: a characterization of data provenance, in *ICDT* (2001)

61. P. Buneman, A. Chapman, J. Cheney, Provenance management in curated databases, in *ACM SIGMOD* (2006)

62. P. Buneman, J. Cheney, S. Vansummeren, On the expressiveness of implicit provenance in query and update languages, in *ICDT* (2007)

63. J.-P. Calbimonte, O. Corcho, A.J.G. Gray, Enabling ontology-based access to streaming data sources, in *Proceedings of the 9th International Semantic Web Conference on The semantic web, ISWC'10*, vol. Part I (Springer, Berlin, 2010), pp. 96–111

64. D. Calvanese, G. Giacomo, D. Lembo, M. Lenzerini, R. Rosati, Tractable reasoning and efficient query answering in description logics: the *DL-lite* family. J. Autom. Reason. **39**(3), 385–429 (2007)

65. D. Carney, U. Çetintemel, A. Rasin, S. Zdonik, M. Cherniack, M. Stonebraker, Operator scheduling in a data stream manager, in *Proceedings of the 29th International Conference on Very Large Data Bases, VLDB '03*, VLDB Endowment, vol. 29 (2003), pp. 838–849

66. J.J. Carroll, C. Bizer, P. Hayes, P. Stickler, Named graphs, provenance and trust, in *Proceedings of the 14th International Conference on World Wide Web* (ACM, New York, 2005), pp. 613–622

67. J.J. Carroll, C. Bizer, P. Hayes, P. Stickler, Named graphs. J. Web Semant. **3**, 247–267 (2005)

68. S. Castano, A. Ferrara, S. Montanelli, G. Racca, Semantic information interoperability in open networked systems, in *ICSNW* (2004)

69. R. Cattell, Scalable SQL and NoSQL data stores. ACM SIGMOD Rec. **39**(4), 12–27 (2011)

70. S. Chandrasekaran, M. Franklin, Remembrance of streams past: overload-sensitive management of archived streams, in *Proceedings of the Thirtieth International Conference on Very Large Data Bases, VLDB '04*, vol. 30, VLDB Endowment (2004), pp. 348–359

71. S. Chandrasekaran, O. Cooper, A. Deshpande, M.J. Franklin, J.M. Hellerstein, W. Hong, S. Krishnamurthy, S. Madden, V. Raman, F. Reiss, M.A. Shah, TelegraphCQ: continuous dataflow processing for an uncertain world, in *First Biennial Conference on Innovative Data Systems Research (CIDR'03)* (2003)

72. F. Chang, J. Dean, S. Ghemawat, W.C. Hsieh, D.A. Wallach, M. Burrows, T. Chandra, A. Fikes, R.E. Gruber, Bigtable: a distributed storage system for structured data. ACM Trans. Comput. Syst. **26**(2), 4:1–4:26 (2008)

73. A. Charalambidis, A. Troumpoukis, S. Konstantopoulos, SemaGrow: optimizing federated SPARQL queries, in *Proceedings of the 11th International Conference on Semantic Systems* (ACM, New York, 2015), pp. 121–128

74. S. Chaudhuri, G. Weikum, Rethinking database system architecture: towards a self-tuning RISC-style database system, in *Proceedings of 26th International Conference on Very Large Data Bases (VLDB)* (2000), pp. 1–10

75. M. Cheatham, Z. Dragisic, J. Euzenat, D. Faria, A. Ferrara, G. Flouris, I. Fundulaki, R. Granada, V. Ivanova, E. Jimenez-Ruiz, P. Lambrix, S. Montanelli, C. Pesquita, T. Saveta, P. Shvaiko, A. Solimando, C. Trojahn, O. Zamazal, Results of the ontology alignment evaluation initiative 2015, in *OM* (2015)

76. A. Chebotko, S. Lu, X. Fei, F. Fotouhi, RDFProv: a relational RDF store for querying and managing scientific workflow provenance. Data Knowl. Eng. **69**(8), 836–865 (2010)

77. J. Chen, D.J. DeWitt, F. Tian, Y. Wang, NiagaraCQ: a scalable continuous query system for Internet databases. SIGMOD Rec. **29**(2), 379–390 (2000)

78. X. Chen, H. Chen, N. Zhang, S. Zhang, SparkRDF: elastic discreted RDF graph processing engine with distributed memory, in *Proceedings of the ISWC 2014 Posters and Demonstra-

tions Track a track within the 13th International Semantic Web Conference, ISWC, Riva del Garda, 21 October 2014, pp. 261–264

79. X. Chen, H. Chen, N. Zhang, S. Zhang, SparkRDF: elastic discreted RDF graph processing engine with distributed memory, in *IEEE/WIC/ACM International Conference on Web Intelligence and Intelligent Agent Technology, WI-IAT,* vol. I, Singapore, 6–9 December 2015, pp. 292–300

80. J. Cheney, S. Chong, N. Foster, M. Seltzer, S. Vansummeren, Provenance: a future history, in *ACM SIGPLAN OOPSLA-09* (2009)

81. J. Cheney, L. Chiticariu, W.-C. Tan, *Provenance in Databases: Why, How, and Where* (Now Publishers Inc., Hanover, 2009)

82. L. Cheng, S. Kotoulas, Scale-out processing of large RDF datasets. IEEE Trans. Big Data **1**(4), 138–150 (2015)

83. E.I. Chong, S. Das, G. Eadon, J. Srinivasan, An efficient SQL-based RDF querying scheme, in *Proceedings of the 31st International Conference on Very Large Data Bases,* VLDB Endowment (2005), pp. 1216–1227

84. P. Ciccarese, E. Wu, G. Wong, M. Ocana, J. Kinoshita, A. Ruttenberg, T. Clark, The swan biomedical discourse ontology. J. Biomed. Inform. **41**(5), 739–751 (2008)

85. P. Ciccarese, S. Soiland-Reyes, K. Belhajjame, A.J.G. Gray, C. Goble, T. Clark, Pav ontology: provenance, authoring and versioning. J. Biomed. Semant. **4**(1), 1–22 (2013)

86. D. Collarana, C. Lange, S. Auer, FuhSen: a platform for federated, RDF-based hybrid search, in *Proceedings of the 25th International Conference Companion on World Wide Web* (International World Wide Web Conferences Steering Committee, Geneva, 2016), pp. 171–174

87. G.P. Copeland, S. Khoshafian, A decomposition storage model, in *Proceedings of the ACM SIGMOD International Conference on Management of Data* (1985), pp. 268–279

88. C. Cranor, T. Johnson, O. Spataschek, V. Shkapenyuk, Gigascope: a stream database for network applications, in *Proceedings of the 2003 ACM SIGMOD International Conference on Management of Data, SIGMOD '03* (ACM, New York, 2003), pp. 647–651

89. I.F. Cruz, C. Stroe, F. Caimi, A. Fabiani, C. Pesquita, F.M. Couto, M. Palmonari, Using AgreementMaker to align ontologies for OAEI 2011, in *OM* (2011)

90. Y. Cui, J. Widom, Lineage tracing for general data warehouse transformations, in *VLDB* (2001)

91. P.P. da Silva, D.L. McGuinness, R. Fikes, A proof markup language for semantic web services. Inf. Syst. **31**(4), 381–395 (2006)

92. C.V. Damásio, A. Analyti, G. Antoniou, Provenance for SPARQL queries, in *Proceedings of the 11th International Conference on The Semantic Web, ISWC'12,* vol. Part I (Springer, Berlin, 2012), pp. 625–640

93. A. Das Sarma, S. Gollapudi, R. Panigrahy, Estimating pagerank on graph streams, in *Proceedings of the Twenty-Seventh ACM SIGMOD-SIGACT-SIGART Symposium on Principles of Database Systems, PODS '08* (ACM, New York, 2008), pp. 69–78

94. E. Daskalaki, D. Plexousakis, OtO matching system: a multi-strategy approach to instance matching, in *CAiSE* (2012)

95. J. David, J. Euzenat, F. Scharffe, C. Trojahn, The alignment api 4.0. Semant. Web J. **2**(1), 3–10 (2011)

96. DBpedia: Towards a Public Data Infrastructure for a Large, Multilingual, Semantic Knowledge Graph. http://wiki.dbpedia.org/

97. J. Dean, S. Ghemawa, MapReduce: simplified data processing on large clusters, in *OSDI* (2004)

98. D. Dell'Aglio, M. Dao-Tran, J.-P. Calbimonte, D. Le Phuoc, E. Della Valle, A query model to capture event pattern matching in RDF stream processing query languages, in *20th International Conference on Knowledge Engineering and Knowledge Management, EKAW 2016,* vol. 10024 (Springer, New York, 2016), pp. 145–162

99. A. Deshpande, Z. Ives, V. Raman et al., Adaptive query processing. Found. Trends Databases **1**(1), 1–140 (2007)

100. L. Ding, Y. Peng, P.P. da Silva, D.L. McGuinness, Tracking RDF graph provenance using RDF molecules, in *International Semantic Web Conference* (2005)

101. R. Dividino, S. Sizov, S. Staab, B. Schueler, Querying for provenance, trust, uncertainty and other meta knowledge in RDF. J. Web Semant. **7**(3), 204–219 (2009)

102. K.M. Dixit, Overview of the SPEC Benchmarks, in *The Benchmark Handbook for Database and Transaction Systems*, 2nd edn. (Morgan Kaufmann, San Francisco, 1993)

103. B. Djahandideh, F. Goasdoué, Z. Kaoudi, I. Manolescu, J.-A. Quiané-Ruiz, S. Zampetakis, Cliquesquare in action: flat plans for massively parallel RDF queries, in *31st IEEE International Conference on Data Engineering, ICDE*, Seoul, 13–17 April 2015, pp. 1432–1435

104. X. Dong, E. Gabrilovich, G. Heitz, W. Horn, N. Lao, K. Murphy, T. Strohmann, S. Sun, W. Zhang, Knowledge vault: a web-scale approach to probabilistic knowledge fusion, in *The 20th ACM SIGKDD International Conference on Knowledge Discovery and Data Mining, KDD '14*, 24–27 August 2014, ed. by S.A. Macskassy, C. Perlich, J. Leskovec, W. Wang, R. Ghani (ACM, New York, 2014), pp. 601–610

105. F. Douglis, J. Palmer, E.S. Richards, D. Tao, W.H. Tetzlaff, J.M. Tracey, J. Yin, Position: short object lifetimes require a delete-optimized storage system, in *Proceedings of the 11th Workshop on ACM SIGOPS European Workshop, EW 11* (ACM, New York, 2004)

106. S. Duan, A. Kementsietsidis, K. Srinivas, O. Udrea, Apples and oranges: a comparison of RDF benchmarks and real RDF datasets, in *SIGMOD* (2011)

107. Dublin Core Metadata Initiative. http://dublincore.org/

108. M. Eckert, F. Bry, S. Brodt, O. Poppe, S. Hausmann, A CEP babelfish: languages for complex event processing and querying surveyed, in *Reasoning in Event-Based Distributed Systems*, ed. by S. Helmer, A. Poulovassilis, F. Xhafa. Studies in Computational Intelligence, vol. 347 (Springer, Berlin, 2011), pp. 47–70

109. M. Eckert, F. Bry, S. Brodt, O. Poppe, S. Hausmann, Two semantics for cep, no double talk: complex event relational algebra (cera) and its application to xchange^{EQ}, in *Reasoning in Event-Based Distributed Systems*, ed. by S. Helmer, A. Poulovassilis, F. Xhafa. Studies in Computational Intelligence, vol. 347 (Springer, Berlin, 2011), pp. 71–97

110. B. Elliott, E. Cheng, C. Thomas-Ogbuji, Z.M. Ozsoyoglu, A complete translation from SPARQL into efficient SQL, in *IDEAS* (2009)

111. A.K. Elmagarmid, P. Ipeirotis, V. Verykios, Duplicate record detection: a survey, in *IEEE TKDE* (2007)

112. O. Erling, I. Mikhailov, RDF support in the virtuoso DBMS, in *Networked Knowledge-Networked Media* (Springer, Berlin, 2009), pp. 7–24

113. J. Euzenat, A. Ferrara, L. Hollink, A. Isaac, C. Joslyn, V. Malaise, C. Meilicken, A. Nikolov, J. Pane, M. Sabou, F. Scharffe, P. Shvaiko, V.S.H. Stuckenschmidt, O. Svab-Zamazal, V. Svatek, C. Trojahn, G. Vouros, S. Wang, Results of the ontology alignment evaluation initiative 2009, in *OM* (2009)

114. J. Euzenat, A. Ferrara, C. Meilicke, J. Pane, F. Schare, P. Shvaiko, H. Stuckenschmidt, O. Svab-Zamazal, V. Svatek, C. Trojahn, Results of the ontology alignment evaluation initiative 2010, in *OM* (2010)

115. J. Euzenat, A. Ferrara, W.R. van Hage, L. Hollink, C. Meilicke, A. Nikolov, F. Scharffe, P. Shvaiko, H. Stuckenschmidt, O. Svab-Zamazal, C. Trojahn, Final results of the ontology alignment evaluation initiative 2011, in *OM* (2011)

116. Febrl project. http://sourceforge.net/projects/febrl/

117. J. Feng, X. Zhang, Z. Feng, MapSQ: a MapReduce-based framework for SPARQL queries on GPU. Preprint (2017). arXiv:1702.03484

118. A. Ferrara, D. Lorusso, S. Montanelli, G. Varese, Towards a benchmark for instance matching, in *OM* (2008)

119. A. Ferrara, S. Montanelli, J. Noessner, H. Stuckenschmidt, Benchmarking matching applications on the semantic web, in *ESWC* (2011)

120. G.H.L. Fletcher, P.W. Beck, Scalable indexing of RDF graphs for efficient join processing, in *Proceedings of the 18th ACM Conference on Information and Knowledge Management* (ACM, New York, 2009), pp. 1513–1516

121. G. Flouris, I. Fundulaki, P. Pediaditis, Y. Theoharis, V. Christophides, Coloring RDF triples to capture provenance, in *Proceedings of the 8th International Semantic Web Conference, ISWC '09* (Springer, Berlin, 2009), pp. 196–212

122. G. Flouris, Y. Roussakis, M. Poveda-Villalon, P.N. Mendes, I. Fundulaki, Using provenance for quality assessment and repair in linked open data, in *EvoDyn* (2012)

123. Fodor and Zagat's Restaurant Guide. http://userweb.cs.utexas.edu/users/ml/riddle/data.html

124. N. Folkert, A. Gupta, A. Witkowski, S. Subramanian, S. Bellamkonda, S. Shankar, T. Bozkaya, L. Sheng, Optimizing refresh of a set of materialized views, in *Proceedings of the 31st International Conference on Very Large Data Bases, VLDB '05*, VLDB Endowment (2005), pp. 1043–1054

125. Freebase. http://www.freebase.com/base/fbontology

126. J. Freire, D. Koop, E. Santos, C.T. Silva, Provenance for computational tasks: a survey. Comput. Sci. Eng. **10**(3), 11–21 (2008)

127. L. Galárraga, K. Hose, R. Schenkel, Partout: a distributed engine for efficient RDF processing, in *23rd International World Wide Web Conference, WWW '14*, Companion Volume, Seoul, 7–11 April 2014, pp. 267–268

128. I. Galpin, C.Y.A. Brenninkmeijer, F. Jabeen, A.A.A. Fernandes, N.W. Paton, An architecture for query optimization in sensor networks, in *Proceedings of the 2008 IEEE 24th International Conference on Data Engineering, ICDE '08* (IEEE Computer Society, Washington, 2008), pp. 1439–1441

129. S. Gao, C. Zaniolo, Provenance management in databases under schema evolution, in *TaPP* (2012)

130. F. Geerts, A. Poggi, On database query languages for k-relations. J. Appl. Log. **8**(2), 173–185 (2010)

131. F. Geerts, A. Kementsietsidis, D. Milano, MONDRIAN: annotating and querying databases through colors and blocks, in *ICDE* (2006)

132. F. Geerts, G. Karvounarakis, V. Christophides, I. Fundulaki, Algebraic structures for capturing the provenance of SPARQL queries, in *Proceedings of the 16th International Conference on Database Theory, ICDT '13* (ACM, New York, 2013), pp. 153–164

133. GeoNames. http://www.geonames.org/

134. T.M. Ghanem, A.K. Elmagarmid, P. Larson, W.G. Aref, Supporting views in data stream management systems. ACM Trans. Database Syst. **35**(1), 1:1–1:47 (2008)

135. Y. Gil, S. Miles, K. Belhajjame, H. Deus, D. Garijo, G. Klyne, P. Missier, S. Soiland-Reyes, S. Zednik (eds.), Prov model primer. W3C Working Group Note NOTE-prov-primer-20130430, World Wide Web Consortium, April 2013

136. B. Glavic, G. Alonso, Perm: processing provenance and data on the same data model through query rewriting, in *ICDE* (2009)

137. B. Glavic, G. Alonso, The perm provenance management system in action, in *Proceedings of the 2009 ACM SIGMOD International Conference on Management of Data, SIGMOD '09* (ACM, New York, 2009), pp. 1055–1058

138. B. Glimm, I. Horrocks, B. Motik, G. Stoilos, Z. Wang, HermiT: an OWL 2 reasoner. J. Autom. Reason. **53**(3), 245–269 (2014)

139. F. Goasdoué, Z. Kaoudi, I. Manolescu, J.-A. Quiané-Ruiz, S. Zampetakis, Cliquesquare: flat plans for massively parallel RDF queries, in *31st IEEE International Conference on Data Engineering, ICDE*, Seoul, 13–17 April 2015, pp. 771–782

140. A. Gómez-Pérez, M. Fernández-López, O. Corcho, *Ontological Engineering: With Examples from the Areas of Knowledge Management, e-Commerce and the Semantic Web (Advanced Information and Knowledge Processing)* (Springer, Secaucus, 2007)

141. J.E. Gonzalez, R.S. Xin, A. Dave, D. Crankshaw, M.J. Franklin, I. Stoica, GraphX: graph processing in a distributed dataflow framework, in *OSDI* (2014)

142. E.L. Goodman, D. Grunwald, Using vertex-centric programming platforms to implement SPARQL queries on large graphs, in *Proceedings of the 4th Workshop on Irregular Applications: Architectures and Algorithms, IA3 '14* (IEEE Press, Piscataway, 2014), pp. 25–32

143. E.L. Goodman, E. Jimenez, D. Mizell, S. al Saffar, B. Adolf, D. Haglin, High-performance computing applied to semantic databases, in *Proceedings of the 8th Extended Semantic Web Conference on The Semantic Web: Research and Applications (ESWC'11), Volume Part II* (Springer, Berlin, 2011), pp. 31–45

144. O. Görlitz, S. Staab, Splendid: SPARQL endpoint federation exploiting void descriptions, in *Proceedings of the Second International Conference on Consuming Linked Data*, vol. 782 (2011), pp. 13–24. CEUR-WS.org

145. C. Goutte, E. Gaussier, A probabilistic interpretation of precision, recall, and F-score, with implication for evaluation, in *ECIR* (2005)

146. B.C. Grau, Z. Dragisic, K. Eckert, J. Euzenat, A. Ferrara, R. Granada, V. Ivanova, E. Jimenez-Ruiz, A.O. Kempf, P. Lambrix, A. Nikolov, H. Paulheim, D. Ritze, F. Schare, P. Shvaiko, C. Trojahn, O. Zamazal, Results of the ontology alignment evaluation initiative 2013, in *OM* (2013)

147. D. Graux, L. Jachiet, P. Genevès, N. Layaïda, SPARQLGX: efficient distributed evaluation of SPARQL with Apache Spark, in *International Semantic Web Conference* (Springer, Berlin, 2016), pp. 80–87

148. J. Gray (ed.), *The Benchmark Handbook for Database and Transaction Systems*, 2nd edn. (Morgan Kaufmann, San Francisco, 1993)

149. A.J.G. Gray, Dataset descriptions for linked data systems. IEEE Internet Comput. **18**(4), 66–69 (2014)

150. T.J. Green, G. Karvounarakis, V. Tannen, Provenance semirings, in *PODS* (2007)

151. T.J. Green, G. Karvounarakis, Z.G. Ives, V. Tannen, Update exchange with mappings and provenance, in *VLDB* (2007)

152. B.N. Grosof, I. Horrocks, R. Volz, S. Decker, Description logic programs: combining logic programs with description logic, in *Proceedings of the 12th International Conference on World Wide Web, WWW '03*, ed. by G. Hencsey, B. White, Y.R. Chen, L. Kovács, S. Lawrence (ACM, New York, 2003), pp. 48–57

153. P. Groth, L. Moreau (eds.), PROV-overview. An overview of the PROV family of documents, W3C Working Group Note NOTE-prov-overview-20130430, World Wide Web Consortium, April 2013

154. P. Groth, A. Gibson, J. Velterop, The anatomy of a nanopublication. Inf. Serv. Use **30**(1–2), 51–56 (2010)

155. R. Gu, S. Wang, F. Wang, C. Yuan, Y. Huang, Cichlid: efficient large scale RDFS/OWL reasoning with spark, in *Proceedings of the 2015 IEEE International Parallel and Distributed Processing Symposium, IPDPS '15* (IEEE Computer Society, Washington, 2015), pp. 700–709

156. R.V. Guha, D. Brickley, S. MacBeth, Schema.Org: evolution of structured data on the web. Queue **13**(9), 10:10–10:37 (2015)

157. Y. Guo, Z. Pan, J. Heflin, LUBM: a benchmark for OWL knowledge base systems. J. Web Semant. **3**(2–3), 158–182 (2005)

158. A. Gupta, I.S. Mumick, Maintenance of materialized views: problems, techniques, and applications, in *Materialized Views* (MIT Press, Cambridge, 1999), pp. 145–157

159. A. Gupta, I.S. Mumick, V.S. Subrahmanian, Maintaining views incrementally. ACM SIG-MOD Rec. **22**(2), 157–166 (1993)

160. R. Gupta, A.Y. Halevy, X. Wang, S.E. Whang, F. Wu, Biperpedia: an ontology for search applications, in *Proceedings of the 40th International Conference on Very Large Data Bases (PVLDB)*, vol. 7 (2014), pp. 505–516

161. S. Gurajada, S. Seufert, I. Miliaraki, M. Theobald, Triad: a distributed shared-nothing RDF engine based on asynchronous message passing, in *International Conference on Management of Data, SIGMOD*, Snowbird, 22–27 June 2014, pp. 289–300

162. C. Gutierrez, C.A. Hurtado, A. Vaisman, Introducing time into RDF. IEEE Trans. Knowl. Data Eng. **19**, 207–218 (2007)

163. L. Haas, D. Kossmann, E. Wimmers, J. Yang, Optimizing queries across diverse data sources (1997). http://ilpubs.stanford.edu:8090/262/

164. H. Halpin, J. Cheney, Dynamic provenance for SPARQL updates, in *The Semantic Web – ISWC 2014*, ed. by P. Mika, T. Tudorache, A. Bernstein, C. Welty, C. Knoblock, D. Vrandecic, P. Groth, N. Noy, K. Janowicz, C. Goble. Lecture Notes in Computer Science, vol. 8796 (Springer International Publishing, Cham, 2014), pp. 425–440

165. M. Hammoud, D.A. Rabbou, R. Nouri, S.-M.-R. Beheshti, S. Sakr, DREAM: distributed RDF engine with adaptive query planner and minimal communication. Proc. VLDB Endow. **8**(6), 654–665 (2015)

166. R. Harbi, I. Abdelaziz, P. Kalnis, N. Mamoulis, Evaluating SPARQL queries on massive RDF datasets. Proc. VLDB Endow. **8**(12), 1848–1851 (2015)

167. S. Harris, N. Gibbins, 3store: efficient bulk RDF storage, in *PSSS1 – Practical and Scalable Semantic Systems, Proceedings of the First International Workshop on Practical and Scalable Semantic Systems*, Sanibel Island, 20 October 2003. CEUR-WS.org

168. S. Harris, N. Lamb, N. Shadbolt, 4store: the design and implementation of a clustered RDF store, in *5th International Workshop on Scalable Semantic Web Knowledge Base Systems (SSWS2009)* (2009), pp. 94–109

169. A. Harth, S. Decker, Optimized index structures for querying RDF from the Web, in *Proceedings of the Third Latin American Web Congress (LA-WEB)* (2005), pp. 71–80

170. O. Hartig, Provenance information in the web of data, in *LDOW* (2009)

171. O. Hartig, Querying trust in RDF data with tSPARQL, in *Proceedings of the 6th European Semantic Web Conference on The Semantic Web: Research and Applications, ESWC*, Heraklion (Springer, Berlin, 2009), pp. 5–20

172. O. Hartig, R. Heese, The SPARQL query graph model for query optimization, in *ESWC'07* (Springer, Berlin, 2007), pp. 564–578

173. O. Hartig, J. Zhao, Publishing and consuming provenance metadata on the web of linked data, in *Provenance and Annotation of Data and Processes* (Springer, Berlin, 2010), pp. 78–90

174. A. Hasan, M. Hammoud, R. Nouri, S. Sakr, DREAM in action: a distributed and adaptive RDF system on the cloud, in *Proceedings of the 25th International Conference on World Wide Web, WWW*, Companion Volume, Montreal, 11–15 April 2016, pp. 191–194

175. A. Hasnain, S. Decker, H. Deus, Cataloguing and linking life sciences LOD cloud. *Research Day 2013 Schedule* (2012), p. 41

176. A. Hasnain, S.S. e Zainab, M.R. Kamdar, Q. Mehmood, C.N. Warren Jr., Q.A. Fatimah, H.F. Deus, M. Mehdi, S. Decker, A roadmap for navigating the life sciences linked open data cloud, in *Joint International Semantic Technology Conference* (Springer, Berlin, 2014), pp. 97–112

177. O. Hassanzadeh, R. Xin, R.J. Miller, A. Kementsietsidis, L. Lim, M. Wang, Linkage query writer. Proc. VLDB Endow. **2**(2), 1590–1593 (2009)

178. P. Hayes, RDF Semantics. World Wide Web Consortium, Recommendation REC-rdf-mt-20040210 (2004)

179. P. Hayes, B. McBride, RDF semantics. W3C Recommendation, February 2004

180. T. Heath, C. Bizer, Linked Data: Evolving the Web into a Global Data Space, in *Synthesis Lectures on the Semantic Web: Theory and Technology*, 1st edn. (Morgan and Claypool, San Rafael, 2011)

181. N. Heino, J.Z. Pan, RDFS reasoning on massively parallel hardware, in *Proceedings of the 11th International Conference on The Semantic Web (ISWC'12), Volume Part I* (Springer, Berlin, 2012), pp. 133–148

182. M.A. Hernandez, S.J. Stolfo, The merge/purge problem for large databases. SIGMOD Rec. **24**(2) (1995)

183. P. Hitzler, M. Krötzsch, B. Parsia, P.F. Patel-Schneider, S. Rudolph (eds.), *OWL 2 Web Ontology Language: Primer*. W3C Recommendation, 27 October 2009. Available at http://www.w3.org/TR/owl2-primer/

184. P. Hitzler, M. Krötzsch, S. Rudolph, *Foundations of Semantic Web Technologies* (Chapman & Hall/CRC, Boca Raton, 2010)

185. J. Hoeksema, S. Kotoulas, High-performance distributed stream reasoning using S4, in *Proceedings of the 1st International Workshop on Ordering and Reasoning* (2011)

186. J. Hoffart, F.M. Suchanek, K. Berberich, G. Weikum, Yago2: a spatially and temporally enhanced knowledge base from wikipedia. Artif. Intell. **194**, 28–61 (2013). Artificial Intelligence, Wikipedia and Semi-structured Resources

187. A. Hogan, J.Z. Pan, A. Polleres, S. Decker, SAOR: template rule optimisations for distributed reasoning over 1 billion linked data triples, in *Proceedings of the 9th International Semantic Web Conference on The Semantic Web, ISWC'10, Volume Part I* (Springer, Berlin, 2010), pp. 337–353

188. W. Hong, M. Stonebraker, Optimization of parallel query execution plans in XPRS. Distrib. Parallel Databases **1**(1), 9–32 (1993)

189. K. Hose, R. Schenkel, WARP: workload-aware replication and partitioning for RDF, in *DESWEB* (2013)

190. W. Hu, J. Chen, C. Cheng, Y. Qu, Objectcoref & falcon-ao: results for oaei 2010, in *OM* (2010)

191. J. Huang, D.J. Abadi, K. Ren, Scalable SPARQL querying of large RDF graphs. Proc. VLDB Endow. **4**(11), 1123–1134 (2011)

192. K. Huppler, The art of building a good benchmark, in *TPCTC* (2009)

193. V. Ingalalli, D. Ienco, P. Poncelet, S. Villata, Querying RDF data using a multigraph-based approach, in *Proceedings of the 19th International Conference on Extending Database Technology, EDBT* (2016), pp. 245–256

194. E. Ioannou, N. Rassadko, Y. Velegrakis, On generating benchmark data for entity matching. J. Data Semant. **2**(1), 37–56 (2013)

195. R. Isele, C. Bizer, Learning expressive linkage rules using genetic programming. Proc. VLDB Endow. **5**(11), 1638–1649 (2012)

196. R. Isele, C. Bizer, Active learning of expressive linkage rules using genetic programming. J. Web Semant. **23**, 2–15 (2013)

197. M. Janik, K. Kochut, Brahms: a workbench rdf store and high performance memory system for semantic association discovery, in *International Semantic Web Conference* (Springer, Berlin, 2005), pp. 431–445

198. Y.R. Jean-Mary, E.P. Shironoshita, M.R. Kabuka, ASMOV: results for OAEI 2009, in *OM* (2009)

199. Y.R. Jean-Mary, E.P. Shironoshita, M.R. Kabuka, ASMOV: results for OAEI 2010 Proceedings 5th ISWC Workshop on Ontology Matching, in *OM* (2010)

200. Q. Jiang, S. Chakravarthy, Queueing analysis of relational operators for continuous data streams, in *Proceedings of the Twelfth International Conference on Information and Knowledge Management, CIKM '03* (ACM, New York, 2003), pp. 271–278

201. Q. Jiang, S. Chakravarthy, H. Williams, L. MacKinnon, *Scheduling Strategies for Processing Continuous Queries over Streams* (Springer, Berlin, 2004), pp. 16–30

202. E. Jimenez-Ruiz, B. Cuenca Grau, I. Horrocks, LogMap and LogMapLt results for OAEI 2012, in *OM* (2012)

203. E. Jimenez-Ruiz, B. Cuenca Grau, I. Horrocks, LogMap and LogMapLt results for OAEI 2013, in *OM* (2013)

204. E. Jimenez-Ruiz, B. Cuenca Grau, W. Xia, A. Solimando, X. Chen, V. Cross, Y. Gong, S. Zhang, A. Chennai-Thiagarajan, LogMap family results for OAEI 2014, in *OM* (2014)

205. E. Jimenez-Ruiz, C. Grau, A. Solimando, V. Cross, LogMap family results for OAEI 2015, in *OM* (2015)

206. N.D. Jones, An introduction to partial evaluation. ACM Comput. Surv. **28**(3), 480–503 (1996)

207. Z. Kaoudi, I. Miliaraki, M. Koubarakis, RDFS reasoning and query answering on top of DHTs, in *Proceedings of the 7th International Semantic Web Conference, ISWC 2008*, Karlsruhe, 26–30 October 2008, ed. by A.P. Sheth et al. Lecture Notes in Computer Science, vol. 5318 (Springer, Berlin, 2008), pp. 499–516

208. G. Karvounarakis, Z.G. Ives, V. Tannen, Querying data provenance, in *Proceedings of the 2010 ACM SIGMOD International Conference on Management of Data* (ACM, New York, 2010), pp. 951–962

209. G. Karvounarakis, I. Fundulaki, V. Christophides, Provenance for linked data, in *Search of Elegance in the Theory and Practice of Computation. Essays dedicated to Peter Buneman* (2013)

210. G. Karypis, V. Kumar, A fast and high quality multilevel scheme for partitioning irregular graphs. SIAM J. Sci. Comput. **20**(1), 359–392 (1998)

211. Y. Kazakov, M. Krötzsch, F. Simančík, The incredible ELK: from polynomial procedures to efficient reasoning with $\mathcal{EL}$ ontologies. J. Autom. Reason. **53**, 1–61 (2013)

212. V. Khadilkar, M. Kantarcioglu, B.M. Thuraisingham, P. Castagna, Jena-HBase: a distributed, scalable and efficient RDF triple store, in *Proceedings of the ISWC 2012 Posters & Demonstrations Track*, Boston, 11–15 November 2012

213. Y. Khan, M. Saleem, A. Iqbal, M. Mehdi, A. Hogan, A.-C. Ngonga Ngomo, S. Decker, R. Sahay, Safe: policy aware SPARQL query federation over RDF data cubes, in *Proceedings of the 7th International Workshop on Semantic Web Applications and Tools for Life Sciences*, Berlin, 9–11 December 2014

214. A. Khiat, M. Benaissa, InsMT/InsMTL results for OAEI 2014 instance matching, in *OM* (2014)

215. A. Khiat, M. Benaissa, M.-A. Belfedhal, STRIM results for OAEI 2015 instance matching evaluation, in *OM* (2015)

216. S. Kikot, R. Kontchakov, M. Zakharyaschev, Conjunctive query answering with OWL 2 QL, in *Principles of Knowledge Representation and Reasoning: Proceedings of the Thirteenth International Conference, KR 2012*, Rome, 10–14 June 2012, ed. by G. Brewka, T. Eiter, S.A. McIlraith (AAAI Press, Palo Alto, 2012)

217. J.-M. Kim, Y.-T. Park, Scalable OWL-Horst ontology reasoning using SPARK, in *2015 International Conference on Big Data and Smart Computing (BIGCOMP)* (IEEE, Piscataway, 2015), pp. 79–86

218. H. Kim, P. Ravindra, K. Anyanwu, From SPARQL to mapreduce: the journey using a nested triplegroup algebra. Proc. VLDB Endow. **4**(12), 1426–1429 (2011)

219. H. Kim, P. Ravindra, K. Anyanwu, Optimizing RDF(S) queries on cloud platforms, in *22nd International World Wide Web Conference, WWW '13*, Companion Volume, Rio de Janeiro, 13–17 May 2013, pp. 261–264

220. J. Kim, H. Shin, W.-S. Han, S. Hong, H. Chafi, Taming subgraph isomorphism for RDF query processing. Proc. VLDB Endow. **8**(11), 1238–1249 (2015)

221. R. Kontchakov, C. Lutz, D. Toman, F. Wolter, M. Zakharyaschev, The combined approach to ontology-based data access, in *IJCAI 2011, Proceedings of the 22nd International Joint Conference on Artificial Intelligence*, Barcelona, Catalonia, 16–22 July 2011, ed. by T. Walsh (IJCAI/AAAI, Menlo Park, 2011), pp. 2656–2661

222. D. Kossmann, The state of the art in distributed query processing. ACM Comput. Surv. **32**(4), 422–469 (2000)

223. S. Kotoulas, E. Oren, F. van Harmelen, Mind the data skew: distributed inferencing by speeddating in elastic regions, in *Proceedings of the 19th International Conference on World Wide Web, WWW '10* (ACM, New York, 2010), pp. 531–540

224. V. Kotsev, N. Minadakis, V. Papakonstantinou, O. Erling, I. Fundulaki, A. Kiryakov, Benchmarking RDF query engines: the LDBC semantic publishing benchmark, in *BLINK* (2016)

225. J. Krämer, B. Seeger, Semantics and implementation of continuous sliding window queries over data streams. ACM Trans. Database Syst. **34**(1), 4:1–4:49 (2009)

226. M. Krötzsch, F. Simančík, I. Horrocks, Description logics. IEEE Intell. Syst. **29**(1), 12–19 (2014)

227. G. Ladwig, A. Harth, Cumulusrdf: linked data management on nested key-value stores, in *SSWS* (2011)

228. G. Ladwig, T. Tran, SIHJoin: querying remote and local linked data, in *The Semantic Web: Research and Applications* (Springer, Berlin, 2011), pp. 139–153

229. F. Lécué, R. Tucker, V. Bicer, P. Tommasi, S. Tallevi-Diotallevi, M.L. Sbodio, Predicting severity of road traffic congestion using semantic web technologies, in *Proceedings of the*

11th Extended Semantic Web Conference (ESWC2014), Anissaras, 25 May–29 May 2014, ed. by V. Presutti, C. d'Amato, F. Gandon, M. d'Aquin, S. Staab, A. Tordai. Lecture Notes in Computer Science, vol. 8465 (Springer, Berlin, 2014)

230. J. Lehmann, R. Isele, M. Jakob, A. Jentzsch, D. Kontokostas, P.N. Mendes, S. Hellmann, M. Morsey, P. van Kleef, S. Auer, C. Bizer, DBpedia – a large-scale, multilingual knowledge base extracted from wikipedia. Semant. Web J. **6**(2), 167–195 (2015)

231. L. Leito, P. Calado, M. Herschel, An overview of XML duplicate detection algorithms, in *Soft Computing in XML Data Management*, vol. 255 (Springer, Berlin, 2010)

232. D. Le-Phuoc, A native and adaptive approach for linked stream data processing. PhD thesis, Digital Enterprise Research Institute, National University of Ireland, Galway, 2013

233. D. Le Phuoc, Operator-aware approach for boosting performance in RDF stream processing. J. Web Semant. **42**, 38–54 (2017)

234. D. Le-Phuoc, A. Polleres, M. Hauswirth, G. Tummarello, C. Morbidoni, Rapid prototyping of semantic mash-ups through semantic web pipes, in *WWW* (2009)

235. D. Le-Phuoc, M. Dao-Tran, J.X. Parreira, M. Hauswirth, A native and adaptive approach for unified processing of linked streams and linked data, in *Proceedings of 10th International Semantic Web Conference* (2011), pp. 370–388

236. D. Le Phuoc, H.N.M. Quoc, C. Le Van, M. Hauswirth, Elastic and scalable processing of linked stream data in the cloud, in *ISWC 2013 (1)* (2013), pp. 280–297

237. D. Le Phuoc, A. Lê Tuán, G. Schiele, M. Hauswirth, Querying heterogeneous personal information on the go, in *ISWC 2014 (2)* (2014), pp. 454–469

238. D. Le Phuoc, H.N.M. Quoc, H.N. Quoc, T.T. Nhat, M. Hauswirth, The graph of things: a step towards the live knowledge graph of connected things. J. Web Semant. **37–38**, 25–35 (2016)

239. J. Leskovec, A. Rajaraman, J.D. Ullman, *Mining of Massive Datasets*, 2nd edn. (Cambridge University Press, Cambridge, 2014)

240. C. Levine, TPC-C: The OLTP Benchmark, in *SIGMOD*, 1997. Industrial Session

241. J. Li, D. Maier, K. Tufte, V. Papadimos, P.A. Tucker, Semantics and evaluation techniques for window aggregates in data streams, in *Proceedings of the 2005 ACM SIGMOD International Conference on Management of Data, SIGMOD '05* (ACM, New York, 2005), pp. 311–322

242. C. Li, L. Jin, S. Mehrotra, Supporting efficient record linkage for large data sets using mapping techniques, in *WWW* (2006)

243. Q. Li, M. Shao, V. Markl, K. Beyer, L. Colby, G. Lohman, Adaptively reordering joins during query execution, in *IEEE 23rd International Conference on Data Engineering, 2007. ICDE* (IEEE, Piscataway, 2007), pp. 26–35

244. J. Li, K. Tufte, V. Shkapenyuk, V. Papadimos, T. Johnson, D. Maier, Out-of-order processing: a new architecture for high-performance stream systems. Proc. VLDB Endow. **1**(1), 274–288 (2008)

245. Y. Liu, P. McBrien, SPOWL: spark-based OWL 2 reasoning materialisation, in *Proceedings of the 4th ACM SIGMOD Workshop on Algorithms and Systems for MapReduce and Beyond, BeyondMR'17* (ACM, New York, 2017), pp. 3:1–3:10

246. Z. Liu, Z. Feng, X. Zhang, X. Wang, G. Rao, RORS: enhanced rule-based OWL reasoning on spark, in *Web Technologies and Applications – 18th Asia-Pacific Web Conference, APWeb, Proceedings, Part II*, Suzhou, 23–25 September 2016, ed. by F. Li, K. Shim, K. Zheng, G. Liu. Lecture Notes in Computer Science, vol. 9932 (Springer, Berlin, 2016), pp. 444–448

247. Z. Liu, W. Ge, X. Zhang, Z. Feng, Enhancing rule-based OWL reasoning on spark, in *Proceedings of the ISWC 2016 Posters and Demonstrations Track Co-located with 15th International Semantic Web Conference (ISWC), CEUR Workshop Proceedings*, Kobe, 19 October 2016, vol. 1690, ed. by T. Kawamura, H. Paulheim (2016). CEUR-WS.org

248. N. Lopes, A. Polleres, U. Straccia, A. Zimmermann, AnQL: SPARQLing up annotated RDFS, in *ISWC'10* (2010), pp. 518–533

249. Y. Low, J. Gonzalez, A. Kyrola, D. Bickson, C. Guestrin, J.M. Hellerstein, Distributed GraphLab: a framework for machine learning in the cloud. Proc. VLDB Endow. **5**(8), 716–727 (2012)

250. S. Lynden, I. Kojima, A. Matono, Y. Tanimura, ADERIS: an adaptive query processor for joining federated SPARQL endpoints, in *On the Move to Meaningful Internet Systems: OTM* (Springer, Berlin, 2011), pp. 808–817

251. L. Ma, Z. Su, Y. Pan, L. Zhang, T. Liu, Rstar: an RDF storage and query system for enterprise resource management, in *Proceedings of the Thirteenth ACM International Conference on Information and Knowledge Management* (ACM, New York, 2004), pp. 484–491

252. S. Madden, M.J. Franklin, Fjording the stream: an architecture for queries over streaming sensor data, in *Proceedings of the 18th International Conference on Data Engineering, ICDE'02* (2002), pp. 555–566

253. S. Madden, M. Shah, J.M. Hellerstein, V. Raman, Continuously adaptive continuous queries over streams, in *2002 ACM SIGMOD International Conference on Management of Data* (2002), pp. 49–60

254. F. Mahdisoltani, J. Biega, F.M. Suchanek, YAGO3: a knowledge base from multilingual wikipedias, in *CIDR 2015, Seventh Biennial Conference on Innovative Data Systems Research, Online Proceedings*, Asilomar, 4–7 January 2015. www.cidrdb.org

255. F. Maier, R. Mutharaju, P. Hitzler, Distributed reasoning with EL++ using MapReduce. Technical report, Department of Computer Science, Wright State University, 2010. http://knoesis.wright.edu/pascal/resources/publications/elpp-mapreduce2010.pdf

256. S. Manegold, I. Manolescu, Performance evaluation in database research: principles and experience, in *EDBT*, 2009. Tutorial

257. M.A. Martínez-Prieto, M. Arias, J.D. Fernandez, Exchange and consumption of huge RDF data, in *The Semantic Web: Research and Applications* (Springer, Berlin, 2012), pp. 437–452

258. A. Mauri, J.-P. Calbimonte, D. Dell'Aglio, M. Balduini, M. Brambilla, E. Della Valle, K. Aberer, Triplewave: spreading RDF streams on the web, in *The Semantic Web – ISWC 2016 - 15th International Semantic Web Conference, Proceedings, Part II*, Kobe, 17–21 October 2016, ed. by P.T. Groth, E. Simperl, A.J.G. Gray, M. Sabou, M. Krötzsch, F. Lécué, F. Flöck, Y. Gil. Lecture Notes in Computer Science, vol. 9982 (2016), pp. 140–149

259. B. McBride, Jena: a semantic web toolkit. IEEE Internet Comput. **6**(6), 55–59 (2002)

260. D.L. McGuinness, F. van Harmelen, OWL Web Ontology Language Overview. https://www.w3.org/TR/owl-features/, February 2004. W3C Recommendation

261. Y. Mei, S. Madden, ZStream: a cost-based query processor for adaptively detecting composite events, in *Proceedings of the 35th SIGMOD International Conference on Management of Data, SIGMOD '09* (ACM, New York, 2009), pp. 193–206

262. A. Metke-Jimenez, M. Lawley, Snorocket 2.0: concrete domains and concurrent classification, in *Informal Proceedings of the 2nd International Workshop on OWL Reasoner Evaluation (ORE-2013), CEUR Workshop Proceedings*, Ulm, 22 July 2013, vol. 1015, ed. by S. Bail, B. Glimm, R.S. Gonçalves, E. Jiménez-Ruiz, Y. Kazakov, N. Matentzoglu, B. Parsia (2013), pp. 32–38. CEUR-WS.org

263. S. Miles, Electronically querying for the provenance of entities, in *Provenance and Annotation of Data*, ed. by L. Moreau, I. Foster. Lecture Notes in Computer Science, vol. 4145 (Springer, Berlin, 2006), pp. 184–192

264. T.M. Mitchell, W.W. Cohen, E.R. Hruschka Jr., P.P. Talukdar, J. Betteridge, A. Carlson, B.D. Mishra, M. Gardner, B. Kisiel, J. Krishnamurthy, N. Lao, K. Mazaitis, T. Mohamed, N. Nakashole, E.A. Platanios, A. Ritter, M. Samadi, B. Settles, R.C. Wang, D.T. Wijaya, A. Gupta, X. Chen, A. Saparov, M. Greaves, J. Welling, Never-ending learning, in *Proceedings of the Twenty-Ninth AAAI Conference on Artificial Intelligence*, Austin, 25–30 January 2015, ed. by B. Bonet, S. Koenig (AAAI Press, Palo Alto, 2015), pp. 2302–2310

265. G. Montoya, H. Skaf-Molli, P. Molli, M.-E. Vidal, Federated SPARQL queries processing with replicated fragments, in *International Semantic Web Conference* (Springer, Berlin, 2015), pp. 36–51

266. L. Moreau, The foundations for provenance on the web. Found. Trends Web Sci. **2**(2–3), 99–241 (2010)

267. L. Moreau, G. Paul, *Provenance: An Introduction to PROV* (Morgan and Claypool, San Rafael, 2013)

268. L. Moreau, B. Clifford, J. Freire, J. Futrelle, Y. Gil, P. Groth, N. Kwasnikowska, S. Miles, P. Missier, J. Myers, B. Plale, Y. Simmhan, E. Stephan, J. Van den Bussche, The open provenance model core specification (v1.1). Futur. Gener. Comput. Syst. **27**(6), 743–756 (2011)

269. M. Morsey, J. Lehmann, S. Auer, A.-C. Ngonga Ngomo, DBpedia SPARQL benchmark – performance assessment with real queries on real data, in *ISWC* (2011)

270. B. Motik, Representing and querying validity time in RDF and OWL: a logic-based approach. Web Semant. **12–13**, 3–21 (2012)

271. B. Motik, B.C. Grau, I. Horrocks, Z. Wu, A. Fokoue, C. Lutz (eds.), *OWL 2 Web Ontology Language: Profiles*. W3C Recommendation, 11 December 2012. Available at https://www.w3.org/TR/owl2-profiles/

272. B. Motik, Y. Nenov, R. Piro, I. Horrocks, Parallel materialisation of datalog programs in main-memory RDF databases, in *Proceedings of the Twenty-Eighth AAAI Conference on Artificial Intelligence*, Qébec City, 27–31 July 2014 (AAAI Press, Palo Alto, 2014)

273. B. Motik, Y. Nenov, R. Piro, I. Horrocks, D. Olteanu, Parallel materialisation of datalog programs in centralised, main-memory RDF systems, in *Proceedings of the Twenty-Eighth AAAI Conference on Artificial Intelligence, AAAI'14* (AAAI Press, Palo Alto, 2014), pp. 129–137

274. B. Motik, Y. Nenov, R. Piro, I. Horrocks, Incremental update of datalog materialisation: the backward/forward algorithm, in *Proceedings of the Twenty-Ninth AAAI Conference on Artificial Intelligence, AAAI'15* (AAAI Press, Palo Alto, 2015), pp. 1560–1568

275. T. Mueller, T. Grust, Provenance for SQL through abstract interpretation: value-less, but worthwhile, in *PVLDB*, vol. 8 (2015)

276. S. Muñoz, J. Pérez, C. Gutierrez, Simple and efficient minimal RDFS. Web Semant. Sci. Serv. Agents World Wide Web **7**(3), 220–234 (2009)

277. R. Mutharaju, Distributed rule-based ontology reasoning. PhD thesis, Wright State University, 2016

278. R. Mutharaju, F. Maier, P. Hitzler, A MapReduce algorithm for EL+, in *Proceedings of the 23rd International Workshop on Description Logics (DL 2010), CEUR Workshop Proceedings*, Waterloo, 4–7 May 2010, vol. 573, ed. by V. Haarslev, D. Toman, G.E. Weddell. CEUR-WS.org

279. R. Mutharaju, S. Sakr, A. Sala, P. Hitzler, D-SPARQ: distributed, scalable and efficient RDF query engine, in *Proceedings of the ISWC 2013 Posters & Demonstrations Track*, Sydney, 23 October 2013, pp. 261–264

280. R. Mutharaju, P. Hitzler, P. Mateti, F. Lécué, Distributed and scalable OWL EL reasoning, in *The Semantic Web. Latest Advances and New Domains – 12th Extended Semantic Web Conference, ESWC 2015. Proceedings*, Portoroz, 31 May–4 June 2015, ed. by F. Gandon, M. Sabou, H. Sack, C. d'Amato, P. Cudré-Mauroux, A. Zimmermann. Lecture Notes in Computer Science, vol. 9088 (Springer, Berlin, 2015), pp. 88–103

281. R. Mutharaju, P. Mateti, P. Hitzler, Towards a rule based distributed OWL reasoning framework, in *Ontology Engineering - 12th International Experiences and Directions Workshop on OWL, OWLED 2015, Co-located with ISWC, Revised Selected Papers*, Bethlehem, 9–10 October 2015. Lecture Notes in Computer Science, vol. 9557 (Springer, Berlin, 2015), pp. 87–92

282. H. Naacke, O. Curé, B. Amann, SPARQL query processing with Apache Spark. Preprint (2016). arXiv:1604.08903

283. M. Nagy, M. Vargas-Vera, P. Stolarski, DSSim results for OAEI 2009, in *OM* (2009)

284. R.O. Nambiar, M. Poess, A. Masland, H.R. Taheri, M. Emmerton, F. Carman, M. Majdalany, TPC benchmark roadmap, in *Selected Topics in Performance Evaluation and Benchmarking* (Springer, Berlin, 2012)

285. T. Neumann, G. Weikum, RDF-3X: a RISC-style engine for RDF. PVLDB **1**(1), 647–659 (2008)

286. T. Neumann, G. Weikum, Scalable join processing on very large RDF graphs, in *Proceedings of the ACM SIGMOD International Conference on Management of Data* (2009), pp. 627–640

287. T. Neumann, G. Weikum, The RDF-3X engine for scalable management of RDF data. VLDB J. **19**(1), 91–113 (2010)
288. A.-C. Ngonga Ngomo, S. Auer, LIMES: a time-efficient approach for large-scale link discovery on the web of data, in *IJCAI* (2011)
289. A.-C. Ngonga Ngomo, D. Schumacher, Borderflow: a local graph clustering algorithm for natural language processing, in *CICLing* (2009)
290. K. Nguyen, R. Ichise, SLINT+ results for OAEI 2013 instance matching, in *OM* (2013)
291. V. Nguyen, O. Bodenreider, A. Sheth, Don't like RDF reification?: making statements about statements using singleton property, in *Proceedings of the 23rd International Conference on World Wide Web* (International World Wide Web Conferences Steering Committee, 2014), pp. 759–770
292. A. Nikolov, A. Schwarte, C. Hütter, FedSearch: efficiently combining structured queries and full-text search in a SPARQL federation, in *International Semantic Web Conference (1)* (2013), pp. 427–443
293. X. Niu, S. Rong, Y. Zhang, H. Wang, Zhishi.links results for OAEI 2011, in *OM* (2011)
294. F. Niu, C. Zhang, C. Ré, J.W. Shavlik, Elementary: large-scale knowledge-base construction via machine learning and statistical inference. Int. J. Semant. Web Inf. Syst. **8**(3), 42–73 (2012)
295. X. Niu, R. Kapoor, B. Glavic, D. Gawlick, Z.H. Liu, V. Krishnaswamy, V. Radhakrishnan, Interoperability for provenance-aware databases using PROV and JSON, in *Proceedings of the 7th USENIX Conference on Theory and Practice of Provenance, TaPP'15* (USENIX Association, Berkeley, 2015), p. 6
296. J. Noessner, M. Niepert, CODI: combinatorial optimization for data integration – results for OAEI 2010, in *OM* (2010)
297. M. Odersky, L. Spoon, B. Venners, *Programming in Scala: A Comprehensive Step-by-Step Guide* (Artima Inc., Walnut Creek, 2011)
298. D. Oguz, B. Ergenc, S. Yin, O. Dikenelli, A. Hameurlain, Federated query processing on linked data: a qualitative survey and open challenges. Knowl. Eng. Rev. **30**(5), 545–563 (2015)
299. OKKAM Project. http://project.okkam.org/
300. C. Olston, B. Reed, U. Srivastava, R. Kumar, A. Tomkins, Pig Latin: a not-so-foreign language for data processing, in *Proceedings of the ACM SIGMOD International Conference on Management of Data, SIGMOD 2008*, Vancouver, 10–12 June 2008, pp. 1099–1110
301. E. Oren, S. Kotoulas, G. Anadiotis, R. Siebes, A. ten Teije, F. van Harmelen, Marvin: distributed reasoning over large-scale Semantic Web data. Web Semant. Sci. Serv. Agents World Wide Web **7**(4), 305–316 (2009)
302. R. Othayoth Nambiar, M. Poess, A. Masland, H.R. Taheri, M. Emmerton, F. Carman, M. Majdalany, TPC Benchmark Roadmap 2012, in *TPCTC* (2012)
303. Z. Ou, G. Yu, Y. Yu, S. Wu, X. Yang, Q. Deng, Tick scheduling: a deadline based optimal task scheduling approach for real-time data stream systems, in *Proceedings of the 6th International Conference on Advances in Web-Age Information Management, WAIM'05* (Springer, Berlin, 2005), pp. 725–730
304. N. Papailiou, I. Konstantinou, D. Tsoumakos, P. Karras, N. Koziris, H2rdf+: high-performance distributed joins over large-scale RDF graphs, in *2013 IEEE International Conference on Big Data* (IEEE, Piscataway, 2013), pp. 255–263
305. N. Papailiou, I. Konstantinou, D. Tsoumakos, P. Karras, N. Koziris, H2RDF+: high-performance distributed joins over large-scale RDF graphs, in *Proceedings of the 2013 IEEE International Conference on Big Data*, Santa Clara, 6–9 October 2013, pp. 255–263
306. N. Papailiou, D. Tsoumakos, I. Konstantinou, P. Karras, N. Koziris, H$_2$rdf+: an efficient data management system for big RDF graphs, in *International Conference on Management of Data, SIGMOD*, Snowbird, 22–27 June 2014, pp. 909–912
307. H.K. Patni, C.A. Henson, A.P. Sheth, Linked sensor data, in *CTS* (2010)
308. P. Pediaditis, G. Flouris, I. Fundulaki, V. Christophides, On explicit provenance management in RDF/S graphs, in *Workshop on the Theory and Practice of Provenance* (2009)

309. P. Peng, L. Zou, L. Chen, D. Zhao, Query workload-based RDF graph fragmentation and allocation, in *Proceedings of the 19th International Conference on Extending Database Technology, EDBT*, Bordeaux, 15–16 March 2016, pp. 377–388

310. P. Peng, L. Zou, M. Tamer Özsu, L. Chen, D. Zhao, Processing SPARQL queries over distributed RDF graphs. VLDB J. **25**(2), 243–268 (2016)

311. J. Pérez, M. Arenas, C. Gutierrez, Semantics and complexity of SPARQL. ACM Trans. Database Syst. **34**(3), 1–45 (2009)

312. A. Potter, B. Motik, Y. Nenov, I. Horrocks, Distributed RDF query answering with dynamic data exchange, in *International Semantic Web Conference* (Springer, Berlin, 2016), pp. 480–497

313. D. Pritchett, Base: an acid alternative. Queue **6**(3), 48–55 (2008)

314. E. Prud'hommeaux, A. Seaborne, SPARQL query language for RDF. www.w3.org/TR/rdf-sparql-query, January 2008. W3C Recommendation

315. R. Punnoose, A. Crainiceanu, D. Rapp, Rya: a scalable RDF triple store for the clouds, in *1st International Workshop on Cloud Intelligence (Colocated with VLDB 2012), Cloud-I '12*, Istanbul, 31 August 2012 (ACM, New York, 2012), pp. 4:1–4:8

316. R. Punnoose, A. Crainiceanu, D. Rapp, SPARQL in the cloud using Rya. Inf. Syst. **48**, 181–195 (2015)

317. B. Quilitz, U. Leser, Querying distributed RDF data sources with SPARQL, in *European Semantic Web Conference* (Springer, Berlin, 2008), pp. 524–538

318. N.A. Rakhmawati, J. Umbrich, M. Karnstedt, A. Hasnain, M. Hausenblas, Querying over federated SPARQL endpoints—a state of the art survey. Preprint (2013). arXiv:1306.1723

319. L. Raschid, S.Y.W. Su, A parallel processing strategy for evaluating recursive queries, in *VLDB*, vol. 86 (1986), pp. 412–419

320. P. Ravindra, V.V. Deshpande, K. Anyanwu, Towards scalable RDF graph analytics on mapreduce, in *Proceedings of the 2010 Workshop on Massive Data Analytics on the Cloud* (ACM, New York, 2010), p. 5

321. P. Ravindra, H. Kim, K. Anyanwu, An intermediate algebra for optimizing RDF graph pattern matching on mapreduce, in *The Semanic Web: Research and Applications – 8th Extended Semantic Web Conference, ESWC, Proceedings, Part II*, Heraklion, 29 May–2 June 2011, pp. 46–61

322. N. Redaschi, UniProt Consortium, UniProt in RDF: tackling data integration and distributed annotation with the semantic web, in *Biocuration Conference* (2009)

323. B. Regalia, K. Janowicz, S. Gao, Volt: a provenance-producing, transparent SPARQL proxy for the on-demand computation of linked data and its application to spatiotemporally dependent data, in *International Semantic Web Conference* (Springer, Berlin, 2016), pp. 523–538

324. K. Rohloff, R.E. Schantz, High-performance, massively scalable distributed systems using the mapreduce software framework: the SHARD triple-store, in *SPLASH Workshop on Programming Support Innovations for Emerging Distributed Applications*, Reno/Tahoe, 17 October 2010, p. 4

325. K. Rohloff, R.E. Schantz, Clause-iteration with mapreduce to scalably query datagraphs in the SHARD graph-store, in *DIDC'11, Proceedings of the Fourth International Workshop on Data-Intensive Distributed Computing*, San Jose, 8 June 2011, pp. 35–44

326. S. Russell, P. Norvig, *Artificial Intelligence: A Modern Approach*, 3rd edn. (Prentice Hall Press, Upper Saddle River, 2009)

327. S.S. Sahoo, A. Sheth, Provenir ontology: towards a framework for eScience provenance management, in *Microsoft eScience Workshop*, October 2009

328. F. Saïs, N. Niraula, N. Pernelle, M.C. Rousset, LN2R – a knowledge based reference reconciliation system: OAEI 2010 Results, in *OM* (2010)

329. S. Sakr, *Big Data 2.0 Processing Systems – A Survey*. Springer Briefs in Computer Science (Springer, Cham, 2016)

330. S. Sakr, G. Al-Naymat, Relational processing of RDF queries: a survey. SIGMOD Rec. **38**(4), 23–28 (2009)

331. S. Sakr, A. Liu, D.M. Batista, M. Alomari, A survey of large scale data management approaches in cloud environments. IEEE Commun. Surv. Tutorials **13**(3), 311–336 (2011)
332. M. Saleem, Q. Mehmood, A.-C. Ngonga Ngomo, FEASIBLE: a feature-based SPARQL benchmark generation framework, in *ISWC* (2011)
333. M. Saleem, A.-C. Ngonga Ngomo, J.X. Parreira, H.F. Deus, M. Hauswirth, DAW: Duplicate-AWare federated query processing over the web of data, in *International Semantic Web Conference* (Springer, Berlin, 2013), pp. 574–590
334. M. Saleem, S.S. Padmanabhuni, A.-C. Ngonga Ngomo, A. Iqbal, J.S. Almeida, S. Decker, H.F. Deus, Topfed: Tcga tailored federated query processing and linking to lod. J. Biomed. Semant. **5**(1), 47 (2014)
335. M. Saleem, Y. Khan, A. Hasnain, I. Ermilov, A.-C. Ngonga Ngomo, A fine-grained evaluation of SPARQL endpoint federation systems. Semantic Web **7**(5), 493–518 (2016)
336. M. Salvadores, G. Correndo, S. Harris, N. Gibbins, N. Shadbolt, The design and implementation of RDFS backward reasoning in 4Store, in *Proceedings of the 8th Extended Semantic Web Conference on The Semantic Web: Research and Applications, ESWC'11*, Volume Part II (Springer, Berlin, 2011), pp. 139–153
337. T. Saveta, E. Daskalaki, G. Flouris, I. Fundulaki, M. Herschel, A.-C. Ngonga Ngomo, LANCE: piercing to the heart of instance matching tool, in *ISWC* (2015)
338. T. Saveta, E. Daskalaki, G. Flouris, I. Fundulaki, M. Herschel, A.-C. Ngonga Ngomo, Pushing the limits of instance matching systems: a semantics-aware benchmark for linked data, in *WWW*, Companion Volume (2015)
339. A. Schätzle, M. Przyjaciel-Zablocki, T. Hornung, G. Lausen, Pigsparql: a SPARQL query processing baseline for big data, in *Proceedings of the ISWC 2013 Posters and Demonstrations Track*, Sydney, 23 October 2013, pp. 241–244
340. A. Schätzle, M. Przyjaciel-Zablocki, S. Skilevic, G. Lausen, S2RDF: RDF querying with SPARQL on spark. CoRR (2015). https://arxiv.org/abs/1512.07021
341. A. Schätzle, M. Przyjaciel-Zablocki, T. Berberich, G. Lausen, S2X: graph-parallel querying of RDF with GraphX, in *1st International Workshop on Big-Graphs Online Querying (Big-O(Q))* (2015)
342. A. Schlicht, H. Stuckenschmidt, MapResolve, in *Web Reasoning and Rule Systems – 5th International Conference, RR 2011*, Galway, 29–30 August 2011. Lecture Notes in Computer Science, vol. 6902 (Springer, Berlin, 2011), pp. 294–299
343. M. Schmachtenberg, C. Bizer, H. Paulheim, Adoption of the linked data best practices in different topical domains, in *The Semantic Web–ISWC 2014* (Springer, Cham, 2014), pp. 245–260
344. A.R. Schmidt, F. Wass, M. Kersten, D. Florescu, M.J. Carey, I. Manolescu, R. Busse, XMark: a benchmark for XML data management, in *VLDB* (2002)
345. M. Schmidt, T. Hornung, M. Meier, C. Pinkel, G. Lausen, SP2Bench: a SPARQL performance benchmark, in *Semantic Web Information Management* (Springer, Berlin, 2009)
346. M. Schmidt, M. Meier, G. Lausen, Foundations of SPARQL query optimization, in *EDBT/ICDT* (2010)
347. R. Schollmeier, A definition of peer-to-peer networking for the classification of peer-to-peer architectures and applications, in *First International Conference on Peer-to-Peer Computing* (2001), pp. 101–102
348. A. Schwarte, P. Haase, K. Hose, R. Schenkel, M. Schmidt, FedX: optimization techniques for federated query processing on linked data, in *The Semantic Web – ISWC* (2011), pp. 601–616
349. Md.H. Seddiqui, M. Aono, Anchor-flood: results for OAEI 2009, in *OM* (2009)
350. B. Shao, H. Wang, Y. Li, Trinity: a distributed graph engine on a memory cloud, in *Proceedings of the 2013 International Conference on Management of Data* (ACM, New York, 2013), pp. 505–516
351. C. Shao, L. Hu, J. Li, RiMOM-IM results for OAEI 2014, in *OM* (2014)
352. M.A. Sharaf, A. Labrinidis, P.K. Chrysanthis, K. Pruhs, Freshness-aware scheduling of continuous queries in the dynamic web, in *WebDB* (2005), pp. 73–78

353. M.A. Sharaf, P.K. Chrysanthis, A. Labrinidis, K. Pruhs, Algorithms and metrics for process-
     ing multiple heterogeneous continuous queries. ACM Trans. Database Syst. **33**(1), 5:1–5:44
     (2008)
354. J. Shi, Y. Yao, R. Chen, H. Chen, F. Li, Fast and concurrent RDF queries with RDMA-based
     distributed graph exploration, in *12th USENIX Symposium on Operating Systems Design and
     Implementation (OSDI 16)* (USENIX Association, Berkeley, 2016), pp. 317–332
355. N. Shivakumar, H. García-Molina, Wave-indices: indexing evolving databases, in *Proceed-
     ings of the 1997 ACM SIGMOD International Conference on Management of Data, SIGMOD
     '97* (ACM, New York, 1997), pp. 381–392
356. K. Shvachko, H. Kuang, S. Radia, R. Chansler, The Hadoop distributed file system, in *MSST*
     (2010)
357. F. Simančík, Consequence-based reasoning for ontology classification. PhD thesis, University
     of Oxford, 2013
358. P. Singla, P. Domingos, Multi-relational record linkage, in *MRDM* (2004). Co-located with
     KDD
359. E. Sirin, B. Parsia, B.C. Grau, A. Kalyanpur, Y. Katz, Pellet: a practical OWL-DL reasoner.
     J. Web Semant. **5**(2), 51–53 (2007)
360. V. Slavov, A. Katib, P. Rao, S. Paturi, D. Barenkala, Fast processing of SPARQL queries on
     RDF quadruples. Preprint (2015). arXiv:1506.01333
361. J.M. Smith, P.Y.-T. Chang, Optimizing the performance of a relational algebra database
     interface. Commun. ACM **18**(10), 568–579 (1975)
362. D. Srivastava, Y. Velegrakis, Intensional associations between data and metadata, in *SIGMOD*
     (2007)
363. U. Srivastava, J. Widom, Flexible time management in data stream systems, in *PODS '04*
     (2004), pp. 263–274
364. S. Staab, R. Studer, *Handbook on Ontologies*, 2nd edn. (Springer, Berlin, 2009)
365. A. Steigmiller, T. Liebig, B. Glimm, Konclude: system description. J. Web Semant. **27**, 78–85
     (2014)
366. M. Stocker, A. Seaborne, A. Bernstein, C. Kiefer, D. Reynolds, SPARQL basic graph pattern
     optimization using selectivity estimation, in *Proceedings of the 17th International Conference
     on World Wide Web* (ACM, New York, 2008), pp. 595–604
367. H. Stoermer, N. Rassadko, Results of OKKAM feature based entity matching algorithm for
     instance matching contest of OAEI 2009, in *OM* (2009)
368. M. Stonebraker, D.J. Abadi, A. Batkin, X. Chen, M. Cherniack, M. Ferreira, E. Lau, A. Lin,
     S.R. Madden, E. O'Neil, P. O'Neil, A. Rasin, N. Tran, S. Zdonik, C-store: a column oriented
     DBMS, in *International Conference on Very Large Data Bases (VLDB)* (2005)
369. P. Stutz, A. Bernstein, W. Cohen, Signal/collect: graph algorithms for the (semantic) web, in
     International Semantic Web Conference (Springer, Berlin, 2010), pp. 764–780
370. P. Stutz, M. Verman, L. Fischer, A. Bernstein, Triplerush: a fast and scalable triple store, in
     *Proceedings of the 9th International Conference on Scalable Semantic Web Knowledge Base
     Systems*, vol. 1046 (2013), pp. 50–65. CEUR-WS.org
371. M. Suchanek, G. Kasneci, G. Weikum, YAGO: a core of semantic knowledge unifying
     WordNet and Wikipedia, in *WWW* (2007)
372. M. Sullivan, A. Heybey, Tribeca: a system for managing large databases of network traffic, in
     Proceedings of the Annual Conference on USENIX Annual Technical Conference, ATEC '98
     (USENIX Association, Berkeley, 1998)
373. Y. Sure, S. Bloehdorn, P. Haase, J. Hartmann, D. Oberle, The SWRC ontology – semantic
     web for research communities, in *EPIA* (2005)
374. I. Tachmazidis, G. Antoniou, G. Flouris, S. Kotoulas, L. McCluskey, Large-scale parallel
     stratified defeasible reasoning, in *ECAI 2012 - 20th European Conference on Artificial
     Intelligence. Including Prestigious Applications of Artificial Intelligence (PAIS-2012) System
     Demonstrations Track*, Montpellier, 27–31 August 2012, ed. by L. De Raedt, C. Bessière, D.
     Dubois, P. Doherty, P. Frasconi, F. Heintz, P.J.F. Lucas. Frontiers in Artificial Intelligence and
     Applications, vol. 242 (IOS Press, Amsterdam, 2012), pp. 738–743

375. I. Tachmazidis, G. Antoniou, G. Flouris, S. Kotoulas, Towards parallel nonmonotonic reasoning with billions of facts, in *Principles of Knowledge Representation and Reasoning: Proceedings of the Thirteenth International Conference, KR*, Rome, 10–14 June 2012, ed. by G. Brewka, T. Eiter, S.A. McIlraith (AAAI Press, Palo Alto, 2012)

376. A. Taheri, M. Shamsfard, SBUEI: results for OAEI 2012, in *OM* (2012)

377. W.C. Tan, Research problems in data provenance. IEEE Data Eng. Bull. **27**(4), 45–52 (2004)

378. W.C. Tan, Provenance in databases: past, current, and future. IEEE Data Eng. Bull. **30**(4), 3–12 (2007)

379. H.J. ter Horst, Completeness, decidability and complexity of entailment for RDF schema and a semantic extension involving the OWL vocabulary. J. Web Semant. Sci. Serv. Agents World Wide Web **3**(2–3), 79–115 (2005)

380. Y. Theoharis, I. Fundulaki, G. Karvounarakis, V. Christophides, On provenance of queries on semantic web data. IEEE Internet Comput. **15**(1), 31–39 (2011)

381. B. Thompson, M. Personick, M. Cutcher, The bigdata® RDF graph database, in *Linked Data Management* (Chapman and Hall/CRC, Boca Raton, 2014), pp. 193–237

382. Transaction Processing Council. http://www.tpc.org/

383. D. Tsarkov, I. Horrocks, FaCT++ description logic reasoner: system description, in *Automated Reasoning, Third International Joint Conference, IJCAR 2006, Proceedings*, Seattle, 17–20 August 2006, ed. by U. Furbach, N. Shankar (Springer, Berlin, 2006), pp. 292–297

384. P.A. Tucker, D. Maier, T. Sheard, L. Fegaras, Exploiting punctuation semantics in continuous data streams. IEEE Trans. Knowl. Data Eng. **15**, 555–568 (2003)

385. O. Udrea, D.R. Recupero, V.S. Subrahmanian, Annotated RDF. ACM Trans. Comput. Log. **11**(2), 10 (2010)

386. J. Urbani, C. Jacobs, *RDF-SQ: Mixing Parallel and Sequential Computation for Top-Down OWL RL Inference* (Springer, Cham, 2015), pp. 125–138

387. J. Urbani, S. Kotoulas, J. Maassen, F. van Harmelen, H.E. Bal, OWL reasoning with WebPIE: calculating the closure of 100 billion triples, in *Proceedings of the 8th Extended Semantic Web Conference (ESWC2010)*, Heraklion, 30 May–3 June 2010 (Springer, Berlin, 2010)

388. J. Urbani, F. van Harmelen, S. Schlobach, H.E. Bal, QueryPIE: backward reasoning for OWL horst over very large knowledge bases, in *10th International Semantic Web Conference*, Bonn, 23–27 October 2011. Lecture Notes in Computer Science, vol. 7031 (Springer, Berlin, 2011), pp. 730–745

389. J. Urbani, S. Kotoulas, J. Maassen, F. Van Harmelen, H. Bal, WebPIE: a web-scale parallel inference engine using MapReduce. J. Web Semant. **10**, 59–75 (2012)

390. J. Urbani, A. Margara, C.J.H. Jacobs, F. van Harmelen, H.E. Bal, DynamiTE: parallel materialization of dynamic RDF data, in *International Semantic Web Conference (1)*, ed. by H. Alani, L. Kagal, A. Fokoue, P.T. Groth, C. Biemann, J.X. Parreira, L. Aroyo, N.F. Noy, C. Welty, K. Janowicz. Lecture Notes in Computer Science, vol. 8218 (Springer, Berlin, 2013), pp. 657–672

391. J. Urbani, A. Margara, C. Jacobs, S. Voulgaris, H. Bal, AJIRA: a lightweight distributed middleware for MapReduce and stream processing, in *2014 IEEE 34th International Conference on Distributed Computing Systems (ICDCS)* (IEEE, Piscataway, 2014), pp. 545–554

392. J. Urbani, R. Piro, F. van Harmelen, H. Bal, Hybrid reasoning on OWL RL. Semant. Web **5**(6), 423–447 (2014)

393. J. Urbani, C. Jacobs, M. Krötzsch, Column-oriented datalog materialization for large knowledge graphs, in *Thirtieth AAAI Conference on Artificial Intelligence* (2016)

394. T. Urhan, M.J. Franklin, XJoin: a reactively-scheduled pipelined join operator, in *Bulletin of the IEEE Computer Society Technical Committee on Data Engineering* (2000), p. 27

395. P. Valduriez, Join indices. ACM Trans. Database Syst. **12**(2), 218–246 (1987)

396. L.G. Valiant, A bridging model for parallel computation. Commun. ACM **33**(8), 103–111 (1990)

397. S. Vansummeren, J. Cheney, Recording provenance for SQL queries and updates. IEEE Data Eng. Bull. **30**(4), 29–37 (2007)

398. S.D. Viglas, J.F. Naughton, Rate-based query optimization for streaming information sources, in *Proceedings of the 2002 ACM SIGMOD International Conference on Management of Data, SIGMOD '02* (ACM, New York, 2002), pp. 37–48
399. S.D. Viglas, J.F. Naughton, J. Burger, Maximizing the output rate of multi-way join queries over streaming information sources, in *VLDB '03* (2003)
400. J. Volz, C. Bizer, M. Gaedke, G. Kobilarov, Discovering and maintaining links on the Web of Data, in *ISWC* (2009)
401. D. Vrandečić, M. Krötzsch, Wikidata: a free collaborative knowledgebase. Commun. ACM **57**, 78–85 (2014)
402. Y.R. Wang, S.E. Madnick, A polygon model for heterogeneous database systems: the source tagging perspective, in *Proceedings of the Sixteenth International Conference on Very Large Databases*, San Francisco (Morgan Kaufmann Publishers Inc., Palo Alto, 1990), pp. 519–533
403. J. Wang, X. Zhang, L. Hou, Y. Zhao, J. Li, Y. Qi, J. Tang, RiMOM results for OAEI 2010, in *OM* (2010)
404. X. Wang, T. Tiropanis, H.C. Davis, LHD: optimising linked data query processing using parallelisation (2013). https://eprints.soton.ac.uk/350719/
405. X. Wang, J. Wang, X. Zhang, Efficient distributed regular path queries on RDF graphs using partial evaluation, in *Proceedings of the 25th ACM International on Conference on Information and Knowledge Management* (ACM, New York, 2016), pp. 1933–1936
406. J. Weaver, J.A. Hendler, Parallel materialization of the finite RDFS closure for hundreds of millions of triples, in *8th International Semantic Web Conference, ISWC 2009*, Chantilly, 25–29 October 2009. Lecture Notes in Computer Science, vol. 5823 (Springer, Berlin, 2009), pp. 682–697
407. R.P. Weicker, An overview of common benchmarks. Computer **23**(12), 65–75 (1990)
408. C. Weiss, P. Karras, A. Bernstein, Hexastore: sextuple indexing for semantic web data management. Proc. VLDB Endow. **1**(1), 1008–1019 (2008)
409. T. White, *Hadoop: The Definitive Guide* (O'Reilly Media, Sebastopol, 2012)
410. G. Wiederhold, Mediators in the architecture of future information systems. Computer **25**(3), 38–49 (1992)
411. K. Wilkinson, K. Wilkinson, Jena property table implementation, in *International Workshop on Scalable Semantic Web Knowledge Base Systems (SSWS)* (2006)
412. K. Wilkinson, C. Sayers, H.A. Kuno, D. Reynolds, Efficient RDF storage and retrieval in Jena2, in *SWDB'03* (2003), pp. 131–150
413. A.N. Wilschut, P.M.G. Apers, Dataflow query execution in a parallel main-memory environment. Distrib. Parallel Databases **1**(1), 103–128 (1993)
414. World Wide Web Consortium, OWL 2 Web Ontology Language (2012)
415. World Wide Web Consortium, SPARQL 1.1 Overview (2013)
416. World Wide Web Consortium, RDF 1.1 Concepts and Abstract Syntax (2014)
417. World Wide Web Consortium, RDF 1.1: On Semantics of RDF Datasets (2014)
418. World Wide Web Consortium, RDF 1.1 Primer (2014)
419. World Wide Web Consortium, RDF Schema 1.1 (2014)
420. E. Wu, Y. Diao, S. Rizvi, High-performance complex event processing over streams, in *Proceedings of the 2006 ACM SIGMOD International Conference on Management of Data, SIGMOD '06* (ACM, New York, 2006), pp. 407–418
421. B. Wu, Y. Zhou, P. Yuan, H. Jin, L. Liu, SemStore: a semantic-preserving distributed RDF triple store, in *CIKM* (2014), pp. 509–518
422. M. Wylot, P. Cudré-Mauroux, DiploCloud: efficient and scalable management of RDF data in the cloud. IEEE Trans. Knowl. Data Eng. **28**(3), 659–674 (2016)
423. M. Wylot, J. Pont, M. Wisniewski, P. Cudré-Mauroux, dipLODocus[RDF]: short and long-tail RDF analytics for massive webs of data, in *Proceedings of the 10th International Conference on The Semantic Web (ISWC'11)*, Volume Part I (Springer, Berlin, 2011), pp. 778–793

424. M. Wylot, P. Cudre-Mauroux, P. Groth, TripleProv: efficient processing of lineage queries in a native RDF store, in *Proceedings of the 23rd International Conference on World Wide Web, WWW '14*, Republic and Canton of Geneva, 2014. International World Wide Web Conferences Steering Committee, pp. 455–466

425. M. Wylot, P. Cudré-Mauroux, P. Groth, A demonstration of tripleprov: tracking and querying provenance over web data. Proc. VLDB Endow. **8**(12), 1992–1995 (2015)

426. M. Wylot, P. Cudré-Mauroux, P. Groth, Executing provenance-enabled queries over web data, in *Proceedings of the 24rd International Conference on World Wide Web, WWW '15*, Republic and Canton of Geneva, 2015. International World Wide Web Conferences Steering Committee

427. B.B. Yao, M. Tamer Özsu, N. Khandelwal, XBench benchmark and performance testing of XML DBMSs, in *ICDE* (2004)

428. P. Yuan, P. Liu, B. Wu, H. Jin, W. Zhang, L. Liu, Triplebit: a fast and compact system for large scale RDF data. Proc. VLDB Endow. **6**(7), 517–528 (2013)

429. M. Zaharia, M. Chowdhury, M.J. Franklin, S. Shenker, I. Stoica, Spark: cluster computing with working sets, in *HotCloud* (2010)

430. K. Zaiss, Instance-based ontology matching and the evaluation of matching systems. PhD thesis, Heinrich-Heine-Universiat Dusseldorf, 2010

431. K. Zaiss, S. Conrad, S.A. Vater, Benchmark for testing instance-based ontology matching methods, in *KMIS* (2010)

432. K. Zeng, J. Yang, H. Wang, B. Shao, Z. Wang, A distributed graph engine for web scale RDF data, in *Proceedings of the 39th International Conference on Very Large Data Bases*, VLDB Endowment (2013), pp. 265–276

433. X. Zhang, Q. Zhong, F. Shi, J. Li, J. Tang, RiMOM results for OAEI 2009, in *OM* (2009)

434. X. Zhang, L. Chen, Y. Tong, M. Wang, EAGRE: towards scalable I/O efficient SPARQL query evaluation on the cloud, in *29th IEEE International Conference on Data Engineering, ICDE*, Brisbane, 8–12 April 2013, pp. 565–576

435. J. Zhao, Guide to the open provenance model vocabulary (2010)

436. J. Zhao, C. Bizer, Y. Gil, P. Missier, S. Sahoo, Provenance requirements for the next version of RDF, in *W3C Workshop RDF Next Steps* (2010)

437. P. Zhao, C.C. Aggarwal, M. Wang, gSketch: on query estimation in graph streams. Proc. VLDB Endow. **5**(3), 193–204 (2011)

438. L. Zhao, S. Sakr, A. Liu, A. Bouguettaya, *Cloud Data Management* (Springer, Cham, 2014)

439. Q. Zheng, C. Shao, J. Li, Z. Wang, L. Hu, RiMOM2013 results for OAEI 2013, in *OM* (2013)

440. Z. Zhou, G. Qi, C. Liu, P. Hitzler, R. Mutharaju, Reasoning with Fuzzy-EL+ ontologies using MapReduce, in *Proceedings of the 20th European Conference on Artificial Intelligence (ECAI 2012)*. Frontiers in Artificial Intelligence and Applications, vol. 242 (IOS Press, Amsterdam, 2012), pp. 933–934

441. Z. Zhou, G. Qi, C. Liu, R. Mutharaju, P. Hitzler, Reasoning with large scale OWL 2 EL ontologies based on MapReduce, in *Web Technologies and Applications – 18th Asia-Pacific Web Conference, APWeb 2016. Proceedings, Part II*, Suzhou, 23–25 September 2016, pp. 429–433

442. A. Zimmermann, N. Lopes, A. Polleres, U. Straccia, A general framework for representing, reasoning and querying with annotated semantic web data. Web Semant. **11**, 72–95 (2012)

443. A.Y. Zomaya, S. Sakr, *Handbook of Big Data Technologies* (Springer, Cham, 2017)

444. L. Zou, M. Tamer Özsu, L. Chen, X. Shen, R. Huang, D. Zhao, gStore: a graph-based SPARQL query engine. VLDB J. **23**(4), 565–590 (2014)

Printed in the United States
By Bookmasters